Praise for
Living Community

At last a community development 'bible' for the uninitiated as well as for those wanting community work accreditation. With *Living Community*, Dave makes another valuable and versatile offering to community development theory and practice.
Jeremy Liyanage, advocate for reconciliation, founder of Bridging Lanka

Living Community is an ideal textbook for school age and mature students who wish to examine their ethical responsibility to the world around them. It is a practical resource for social workers, community organisers, and human rights advocates, as well as offering the layperson no nonsense pragmatic options for how to become more involved in one's community.

Using a method of Socratic questioning, *Living Community* concerns the reader with developing themselves as active, participating, and responsible members of the community. It encourages the reader to develop their own definitions and meanings regarding the complexity of the relationship between self and community, and thus echoes Plato's Republic in many ways, as *Living Community* asks the question: "What is the ideal society and how do we make it so?"

Living Community asks us to see the world as not outside or 'around us' but as a living and ever-changing connection between all humans, where the world, and all people, and everything, is one. This 'we are all one machine' approach dissolves the isolation of the self, and is the first step to seeing a world where all humans are the same. Once this idea of the self as a component in a greater whole is grasped, the next step *Living Community* takes is understanding that the only person we can change is our self, but by doing so we inevitably change the world.
Evelyn Hartogh, legendary LGBT performance artist and activist

Living Community

an introductory course
in community work

Dave Andrews

Tafina Press

Copyright © 2007 Dave Andrews

The author asserts the moral right
to be identified as the author of this work

First published in Australia in 2007

This re-authored and updated edition published 2019

Published by
Tafina Press
7 Drake St
West End, Q. 4101
Australia

ISBN-10: 0-9757658-7-6
ISBN-13: 978-0-9757658-7-6

All rights reserved.
No part of this book may be transmitted or reproduced in any form or by any means, including but not restricted to photocopying, recording, or by any information storage and retrieval system, without written permission from the publisher; except for brief quotations in printed reviews.

Typeset in Aldine 401

Contents

Introduction ix

Facilitator's Guide xvi

Part One Principles of Living Community 1

Session 1	Introduction to Community	2
Session 2	Possibilities and Problems	12
Session 3	Community Development	26
Session 4	Breaking through the Barrier of Fear	36
Session 5	Breaking through the Barrier of Futility	44
Session 6	Breaking through the Barrier of Selfishness	54
Session 7	Breaking through the Barrier of Spitefulness	64
Session 8	Building Bridges to People	75
Session 9	Building Bridges on Relationships	87
Session 10	Building Bridges through Groups	99
Session 11	Building Bridges for Cooperation	108
Session 12	Bringing About Personal Hope	117
Session 13	Bringing About Social Empowerment	130
Session 14	Bringing About Problem Resolution	142
Session 15	Bringing About Real Transformation	152

Part Two Community Work Practices 169

Session 16	Working within a Vocational Framework	170
Session 17	Working within an Ethical Framework	183
Session 18	Working within a Cultural Framework	197
Session 19	Working within a Legal Framework	212
Session 20	Community Work Skill 1: Communicating	218
Session 21	Community Work Skill 2: Negotiating	228
Session 22	Community Work Skill 3: Facilitating	237
Session 23	Community Work Skill 4: Supporting	248
Session 24	Community Work Skill 5: Researching	258
Session 25	Community Work Skill 6: Planning (A)	264
Session 26	Community Work Skill 6: Planning (B)	271

Session 27	Community Work Skill 7: Budgeting	282
Session 28	Community Work Skill 8: Reporting	289
Session 29	Community Work Skill 9: Promoting	300
Session 30	Community Work Skill 10: Persevering	310
Appendix A	The UN Declaration of Human Rights	318
Appendix B	Readings	324

Foreword

David Busch

This is written as a text book, but unlike any text book I've read.

It doesn't keep its subject matter at arm's length, writing about it as object, in the third person, enabling the reader to stay safely external and scrutinising.

In a strange way the book reads me. It challenges me about instrumental friendships—about making the focuses of my life everywhere else other than the very place where I live. It plunges me deeper into my own life and it calls forth a response that means I may not be the same person at the end of this book than when I started.

It is an easy read, but not a comfortable one. It is very engaging and absorbing, yet you constantly have to put it down because you need time to assimilate and wrestle with the ideas that clash with—or sometimes clarify—your own preconceptions. It is gently affirming yet demanding. Optimistic, even idealistic, yet thoroughly realistic.

May I commend this to you as a book that takes seriously what it is to be truly human, from the pen of someone who tries harder than most to live it. May it sow many seeds of hope in the grounds of despair and indifference in our cities, towns and neighbourhoods. God knows that we need it.

Introduction

About the Course

Living Community is an introductory course on practical community work. It can be studied formally as a subject at college, or informally in your own community.

In his study of community, David Clark says:

> community [is] essentially a sentiment which people have about themselves in relation to themselves: a sentiment expressed in action, but still basically a feeling. People have many feelings, but there are two essentials for the existence of community: a sense of significance and sense of solidarity. The strength of community within any given group is determined by the degree to which its members experience both a sense of solidarity and a sense of significance within it. [1]

According to psychologist Scott Peck:

> If we are going to use the word meaningfully we must restrict it to a group of individuals who have learned to communicate honestly with each other, whose relationships go deeper than their masks of composure, and who have developed some significant commitment to 'rejoice together, mourn together', 'delight in each other, make others' conditions our own'. [2]

After researching five different intentional communities, sociologist Luther Smith wrote:

> The primary indicator of communal well-being is that members feel their fellowship approximates the qualities of a caring family. Hardship and failures will be the occasion for creative solutions and increased resolve. They do not break the spirit of a community. But loss of mutual respect and steadfast caring strikes a deathblow at the very heart of a community. [3]

Thus it is our hope that this training will provide you with the opportunity to explore the sense of significance and solidarity, which is at the heart of community. Hopefully through this learning experience, you will develop a sense of deep mutual respect with people around you, as in a healthy extended family in which you will be free to 'rejoice together and mourn together'. [4]

---

1 Clark, D. *Basic Communities* (London: SPCK 1975), pp 4-5.
2 Peck, S. *The Different Drum* (London: Rider and Co. 1988), p 59.
3 Smith, L. *Intimacy And Mission* (Herald Press, 1994), pp 98-100.
4 *Research in Organisational Change and Development*, Vol 1 (JAI Press, 1987), pp. 129–169.

The two dimensions of the course

The *Living Community* course has an inner dimension and an outer dimension. The outer dimension, the 'body' of the course, is the Australian National Training Authority's body of community development knowledge, skills, principles, practices, and competencies. The inner dimension, or 'soul', is our passion for in-situ, spiritual, experiential, personal, relational, ethical, action-reflection community work education.

The outer dimension: The body of the course

The content of this course addresses two units of competency from the Community Services Training Package (CHC02) endorsed by the Australian National Training Authority:

- CHCCD1A, which focuses on support for community participation.
- CHCCD9A, which focuses on support for community leadership.

Underpinning knowledge of community work

The underpinning knowledge presented includes:

- Health promotion (as per the Ottawa Charter)
- Local, state and federal strategies/legislation
- The nature and the structure of the community
- Significant cultural awareness—practices and protocol
- Impact of cultural attitudes on organisational planning
- Community development principles and practices
- Community development strategies, tactics, and methods
- Strategies for encouraging community input and participation
- Organisational systems, guidelines and practice
- Concepts of effective community leadership
- Availability of skills development training
- Support mechanisms and structures in context
- Organisational budget and funding allocation
- Funding sources and their policies

Underpinning skills of community work

The underpinning skills presented include:
- Formal and informal networking
- Liaising with a range of people
- Researching community issues
- Developing community policies
- Facilitating community meetings
- Negotiating community agreements
- Preparing community budgets
- Marketing community activities
- Evaluating community programs
- Writing community reports

Practical content and process

This course will give you the opportunity to

- Clarify your understanding of a spiritual approach to community
- Consider general theories in relation to your particular community
- Experiment with an experiential approach to community work
- Discover a personal and relational approach to community work
- Develop an ethical, action-reflection approach to community work
- Analyse the issues involved in doing sensitive community work
- Appreciate sensitive responses which enhance both dignity and solidarity
- Identify and develop opportunities for community leadership
- Provide support for leadership structures and processes in the community
- Provide support for leadership training and learning in the community

- Demonstrate your capacity to undertake a range of activities to ensure appropriate participation in community activities
- Undertake a range of activities to ensure appropriate participation by groups and individuals in community activities
- Develop an appropriate range of skills, such as
    - networking
    - liaising
    - negotiating
    - facilitating
    - researching
    - writing
    - evaluating
    - budgeting
    - promoting
    - persevering

The inner dimension: The soul of the course

An in-situ course

Formal community work training is usually conducted in a college, while non-formal community work training is usually conducted in the context of the community. This course seeks to provide *in-situ* community work training that can be done formally for credit or informally for interest, in the context of the community.

A spiritual course

This course seeks to provide people with the opportunity to explore a dynamic *spirituality* that is essential for developing a healthy community. We believe that the practice of a radical spirituality of compassion, as advocated in all the major world religions, is not merely our best hope for developing a healthy community—it is our only hope.

An experiential course

This course seeks to provide the opportunity for people to experience the 'sentiment', the 'sense of significance and solidarity' at the heart of community: an opportunity to *experience* the training to develop 'deep mutual respect' for one another, as in a 'healthy extended family'.

A personal course

Community work is a *personal* issue - it begins with us! Either we can complain about the way things are, or we can change the way they are, starting with ourselves. This course can give people that start.

A relational course

Community work is both a personal and a *relational* issue. Change may start with us, but if it stops with us, it will stop altogether! This course can help us to help one another make the needed change together.

An ethical course

Community work is at heart an essentially *ethical* activity. There are no short cuts. There are no quick fixes. We cannot develop our community unless we 'do unto others as we would have them do unto us'.

An action-reflection course

This course will encourage us to remember that anything worth doing is worth doing badly to begin with; but if we want to do good, we should try to do it better than we did before. We all need to develop the capacity to reflect critically on our actions.

Content and Outcomes

The content of *Living Community* is divided into 30 sessions. Part I (Sessions 1 to 15) helps people understand the foundation principles of practical community work. Building on those foundations, Part II (Sessions 16 to 30) then sets out the practices of community work in such a way as to enable people to use these skills in their own particular contexts.

When you complete *Living Community*, you will be able to:

- demonstrate a developed understanding of community and of community work
- articulate a broad understanding of general theories related to community work
- analyse with insight the issues involved in doing practical community work
- identify and develop opportunities for practical community leadership
- appreciate sensitive responses which enhance dignity and solidarity

- practise a co-operative approach to community work

Learning strategies and learning partners

Living Community includes processes, exercises, a set text, study notes, additional readings, and a simple series of community tasks that you can work through, step by step, in the context of your own community.

This course includes a set of instructions to assist you in self-managed study. However, no course on community work could possibly be done in total isolation. So you will need a learning partner for this course. It doesn't matter if it is a new acquaintance or an old friend. What matters is that it is someone you believe you can work with, someone you feel comfortable with, you can collaborate with, and be accountable to.

A learning partner does not need to be present when you do most of the study sessions. But there are some sessions where it is absolutely essential that you have one or two learning partners with you, in order to be able to explore with integrity the subject you are studying. The learning partners for these sessions need not be learning partners you have chosen for the whole course, but any helpful people who might be available.

Learning responsibilities and resources for informal study

1. You alone are responsible for your own learning. To get the most out of your study of *Living Community,* you need to follow the instructions in each session on a weekly basis—including reading the materials, talking things over with a learning partner, answering the questions, completing the set community tasks and writing up the working notes.

2. To do all the work the course entails, you need to set aside at least 2½ hours for each session, and a further 2½ hours for the tasks associated with each session. It would take about 5 hours a week.

3. At the end of each session, we have set Community Tasks that you are encouraged to do. These tasks provide the simple activities that are the basis for the action and reflection at the heart of the course.

4. You are encouraged to keep Working Notes made up of informal personal reflections on specific lessons you learn from this course through your engagement with community development theory and practice in your

community. *Working Notes* are not an objective reporting of events, *per se*, but more subjective, personal reflections on some of the thoughts, feelings and issues that the course raises for you to consider.

5. While reading widely on the topic of community development is strongly encouraged, we have tried to provide enough resources for you to read without having to access a library. The Readings (listed in Appendix B) have been provided at http://www.daveandrews.com.au

In addition to *Living Community*, you will need additional materials to complete the course. The articles, stories and assignment guidelines are all available on http://www.daveandrews.com.au

Facilitator's Guide
Training Resources and Responsibilities

Your responsibilities are:

- To help students clarify their understanding of material related to community and community work;
- To consider general theories related to community work in the context of today's world;
- To analyse the issues involved in doing practical community work;
- To appreciate sensitive responses which enhance dignity and solidarity in:
    - ❖ the principles of practical community work
    - ❖ the practices of practical community work
    - ❖ the opportunities for community leadership
    - ❖ leadership structures and processes in the community
    - ❖ leadership training and learning in the community
    - ❖ a range of activities to ensure participation in community activities

You need to encourage students to study *Living Community*, following the instructions in the each session (including reading the materials, talking things over with a learning partner, answering the questions, and writing up the Working Notes) on a weekly basis where possible.

If students are studying the course for accreditation, you will also need to encourage them to:

- Participate in a Residential Intensive (if required)
- Complete the weekly Community Tasks
- Complete the weekly Working Notes
- Complete the Essays and Reports

Students should be encouraged to set aside at least 2½ hours for each session, 2½ hours for the tasks associated with each session, 3 hours per week for additional reading, and 2 hours for writing. This means that students should aim to dedicate at least 10 hours a week to this course.

The best way of encouraging students is to meet with them at least once a week every week for a couple of hours. If that is not possible, you may want to consider staying in touch with them by phone and/or email, and organise a Residential Intensive once or twice during the course.

A Residential Intensive is a two to three day face-to-face facilitated learning experience.

What a residential intensive is	What a residential intensive is not
One important aspect of their learning experience.	The main learning event for this course.
An opportunity to withdraw briefly from their context to reflect on and discuss the themes and emphases of this course, after which they will return to their in-situ engagement.	The place to be provided with the content of the course.
A gathering of fellow travellers who have unique and valuable perspectives and contributions to make to each other's learning.	A place for students to be lectured to by 'an expert'.
A facilitated, interactive process.	A passive, receptive process.
A 'whole-of-person' engagement.	An academic exercise only.[1]

The Community Tasks that need to be completed are at the end of each session. These tasks provide the simple activities that are the basis for the action and reflection at the heart of the course. The Reports that students are expected to write are based on the Working Notes they keep on these Community Tasks.

The Working Notes are to be made up of informal (but legible) personal reflections on specific lessons that students learn from this course, through their engagement with community development theory and practice in their community. The Working Notes are not the Reports but form the basis for the student's Reports. Working Notes are not an objective reporting of events, *per se*, but more subjective, personal reflections.

Note: Working Notes should **not** be graded but should be submitted as evidence of the student's personal learning progress.

Two formal Reports are to be submitted, one for each half of the course, framed around:

- the weekly tasks attempted
- strategies tried
- successes
- failures
- lessons learned along the way

The Reports should demonstrate the student's theoretical and practical understanding of community work within the framework of the student's personal world view. Reports should be based on the weekly Working Notes they keep on their Community Tasks. Honesty, authenticity and creativity in these presentations should be rewarded. But students should be reminded that while they may be personal and practical, these Reports are assessable pieces of work. References and research need to be adequately cited, and a Bibliography appended.

Reports by degree students should be 2,000 words, diploma students should be 1,500 words and certificate students should be 1,000 words.

Two Essays are to be written, one for each half of the course, each essay demonstrating an in-depth understanding of one aspect of compassionate community work. Students may either suggest a topic for approval to the facilitator, or choose one of the following suggested topics:

- the principles of practical community work
- the practices of practical community work
- gender equity and community work
- indigenous people and community work
- migrants and refugees and community work
- disadvantaged people and community work
- community work as a personal journey
- community work with local groups (clubs, churches etc)

Essays by degree students should be 3,000 words, by diploma students should be 2,500 words and by certificate students should be 2,000 words.

Facilitators need to understand that not all students have access to good libraries. While library research is strongly encouraged where possible, we have tried to provide the resources needed for students to be able to complete essay writing without accessing a library. Additional Articles have been provided on the website: http://www.daveandrews.com.au

Part One

Principles of Living Community

Session 1

Introduction to Community

Objectives

- To establish guidelines for the conduct of the course
- To introduce the course, its content and process
- To establish learning partnerships for the course
- To introduce the underpinning concept of community

Time

2 hours in session, and 3 hours in community

Guidelines

10 minutes

Living Community includes processes, exercises, a set text, study notes, additional readings, and a simple series of community tasks that you can work through, step-by-step, in the context of your own community. If you have not read **An Introduction to** *Living Community* at the beginning of this book, you need to read it before you proceed.

If you want to work through the book informally, you will need to read carefully section 3 in the Facilitator's Guide, **Learning Responsibilities and Resources for Informal Study.**

If you want to work through the book formally for accreditation, you will need to read the whole Facilitator's Guide, which gives an idea of the formal study requirements.

Learning partners

You will need to find a learning partner for this course. For details and guidelines see the Facilitator's Guide above, **Learning Responsibilities and Resources for Informal Study.**

Community tasks

At the end of each session you will be assigned a community task. These tasks provide the simple activities that are the basis for the action and reflection at the heart of the course. These tasks will form the basis of your working notes and any report(s) you may write.

Working notes

You will keep these notes in the context of learning activities. These "rough scribblings" are part of your permanent record of the underpinning knowledge and skills presented during the training sessions, and you should file them in a suitable folder as part of a portfolio of your learning. These documents don't have to be neat, but they must be readable. If you are doing the course for accreditation your working notes won't be assessed for a mrak or grade, but you will be required to submit them to document your learning experience.

Expectations

10 minutes

- What are your expectations of this course? What do you hope to get out of it?
- How realistic are those expectations? (Check them against the course content.)
- How can you make the most of the course? What do you need to put into it?
- If you feel the course will help you meet your goals, then let's get started . . .

Introduction

10 minutes

- ☐ Reflect on the following:
    - ❖ Where have you lived in the past ten years?
    - ❖ What community or communities you have been a part of?
    - ❖ What is your most positive memory of a healthy community experience?

If there are more than one of you, talk about it. If you are on your own, jot down a few notes about the final question above.

Vision exercise
15 minutes

- ☐ Draw a picture of your ideal community—the kind you'd like to be a part of.
- ☐ This exercise is not an art competition and is not for assessment. But you need to keep a copy of your picture in your Working Notes.
- ☐ When you have finished, consider the community in the picture. Look at your picture and listen to what it says to you about the kind of community that deep down you'd really like to be a part of.
- ✎ Then write down what it says to you about your ideal community. Keep a copy of what you write, in your Working Notes.

Values exercise
35 minutes

- ☐ Make a list of all the values that you would consider as crucial to the development of your ideal community.
- ☐ Then make a list of what you would nominate as the **top four** priority values that you think are most important for the development of your ideal community.
- ☐ Then answer the following questions. Make sure you record your conclusions in your Working Notes.

- What are the values you nominated as top priority?
- Why do you consider these values as so important?
- What are the similarities between your own values and the values that other people have listed below? What are the differences?
- What values that other people have listed, would you like to add to your list?
- What values have you listed, that you would like to take off your list?
- What would you nominate as your top four values now?
- Are they the same, or different? Explain the reasons for your selections and changes.

Examples of values other people have nominated include:

- Faith
- Love
- Respect
- Support
- Honesty
- Safety
- Hope
- Acceptance
- Compassion
- Help
- Equality
- Freedom

✍ Record your reflections in your Working Notes.

Other Views
20 minutes

Now that you have clarified your own view of an ideal 'community', you may be interested in comparing and contrasting your own view with those of others.

When we talk to people about the possibility of making their dream of community come true, they respond very positively. According to the sociologists Bell and Newby, it seems 'everyone—even sociologists—has wanted to live in a community.' [1]

Some say it is because community is a 'touchy feely' word, like heaven, love, romance, friendship, marriage or family, and the concept has 'warm fuzzy' connotations. Certainly, according to Williams, in his book *Keywords*, 'the word "community", unlike all other terms of social organisation, (such as "group", "party", "network", "association", or "institution") is never used unfavourably.' [2]

Some say that the reason the word 'community' is seldom used unfavourably is that we have forgotten how parochial and oppressive communities can be. According to Bryson and Mowbray,

> In drawing on the historical notion of community, the Nelsonian touch is applied by communitarians, [turning a blind eye] to the tensions and conflicts that were ordinary parts of their archetypal communities. Gross inequalities, rigid status, blood feuds, intolerance, bondage and ignorance are carefully forgotten, so that "real community" is seen only in terms of cooperation ... [3]

And for some, that may be so. But the reason the word 'community' is seldom used unfavourably by the people we talk to, is not that we have

---

[1] Bell, C. and Newby, H. *Community Studies*. Allen and Unwin London 1971, p. 2
[2] Williams, R. *Keywords: A Vocabulary Of Culture And Society*. Fontana London 1976, p.66
[3] Bryson, L. and Mowbray, M. "Community: The Spray-On-Solution." *Australian Journal of Social Issues*, Vol.16 No.1 p.256

forgotten how parochial and oppressive communities can be. Quite the contrary. We remember very acutely the tensions and conflicts, that so often have characterised our communities. Yet for us, the word 'community' is essentially a qualitative term which refers to the way we ought to be, liberated from intolerance, bondage and ignorance, rather than the way we are, circumscribed by gross inequalities, rigid status, and blood feuds.

According to Nisbet, our use of the word is quite typical. Whether we are talking about Confucius, Aristotle, Ibn Khaldun or Thomas Aquinas, the notion of community has always been a normative prescription of an ideal for the world, rather than an empirical description of the real world. [1]

According to Bellah, this notion of community, which we speak about in qualitative terms, may be 'resisted as absurdly utopian ... But the transformation of which we speak is both necessary and modest. Without it, indeed, there may be very little future to think about at all.' [2]

In the spectrum of social science research, the term 'community' is not only one of the most common, but also one of the most crucial concepts for the welfare of our society.

Yet there is a lot of confusion about the meaning of the term. As long ago as 1955, Hillery noted no less than ninety-four different definitions of 'community'. And more than a decade later, Stacey stated that 'certainly confusion continues to reign over the uses of the term'. [3] So much so, Gowdy once said in frustration, 'it is doubtful whether the concept of "community" refers to a useful abstraction' [3].

After much study, however, Hillery was able to distinguish three distinctive common elements among the myriad of definitions that he had tabulated. Later Wirth, then Gowdy, confirmed Hillery's findings. They found that, to increasing degrees of significance, a common physical location, a common social connection, and a quality of common reciprocal interaction, were the components most likely to constitute community. [4]

Clark, picking up on the quality of conscious reciprocal interaction as the most important component in community, says in his study of *Basic Communities*:

> community [is] essentially a sentiment which people have about themselves in relation to themselves: a sentiment expressed in action, but still basically a feeling. People have many feelings, but there are two essentials for the existence of community: a sense of significance and sense of solidarity ... The strength of community within any given

---

1 Nisbet, R., *The Sociological Tradition*. Heinemann London 1966 ch.3
2 Bellah, R.et.al., *Habits of the Heart*, Uni. of Cal. Press Berkely 1985 p 286
3 Hillery, G. "Definitions of Community: Areas of Agreement" *Rural Sociology* no. 20, 1955
4 Gowdy, 1982, p 374

group is determined by the degree to which its members experience both a sense of solidarity and a sense of significance within it.[1]

Toennies argues that while the quality of interaction required to produce a 'society' involves only transient, impersonal, unidimensional, secondary relationships, the quality of interaction required to produce a 'community' involves permanent, personal, multi-faceted, primary relationships.[2]

Toennies thinks that 'community' is probably only possible for people in kinship groups. But Daley and Cobb think that while 'community' may be easier in homogeneous groups, it may be broader, deeper, higher, and wider in heterogeneous groups.[3] Certainly that's the experience of most people.

Scott Peck says that

> if we are going to use the word meaningfully we must restrict it to a group of individuals who have learned to communicate honestly with each other, whose relationships go deeper than their masks of composure, and who have developed some significant commitment to 'rejoice together, mourn together', delight in each other, make other's conditions our own.[4]

Luther Smith says

> The primary indicator of communal well-being is that members feel their ... fellowship approximates the qualities of a caring family. Hardship and failures ... will be the occasion for creative solutions and increased resolve. They do not break the spirit of a community ... But loss of mutual respect and steadfast caring strikes a death blow at the very heart of a community!

A healthy community is:
- A safe space,
- A place where people are accepted as people,
- A place where both similarities and differences are respected,
- A place where everyone is important, and no-one is expendable,
- A place where people can participate in decisions that impact them,
- A place where people seek to do justice to the most disadvantaged—not only those inside the group, but also those outside the group.

---

1 Clark, D., *Basic Communities*, SPCK, London 1975, pp 4-5
2 Toennies, F., *Community and Society*, Harper, New York 1957, pp 12-29
3 Cobb, J. and Daley, H., *For the Common Good*, Beacon Press, Boston 1992, p 170
4 Peck, S. *The Different Drum*, Rider and Co., London 1988, p 59

Living Community: Session 1

Having read these views, answer the following questions:

1. What are the values that characterise a 'healthy community'?
2. How do they compare/contrast with the values you selected?
3. What are the values in your community that are most healthy?
4. What are the values in your community that are least healthy?
5. How do you think you can nurture healthy values your community?
6. What are you doing that you need to keep doing to help this take place?
7. What are you doing that you need to change in order to help this happen?

✍ Record your reflections in your Working Notes.

A Place Called Heaven
10 minutes

❐ Read the story of *A Place Called Heaven* by Paulo Coelho.

Once upon a time, a man, his horse and his dog were travelling along a road. As they passed by a huge tree, it was struck by lightning, and they all died. But the man failed to notice that he was no longer of this world and so he continued walking along with his two animal companions. (Sometimes the dead take a while to register their new situation).

It was a long, uphill walk, the sun was beating down on them and they were all sweating and thirsty. At a bend in the road they saw a magnificent marble gateway that led into a gold-paved square, in the centre of which was a fountain over-flowing with crystal-clear water. The man went over to the guard at the entrance.

'Good morning.'
'Good morning,' the guard replied.
'What is this lovely place?'
'It's Heaven.'
'Well, I'm very glad to see it, because we're very thirsty.'
'You're welcome to come in and drink all the water you want.' And the guard indicated the fountain.
'My horse and dog are also thirsty.'
'I'm terribly sorry,' said the guard, 'but animals are not allowed in here.'

The man was deeply disappointed for he really was very thirsty, but he was not prepared to drink alone, so he thanked the guard and went on his way.

Exhausted after more trudging uphill, they reached an old gateway that opened onto a dirt road flanked by trees. A man, his hat pulled down over his face, was stretched out in the shade of one of the trees, apparently asleep.

'Good morning,' said the traveller. The other man greeted him with a nod.

'We're very thirsty—me, my horse and my dog.'

'There's a spring over there amongst those rocks,' said the man indicating the spot. 'You can drink all you want.' The man, his horse and his dog went to the spring and quenched their thirst. The traveller returned to thank the man. 'Come back whenever you want,' he was told.

'By the way, what's this place called?'

'Heaven.'

'Heaven? But the guard at the marble gateway told me that was Heaven!'

'That's not Heaven, that's Hell.'

The traveller was puzzled.

'You shouldn't let others take your name in vain, you know! False information can lead to all kinds of confusion!'

'On the contrary, they do us a great favour, because those who stay there have proved themselves capable of abandoning their dearest friends.'

- From *The Devil And Miss Prym*

- What does this story say to you about the nature of 'true' community?

✍ Record your reflections in your Working Notes.

Conclusion

10 minutes

☐ Plan to begin each session from now on with a review of the work from the previous session. This will include a review of your response to the issues raised in the course notes and the follow-up readings—and your experience of trying to do a series of set community tasks.

> • Your working notes serve as a journal of reflections on your experiences, thoughts and feelings about your experiments, and your growing understanding of the nature of community and community development. You should aim to write at least one hundred words each week, incorporating all aspects of your learning experiences. Keep your working notes handy at all times, as learning experiences are not always predictable or scheduled.

The follow-up reading for this session is

> Pages 52-68 from ***Building A Better World,*** Albatross, Sutherland, 1996. (Reading 1)

The set community tasks for this session are:

- Finding a learning partner,
- Observing your community,
- Talking over your observations with your learning partner.

Finding a learning partner

- ☐ You need to identify a learning partner, then get together with him or her and discuss the partnership.
- ☐ As a starting point, address the following questions with your learning partner. Record conclusions in your Working Notes.

> - What would be signs of a good partnership?
> - How could you tell whether it was working well?
> - How could you say if it wasn't working so well?
> - What do you think you need most help with?
> - What do you feel you can help most with?

Observing your community

- ☐ Observe 'your community' this week. It may be your family, your locality, your church, your sports club, your craft group, your trade union, your workplace or your market place. Wherever it is, find an unobtrusive place to sit, and just observe the people and their relationships in 'your community'.

- ❖ What do you see?
- ❖ What do you hear?
- ❖ What conclusions can you draw about your community based on your observations?

Meeting with your learning partner

☐ Then meet with your learning partner over a cuppa and discuss your observations of your community in the light of the issues raised in this session.

✎ Record your actions, reflections, and conclusions in your Working Notes.

Session 2

Possibilities and Problems

Objectives

- To review your understanding of the concept of a healthy community
- To introduce the structure of community networks
- To explore the significance of these for the production of 'social capital'.
- To consider the possibilities, as well as the problems, with the resources provided by social capital for community development

Review

15 minutes

- ☐ Review your work from Session 1.
- ☐ Review the issues raised in course notes in the previous session, particularly your understanding of the nature of a healthy community.
- ☐ Review the reading:
     Pages 52-68 from ***Building A Better World,*** Albatross, Sutherland, 1996. (Reading 1)
- ☐ Review the tasks:
    1. Did you identify a learning partner? If so, good. If not, find someone to fulfil this role.
    2. Did you get together with this person to discuss the learning partnership? If so, what terms did you agree on?
    3. What 'community did you observe? Were you able to find an unobtrusive place to sit and observe the people and their relationships?

> 4. What are the most important things you learned about community from your observation?
> 5. What were the results of getting together with your learning partner to discuss your observations of your community in the light of the issues raised in class and clarified in the reading?

The famous German martyr-theologian, Dietrich Bonhoeffer, was quoted in the reading (p 63) as saying, 'Those who love community, destroy community. Those who love people, build community.'

If what he says is true, if we try to build community at the expense of the people in it, we will destroy the very community we are trying to build. It is only as we lay aside our obsession with building perfect communities and simply love the people in them as sincerely as we can, that we will be able to build healthy people-friendly communities!

✍ Record your reflections in your Working Notes

The possibilities of community

35 minutes

> - Have you heard of 'social capital'?
> - If so, what do you understand the term to mean?

✍ Record your reflections in your Working Notes.

With the help of Eva Cox, Hugh Mackay and Robert Putnam, you can expand your understanding of the concept of 'social capital'.

In *A Truly Civil Society*, Eva Cox says there are four types of capital that are essential to our well-being:

- **Physical capital** – our land, water and air
- **Human capital** – our knowledge and skills
- **Social capital** – our networks and relations
- **Financial capital** – our dollars and cents [1]

She says too much attention has been paid to financial capital; that ours is a culture of 'economic correctness' rather than political correctness. She

---

1 E. Cox, *A Truly Civil Society*, p15

says we need to pay much more attention to physical, human and social capital. At this point we want to pay attention to 'social capital'.

According to social scientist Robert Putnam, the term 'social capital' was coined by Lyda Hanifan who said that it was made up of

> those tangible substances [that] count for most in the daily lives of people: namely good will, fellowship, sympathy, and social intercourse among the individuals and families who make up a social unit ... The individual is helpless socially, if left to himself ... If he comes into contact with his neighbour, and they with other neighbours, there will be an accumulation of social capital, which may immediately satisfy his social needs and which may bear a social potentiality sufficient to the substantial improvement of living conditions in the whole community. The community as a whole will benefit by the co-operation of all its parts, while the individual will find in his associations the advantages of the help, the sympathy, and the fellowship of his neighbours.[1]
>
> Social capital is based on a sense of mutual obligation. It can be either 'specific' or 'general'. If it is specific, the reciprocity is specific: I'll do this for you if you do that for me. If it is general, the reciprocity is generalised: if we do what we can to help other people now, then someday, when we need help, someone may help us.[2]

The Golden Rule, enunciated in the Scriptures, is a classic example of generalised reciprocity that is the basis of social capital in community. We are to 'do unto others as we would have them (sooner or later) do unto us'. (Luke 6.31)

Social capital functions as a 'favour bank'. It is both a private good, in that it benefits us, and a public good, in that it benefits others as well.[3] We need to remember there's pure gold in that Golden Rule. Social capital often is more important than economic capital in ensuring our welfare.[4]

As social scientist, Hugh Mackay, says 'We are social creatures—we thrive on our personal connections with each other. We are at our best when we are fully integrated with the herd; and at our worst when we are isolated.'[5]

Community networks of mutual obligation improve our quality of life to a significant degree on a whole range of different levels.

---

1 R. Putnam, *Bowling Alone*, p19
2 Putnam, p 20-21
3 Putnam, p 291-347
4 Putnam, p 20
5 Putnam, p 256

Community networks affect honesty

Through density, frequency and continuity of connections, and the accountability that those connections require, community encourages honesty. Long-term credibility is worth more than potential gains from short-term treachery.

There is more cheating on tax returns and insurance claims, and there are more cars returned to second-hand dealers, in communities where people are not connected.[1]

Community networks affect safety

Through connecting, checking, mentoring, and supervising, vandalism, graffiti, street crime, and gang violence can all be reduced. An absence of trust between neighbours and an unwillingness to intervene when people cause trouble increases the level of violence in neighbourhoods.[2]

Community networks affect prosperity

On the one hand, where people trust one another, there is a significant reduction in 'transaction costs', from security to insurance.[3] On the other hand, where people are not connected to one another, they are less likely to get jobs, promotions, bonuses, and other benefits.[4]

Community networks affect charity

The most common reason for giving is being asked and the most common reason for not giving, not being asked. People are not likely to be asked if they are not in contact with others. Those not in clubs and churches are ten times less likely to give than others.[5]

Community networks affect generosity

People are more likely to help others if they have received help, and they are more likely to have received help if they are connected to clubs and churches. They are less likely to give and receive help in big cities rather than small towns.[6]

---

1 Putnam, p 136-8
2 Putnam, p 308-9, 313
3 Putnam, p 147
4 Putnam, p 319
5 Putnam, p 119-121
6 ibid.

Community networks affect democracy

The research shows lack of participation in political processes and structures causes poor, corrupt governance, not the other way round. Without participation, governance is more corrupt and less focused on community issues. [1]

Community networks affect equality

Networks of reciprocity enhance equality, while disparity undermines solidarity. Income is evenly distributed where networks are strong. [2] As networks weakened in Australia, the gap between the rich and the poor widened. The richest 10% now own almost 50% of the nation's wealth, while the poorest 30% own less than 10%. [3]

Community networks affect health

Because of the encouragement of healthy norms, assistance in ill health, and advocacy for proper health-care, people who are connected to networks are less likely to have heart attacks, strokes, cancer—even colds! Disconnected people are two to five times more likely to die prematurely from all causes of death. [4]

Community networks affect happiness

The best single indicator of happiness is connectedness. Those who have little connection with family and friends are more likely to experience loneliness, low self-esteem, sadness, eating and sleeping disorders, and depression. [5]

☐ Consider how the presence or absence of community networks might affect our lives …

- What are two or three examples of how the presence—or the absence—of community networks has significantly affected the quality of your life?

✎ Record your reflections in your *Working Notes*.

---

1 Putnam, p 347
2 Putnam, p 359
3 H. Mackay, *Turning Points*, p52
4 Putnam, p 327
5 Putnam, p 332

☐ Read what you have written, then consider the actual - or potential - importance of local community networks. How important do you think they are?

✍ Don't forget to record your reflections in your Working Notes.

The problems of community

60 minutes

The quiet crisis

Many people in Australia have the feeling that the fabric of society is unravelling. As Hugh Mackay, one of our most well known psychosocial researchers says, 'our sense of community is under threat'.[1]

On the political scene

People are better informed, but are less involved. Where involved, they are involved in a more autonomous manner. They are more likely to write a letter of protest than they are to take part in a protest march.[2]

On the civic scene

There has been an increase in civic organisations, but by and large they are professionally-staffed, nationally-focused civic organisations rather than self-managed, locally-based, civic organisations. Membership is more a matter of paying a subscription than of participating in the organisation, more a product of direct-mail marketing than direct-action membership.[3]

On the work scene

People spend more time at work, and though the recent emphasis on team dynamics has opened up the possibility of an increase in some people's participation at work, the trends in downsizing, contracting-out, and casualising, along with the dwindling of workplace associations like unions, have undermined many people's level of participation at work.[4]

---

1 Mackay, p 257
2 Putnam, p 44-45
3 Putnam, p 50-53
4 Putnam, p 50-53

But nothing has undermined their level of participation more than unemployment. Up to 2 million Australians are now either unemployed or under-employed. [1]

On the home scene

People see more sport, but play sport less. They listen to more music, but play music less. They watch *Home and Away*, *Neighbours* and *Friends* more, but have fewer meals together as families, visit neighbours less, and entertain friends less. [2]

Take some time and ask yourself the question…

- **What are the causes of this crisis in community?**

  ☐ Write a list of underlying causes, and the reasons that you have for selecting them.

  ✎ Don't forget to keep a record of your lists in your *Working Notes*.

Now, consider your lists in the light of the reasons that Hugh Mackay and Robert Putnam cite. Hugh Mackay cites a number of (micro) reasons for these trends:-

Mobility: Mobility creates inherent instability and insecurity. 'Australians move—on average—once every six years.' [3]

Break-up of marriages: 40% of all marriages end up in divorce. [4]

Breakdown of families: 20% of children live with only a single parent. [5]

Fragmentation of households: Single-person households already constitute 24% of the total. If current trends continue, by 2006 they will be the most common type. [6]

Perception of rising crime rate: 'Generally assumed to be worse than the actual situation, inhibits people from moving freely around their own neighbourhood'. [7]

---

1 Mackay, p 55
2 Putnam p 98 ff.
3 Mackay, p 258
4 Mackay, p 144
5 Mackay, p 257
6 Mackay, p 251-2
7 Mackay, p 258

Robert Putnam cites other (macro) reasons for these trends:

The rise and fall of local churches

According to Putnam, churches have traditionally developed up to 50% of small groups in a local community [1] and facilitated connections that made sharing 10 times more likely! [2]

But while interest in religion still continues, interest in religious institutions like the church, is on the decline. [3] And those churches not on the decline tend to be more inward-looking than outward-looking, and more likely to be involved in the church than in the locality, or in church activities in the locality. [4]

Kaldor says churches contribute to community through denominational agencies—which in Australia are the largest non-government providers of social services, including family welfare, aged care, child care, youth, unemployment, and disability services. But, as Putnam says, by and large these denominational agencies are run by professionally-staffed, nationally- or regionally-focused organisations, rather than self-managed, locally-based organisations. So involvement of most church people is more a matter of association than of participation. [5]

Kaldor says churches also contribute to community through congregational activities: 60% provide material assistance, 40% provide personal counselling and 30% provide support groups. The number of small groups has actually grown in recent years. 40% of people claim to be in church groups, home groups, cell groups, support groups encounter groups, and self-help groups. But, as Robert Wuthnow says in *Sharing the Journey*,

> small groups may not be fostering community as effectively as many of their proponents would like. Some small groups merely provide occasions for individuals to focus on themselves in the presence of others. The social contract binding members together asserts only the weakest of obligations. Come if you have time. Talk if you feel like it. Respect everyone's opinion. Never criticise. Leave quietly if you become dissatisfied ... [6]

A New Society study of volunteers, compared to non-volunteers, showed that volunteers are more likely to perceive themselves as religious, and to have had profound religious experiences—and three times more likely

---

1 Putnam, p 148-9
2 Putnam, p 119-121
3 Putnam, p 74
4 Putnam, p 77-8
5 Putnam, p 51-53
6 R. Wuthnow, *Sharing the Journey*, p 3-6

than non-volunteers to attend church at least monthly. A study conducted by Kaldor et al. in 2001 on behalf of the Church National Life Survey confirmed these results.[1] He says church attenders are more likely to be involved in voluntary work than non-attenders.

But not all is as good on the church front as it may appear to be.

- Most care is provided by older members, not by the younger generation.
- Regional, not local, churches are in vogue. And the larger the church, the less likely for its members to be involved in the wider community. They are more likely to be involved in organised, in-house, at-church activities.
- Greater church involvement does not necessarily lead to greater insularity from the community, but many growing churches are more inward looking than outward-looking, encouraging people to be involved in the church rather than in the locality, or only in church-managed programs organised in the locality.
- 20% of people in church said they had contact with more than ten people in their locality outside their church for more than fifteen minutes per week. However, 23% of people in church said they had contact with only one or two people in the locality for more than fifteen minutes per week—and 16% had not made any contact all!
- 28% of people in church said they were involved in serving people outside the church in the locality in which they were located in some capacity or other. However, 72% of people weren't involved in the community at all.

Urbanization and suburbanisation

Movement from small towns to big cities always reduces the levels of community connections people have. However, moving to suburbia is likely to reduce those connections even more.[2]

Firstly, as Lewis Mumford observed, 'suburbia is the collective effort to live a private life'.[3]

---

[1] P. Kaldor et al, p 54-60
[2] Putnam, p 205
[3] Putnam, p 210

Secondly, the separation of the place where we live from the place where we work, where we play, and where we pray, segments rather than integrates our public lives.[1]

Thirdly, the time spent commuting between these separate places affects our involvement in the community very adversely. Each 10 minutes spent commuting cuts down community involvement by 10% and adversely affects not only the commuters, but also family and friends associated with them.[2]

Technology - particularly television

Though those who watch the news on television are more likely to be involved in the community than those who do not, those who watch talk shows and game shows and soap operas are less likely to be involved.[3]

Firstly, TV takes time. On average people now watch television four hours per day.[4]

Secondly, TV induces passivity. The more people watch TV, the more likely they are to want to rest and/or sleep.[5]

Thirdly, TV provides a sense of pseudo-community, e.g. *Home and Away, Neighbours, Friends* and *Cheers*.[6] Consequently, each extra hour per day of watching television reduces community involvement by roughly 10%.[7]

The decline of a great civic generation

The older generation, born in the 20s and 30s and brought up with a great sense of responsibility through the hardship of depression and war, built civic society as we know it today; and civic society is declining as that great civic generation is in a decline[8] (see Figure 1 showing membership of Parents and Teachers Associations in the USA).

---

1 Putnam, p 214
2 Putnam, p 212-13
3 Putnam, p 243
4 Putnam, p 222
5 Putnam, p 237
6 Putnam, p 242
7 Putnam, p 228
8 Putnam, p 250 ff

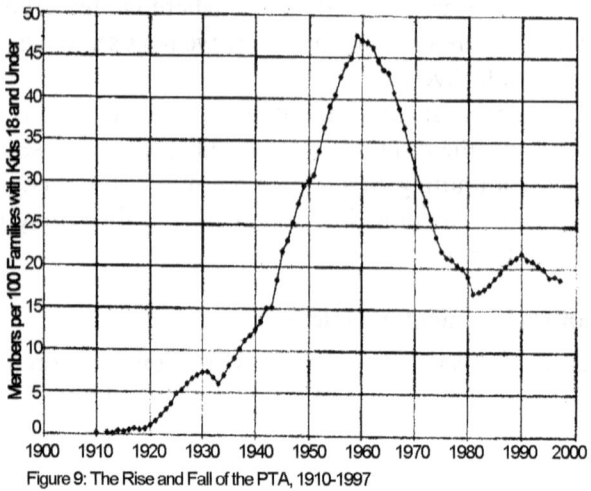

Figure 1

The rise of the great consumer generation

The consumer generation is more preoccupied with materialistic rather than non-materialistic values. Materialistic values include an orientation towards

- body image and appearance,
- private property and finance,
- public recognition and success. [1]

Non-materialistic values include an orientation towards

- personal acceptance and development
- social relationships and responsibilities,
- communal connections and contributions. [2]

As Tim Kasser shows in *The High Price of Materialism*, materialistic people

- are more narcissistic, obsessive, and paranoid
- are more passive-aggressive and over-controlling
- are more unlikely to be self-actualised and satisfied
- are more likely to use/misuse/abuse substances
- are more likely to be abusive (insulting, swearing)
- are more likely to be aggressive (pushing, shoving)

---

1 T. Kasser, *The High Price of Materialism*, p 10
2 Kasser, p 10

- do not invest in marriages, families and communities
- make hostile choices causing tragedy to the commons
- their relationships are shorter, less positive, more negative and more likely to produce a sense of alienation. [1]

Eva Cox in *A Truly Civil Society* says government policies are also destroying our community connections.

- **Privatisation:** 'The loss of public capital makes people feel poorer'. [2]
- **Competition:** 'The move towards competition in the provision of public services ... the cost-cutting and cut-backs ... contribute to widespread anxiety.' [3]
- **Targeting:** 'The targeting of social security payments, once viewed as universal, is now selective—and leaves out some people.' [4]
- **Elitism:** 'These days there are many walled and gated communities built with the intention of excluding those who do not have desirable characteristics.' [5]
- **Nationalism:** 'Nationalism, tribalism, and racism are used to invoke an other who is a threat.' [6]

Cox says 'we increase social capital by gossip[ing], relat[ing] and working together voluntarily in egalitarian organisations.' [7]

> If the social system isolates people, discourages informal and formal contact, or just fails to offer the time and space needed for social contact, then social capital is under threat. We become vulnerable to social bankruptcy when our social connections fail. [8]

The role of the Internet?

Robert Putnam says the role of the Internet is still uncertain. Is it like television, which adversely affects the development of community

---

1 Kasser, pp 12-90 passim
2 Cox, p 74
3 Cox, p 74
4 Cox, p 73
5 Cox, p 36
6 Kasser, p 62
7 Kasser, p 63
8 Cox, p 16-17

networks? Or like the telephone, which reinforces the community networks we are developing? [1]

The positive signs include

- Broader, wider connections
- Access to more information
- More forthright conversation
- Potential for mobilization, [2] e.g. the Campaign to Ban Landmines

The negative signs include

- The reduction of personal 'communication' to impersonal 'information' exchange
- The development of 'cyberarpartheid'—the growing digital rich-poor divide
- The development of 'cyberbalkanisation'—with 'cyber-ghettoes' based on interests rather than 'cybercommunities' based on respect
- The development of 'virtual communities' rather than real communities. [3] You still need a real person to look after you when you're sick!

At best the Net can help us, but we still need to reweave the tattered fabric of community with our own hands, face to face, in flesh and blood.

- Let's consider these perspectives and the questions they raise.

> - Which of this information is new to you?
> - Does it confirm or conflict with your perspective?
> - What do you agree with? What do you disagree with?
> - What are the signs of community unravelling that worry you most?
> - What contribution do you think the Internet will make to real community?

✍ Record your reflections in your Working Notes.

---

1 Putnam, p 166-68
2 Putnam, p 172
3 Putnam, p 171-178

Conclusion

10 minutes

The follow-up reading for this session is:

> Pages 1-12 of An Interview with Robert Putnam on *The Potential and Problems of Community,* 26/09/01, Radio National ABC Radio (Reading 4).

The set community tasks for this session are:

- ❏ Talk with three people in your community this week— one older, one middle-aged and one younger—about their 'sense of community'.
- ❏ Ask them to talk about any experiences of community they may have; whether they feel the sense of community in society is stronger or weaker than it used to be; whether they think this is just their own experience or whether they think others feel the same; and if so why?
- ❏ Then get together with your learning partner and discuss how your findings compare or contrast with the research that you learned through this session and the interview with Professor Robert Putnam.
- ✍ Record your actions, reflections, and conclusions in your *Working Notes*.

Session 3

Community Development

Objectives

- To review your understanding of community networks and the significance of these for the production of 'social capital'.
- To review the potential, as well as the problems, with 'social capital' in society as a resource for community development.
- To introduce the community development approach, some community development principles, community development strategies and tactics.

Review

15 minutes

☐ Review your work from Session 2.
☐ Review the issues raised in course notes in the previous session, particularly your understanding of the nature of 'social capital'.
☐ Review the reading:

> Pages 1-12 of An Interview with Robert Putnam on *The Potential and Problems of Community* (Reading 2).

☐ Review the tasks:
1. Did you talk with three people in your community this week—one older, one middle-aged and one younger—about 'their sense of community'?
2. Did you ask them to talk about any experiences of community they may have; whether they feel the sense of community in society is stronger or weaker than it used to be; whether they think that is just their own experience or whether they think others feel the same; and if so why?

3. What conclusions did you reach, based on these conversations?
4. What was the result of the meeting with your learning partner, discussing how your findings compared and/or contrasted with the social trends discussed in the previous session?

☐ We always need to be mindful of the fact that, as Robert Putnam says, 'It's the day-to-day social connections through membership of organisations, through voluntary work, through having friends over to your house, that make for strong community.'

Community development

15 minutes

Tony Kelly, recently retired Senior Lecturer in Community Work, at the University of Queensland, says:

> Community development is not a science.
>
> Community Development describes a way of working with people that is based on a set of values. These values emphasises the right (and the responsibility) of people to participate in decisions that will affect their lives.
>
> Community Development is concerned first and foremost with poverty and power. It is concerned with giving people—particularly the poorest—the knowledge, skills, opportunity and resources so that they can control their own lives. It emphasis the process that enables maximum decision making for people where they are—at the grass-roots where they live.
>
> A Community Development worker is anyone with these values who works with people where they live. A Community Development worker therefore can work with the people on any task that the community sees as important. In this sense, the choice of the task is of secondary importance, the way in which the task is approached is of primary importance.

☐ In order to reflect on Tony Kelly's definition of community development, ask yourself the following series of questions (and note your answers).

Living Community: Session 3

1. What do you think of Tony Kelly's definition of community development?
2. Which of these ideas are most important for developing your community?
3. How do you think these themes may apply to the work that you want to do?

✎ Record your reflections in your *Working Notes*

Community development principles

20 minutes

A Community Forum of the YMCA in Fiji wrote the following list of Community Development Principles (see opposite).

❐ Read the list of principles.
❐ Circle the numbers of the ones that you agree with, and put a cross on the ones that you disagree with.

- What are the principles you disagree with?
- Why do you disagree with them?
- What are the principles you agree with?
- Why do you agree with them?
- Are there any principles that you agree with that correspond to some of the ones that you disagree with? If so what do you make of that?
- Which of the principles you agree with do you practise well? (Give examples)
- Which principles you agree with do you need to develop more? (Give examples)

✎ Record your reflections in your *Working Notes*

The Fiji Community Forum List of Principles

1. People are more important than things; people are more important than programs.

2. Growth comes from within people; all people have talents waiting to be developed.

3. People grow in responsibility as they are helped to accept greater responsibilities.

4. The most effective venue for training the community takes place in the community.

5. Learning becomes most relevant when it's built on the basis of people's experience.

6. As communities are integrated, they are best served by integrated development rather than departmentalised units working in isolation from one another.

7. The most effective agent to act as a helper is a person who strongly identifies with the community and who develops a relationship based on trust.

8. Communities know their problems and the solutions to their problems that will work better than others.

9. The energy a community will put into any activity will be in proportion to their involvement in the planning of that activity.

10. The pace of development will be determined by the community; a particular change will only become permanent if a community is really ready for it.

11. People should be helped only in so far as it enables them to become more self-reliant.

12. There are resources in each community that are under-utilised waiting to be released.

Living Community: Session 3

Community development strategy

30 minutes

Community development strategy involves always working in a team of three or more. See Figure 2.

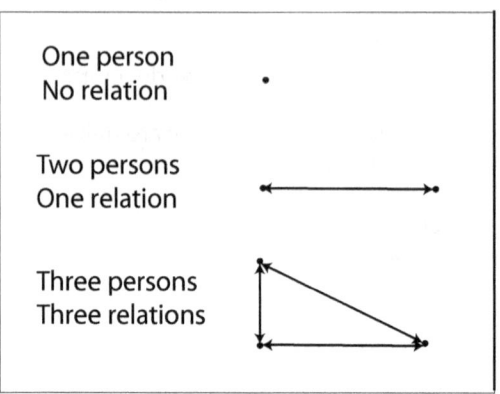

Figure 2

A team of three is a building block for building community for at least three reasons:

1. **A team of three—of me-you-we—creates the stability and security** that is necessary for community development. If the relationship between two breaks down the relationship they have with a third person can hold them together. See Figure 3.

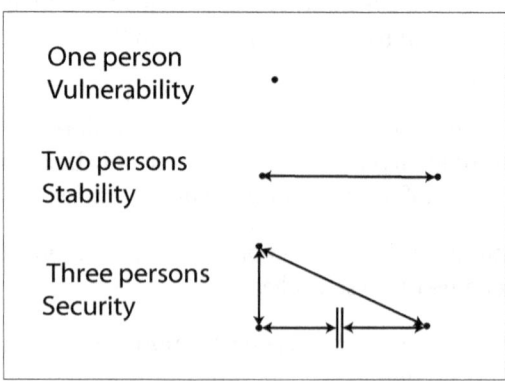

Figure 3

2. **A team of three—of me-you-we—creates the subjectivity and objectivity** that is necessary for community development. When a relationship breaks down between two people, an objective third party can help them sort out their conflict and solve their problems. See Figure 4.

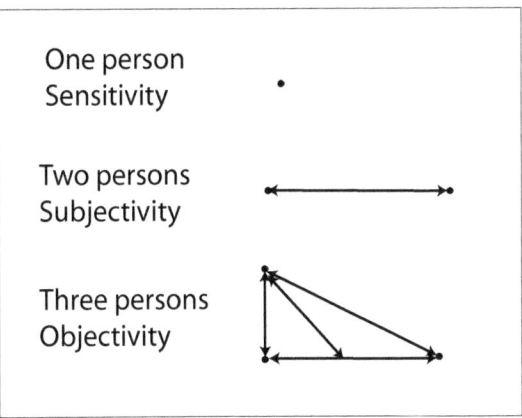

Figure 4

3. **A team of three—of me-you-we—creates the possibility for the opportunity** necessary for community development. An individual can raise the issue of community; a couple can talk about the significance of relationships for community; but it takes a network of at least three people to create the psycho-social space in their relationships for people to actually experience community. See Figure 5.

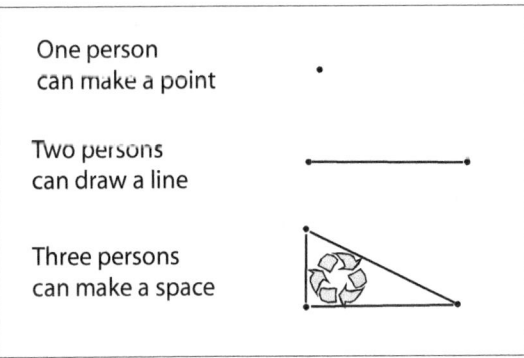

Figure 5

- Take a few minutes just to write down on a piece of paper, in your own words, three reasons why a team of three is a building block for building community.
- There are very important structural implications of this development strategy.

Three of the most common kinds of local development programs are:
- Individual development
- Institutional development
- Community development

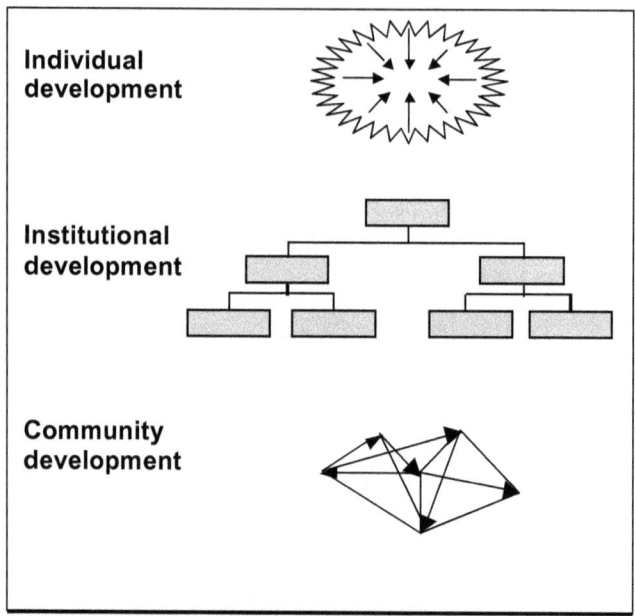

Figure 6

1. What are the similarities between these approaches?
2. What are the differences between these approaches?
3. Which of these approaches is a 'me-you-we' approach?
4. What is different about 'me-you-we' community development, and what difference, if any, does it make?

Consider, for example, developing a neighbourhood visiting program.

1. What would an individual visiting program look like?
2. What would an institutional visiting program look like?
3. What would a community development visiting program look like?

✎ Record your reflections in your Working Notes

Community development tactics
40 minutes
Consider a range of community development tactics used today.

Tactic One - Community relief
Precept - You help people yourself.
Proverb - 'You give them a fish!'

Tactic Two - Community education
Precept - You train people to help themselves.
Proverb - 'You teach them to fish themselves!'

Tactic Three - Community confrontation
Precept - You challenge groups who won't help.
Proverb - 'You give the powers-that-be a serve!'

Tactic Four - Community formation
Precept - You develop a way of helping one another.
Proverb - 'You develop a little fishing co-operative!'

Tactic Five - Community transformation
Precept - People adopt that way as their way of life.
Proverb - 'The fishing community becomes co-operative.'

1. Which tactic do you think is most important?
2. If you nominated one, what reasons do for you have for your choice ?

✎ Record your reflections in your Working Notes.

- Actually, no one tactic is more important than another! What is really important is not a particular tactic, but the appropriate use of that tactic.

Living Community: Session 3

- Which of these tactics do community groups tend to use *more*?
- Which of these tactics do community groups tend to use *less*?
- ☐ Rate the tactics 5, 4, 3, 2, 1, where 5 stands for the tactic you think community groups and organisations actually use *most*; and 1 stands for the tactic you think they use *least*.

✎ Record your reflections in your Working Notes.

Most people usually rate 'community relief' as 5, 'community education' as 4, 'community confrontation' as 3, 'community development' as 2, and 'community transformation' as 1. That is probably a reasonably accurate rating.

The questions we need to ask are:-

- Why do groups tend to use a community relief tactic most?
- Why do groups tend to use a community transformation tactic least?

✎ Record your reflections in your Working Notes.

There are a number of reasons that we can give, like time, effort, speed, ease, specificity, and so on. However, the most critical reason of all is **control**.

1. Why do we tend to use tactics that we can control more?
2. What is the strength of using tactics we can control more?
3. What is the weakness of using tactics we can control more?
4. Why is it so important to work for community transformation?
5. Which tactics can undermine community transformation? How?
6. Which tactics can undergird community transformation? How?

✎ Record your reflections in your Working Notes.

We need to learn what tactics are most appropriate in a given situation, and how to develop an integrated response that combines all the appropriate tactics needed to address the given situation systematically.

Pick an issue that your community is confronted with, and consider what tactics you could use to deal with it. All five strategies have their time and place. Therefore, you will need to think carefully about which of the processes is most appropriate for addressing the issue. It may be a number of options—indeed a combination of options—are needed to solve the problems.

Then take time to evaluate the strengths and weaknesses of your proposals.

✐ Record your reflections in your Working Notes.

Conclusion

10 minutes

The follow-up reading for this session is:

> The *Ottawa Charter for Health Promotion* (Reading 3).

The set community tasks for this session are:

- ❐ Attend a large gathering and a small group meeting in your community.
    - ❖ Which community principles do you practise most?
    - ❖ Which community principles do you need to practise more?
- ❐ Get together with your learning partner over a cuppa and discuss how you could practice a community development approach more in your community.
    - ❖ How could you incorporate the community development strategy into your community development work more systematically?
    - ❖ What community development tactics do you need to try?
- ✐ Record your actions, reflections, and conclusions in your Working Notes.

Session 4

Breaking through the Barrier of Fear

Objectives

- To review your understanding of the community development approach, some community development principles, community development strategies and tactics.
- To consider how you might overcome barriers that might block your progress towards community development—starting, as we all do, with fear.

Review

15 minutes

- ☐ Review your work from Session 3.
- ☐ Review the issues raised in course notes in the previous session, particularly your understanding of community development.
- ☐ Review the reading:
    The Ottawa Charter for Health Promotion (Reading 3).
- ☐ Review the tasks:
    - ❖ After attending a large gathering and a small group meeting in your community, which community principles do you think you practise most and which community principles of do you think you need to practise more?
    - ❖ What were the results of getting together with your learning partner and discussing how you could practice a community development approach more in your community?
    - ❖ What did you conclude as to how you could incorporate the community development strategy into your community development work more systematically; and what community development tactics do you need to try more consistently?

✎ Record your reflections in your Working Notes

The Fearless Ideal

15 minutes

☐ Read the story of 'The Bandit and The Saint' by Paulo Coelho.

Once, many years ago, a hermit—who later came to be known as St Savin—lived in one of the caves hereabouts. At the time, Viscos was little more than a frontier post populated by bandits fleeing from justice, by smugglers and prostitutes, by confidence tricksters in search of accomplices even by murderers resting between murders. The wickedest of them all, an Arab called Ahab, controlled the whole village and the surrounding area, imposing extortionate taxes on the local farmers who still insisted on maintaining a dignified way of life.

One day, Savin came down from his cave, arrived at Ahab's house and asked to spend the night there. Ahab laughed: 'You do know that I'm a murderer who has already slit a number of throats, and that your life is worth nothing to me?'

'Yes, I know that,' Savin replied, 'but I'm tired of living in a cave and I'd like to spend at least one night here with you.'

Ahab knew the saint's reputation, which was as great as his own, and this made him uneasy, for he did not like having to share his glory with someone so weak. Thus he determined to kill him that very night, to prove to everyone that he was the one true master of the place.

They chatted for a while. Ahab was impressed by what the saint had to say, but he was a suspicious man who no longer believed in the existence of Good. He showed Savin where he could sleep and continued menacingly sharpening his knife. After watching him for a few minutes, Savin closed his eyes and went to sleep.

Ahab spent all night sharpening his knife. Next day, when Savin awoke, he found Ahab in tears at his side.

'You weren't afraid of me. For the first time ever, someone spent a night by my side trusting that I could be a good man, one ready to offer hospitality to those in need. Because you believed I was capable of behaving decently, I did.'

From that moment on, Ahab abandoned his life of crime and set about transforming the region. Viscos ceased being merely a frontier post, inhabited by outcasts, and became an important trading centre on the border between two counties.

❖ From *The Devil And Miss Prym*

- What does this story say about the importance of fearlessness?
- How significant do you think it is that the story is actually a fantasy?

✍ Record your reflections in your Working Notes

The fearful reality

15 minutes

☐ Read the following reflections on fear.

Some time back, we spent a number of weeks talking to a group about becoming involved in their community. Discussions had gone well and the congregation had quickly identified a range of isolated people in their community that they could get involved with. However, when it came to putting their plan into operation, their enthusiasm suddenly evaporated.

'Why?' we asked them in astonishment. 'Because we are scared,' they replied. 'If we visit those people, chances are they will visit us. Then we'll never get rid of them. They'll just keep hanging around the house like a bad smell.' They wanted to get involved, but they were afraid.

Fear of the unknown. Fear of others. Fear of ourselves. Fear of success. Fear of failure. Fear of risking private space. Fear of losing personal security. Fear of fear itself. We are all full of fears. And each and every fear stands like a street corner bully ready to take us apart if we dare to cross the line and actually get involved in the community.[1]

- Does that reading ring any bells for you?
- In what situations are you most afraid?
- How could that fear affect your involvement in the community?

✍ Record your reflections in your Working Notes.

Facing our fear

30 minutes

We need to face our fears.[2] Many of our fears are fears of the unknown. They are based on ignorance or prejudice rather than reality. Simply coming to terms with the facts can dispel these fears. Usually, simply getting to know our neighbours can dispel our fear of getting involved with them.

A little while ago a friend wanted to get involved with a person in the community with a disability. But he was afraid of getting involved

---

1 Andrews, p 97
2 Adapted from *Not Religion But Love*, p 98-101

because he felt awkward around people with disabilities. He didn't know anybody with a disability and he didn't know how to relate to anybody with a disability. He was embarrassed to admit it, but he was actually quite scared. However, after we were able to introduce him to a neighbour with a disability and they were able to spend some time together, he discovered to his delight that his neighbour with a disability was pretty much like him. His fear, based on ignorance, totally disappeared in the light of his discovery of their common humanity.

Think of two or three examples of fears that you have had (or your friends have had) that were dispelled by coming to terms with the facts. Consider those examples for a while, exploring any connections between these fears you experienced in the past and any fears you anticipate you may have in the future.

We can deal with some of our fears pretty easily by knowing the facts. But we cannot deal with all of our fears are so easily. Some fears have no basis in reality but others do. Simply coming to terms with the facts can't dispel these fears—because the facts themselves are very frightening. The more you know about these situations, the more scared you are. These fears shouldn't necessarily stop us from getting involved—because there may be people who need our help—but these fears should slow us down and make us much more careful about the way we consider getting involved.

❐ Read the following story:

One night I was walking down the street and came across a man being attacked by a couple of hoods who were stabbing him with the jagged shards of a broken bottle. His face was already covered in blood and the hands he used to protect his face were already badly cut and bleeding. I thought, 'If someone doesn't do something soon, this chap could be cut to pieces'. I looked up and down the street. But no one else was around.

I knew it was up to me to do something myself but, I must confess, I was tempted to just to walk on by pretending I hadn't seen anything warranting my attention, let alone my intervention. I was afraid, terribly afraid, and my fear was well founded. It had a strong basis in fact. There were two men across the road trying to kill someone and if I tried to help him, chances were that I could be killed too. After all, there were two of them; and only one of me. They looked like street fighters and I looked like the wimp that I was. I had no weapon and wouldn't know how to use one even if I had one and they had shards of sharp glass that they wielded as wickedly as the grim reaper himself might have swung his scythe.

Fears such as these should not be dismissed because fears based on reality act as a basic reality test for our intentions. Believe it or not, on a number of occasions, when confronted with people who wanted to kill him, even Christ decided that it was better for him to run away and fight another day than to die for nothing at all. (Luke 4:29-30) And sometimes there are situations it might be better for us to run away from too—and the faster the better!

However, this was not one of those times. This time someone's life was at stake. Christ would not have run away on this occasion. And neither—really—could I. So I wrapped the tattered rags of my makeshift courage around me, and, with trembling hands, wobbly knees, and a heart ringing like an alarm bell, crossed the road to intervene in the fight. I didn't rush over and try to crash tackle the assailants. That only ever works in the movies and even then it doesn't work all the time.

I simply walked to within ten metres of the melee, stopped, and said from a safe distance the most inoffensive thing I could think of the time, which was, 'G'day.' The antagonists immediately turned in my direction. Now I had their attention I tried to distract them from further hurting their victim. But the trick was to do it without them harming me instead. So I said to them in as friendly a tone as I could muster, 'Can I help you?'

The aggressors looked at one another, then at me, and laughed. They thought it was a big bloody joke. 'Does it look like we need any help?' they asked facetiously. 'No.' I said very carefully. 'It doesn't look like you need any help. But, it looks like he might need some help. What d'you reckon?' By now they had stopped stabbing their prey, and, in answer to my question, they shrugged their shoulders, and said, 'Well you help him then!' And with that, they walked off and left me to care for the mutilated man on the side of the road. He was seriously injured but at least he was still alive. And so was I.

I've intervened in many violent situations in my life. Sometimes I've been beaten up so badly I've had to be hospitalised. One time I had to be rushed in for emergency surgery. But that was when I was younger and intervened more aggressively and unconsciously escalated the spiral of violence in the situation. Now I'm older, I'm a little wiser.

These days I am very wary about intervening. And when I do, I am very careful to do it as peacefully as I possibly can. My fear doesn't usually stop me but it does usually slow me down. This is exactly what fear ought to do. Not stop us. But slow us down. And make us more careful about the way we go about the task of getting involved with people.

Have you heard any stories, read any reports, or seen any incidents yourselves of where people have been able to intervene *successfully* in a fearful situation?

If you can think of your own such story, then use that for reflection. If not, use the story above as the basis for your consideration of the following questions.

1. What was the cause of fear in the situation?
2. What was the effect of fear in the situation?
3. How did the people in the situation deal with their fear?
4. How did the people deal with the situation in spite of their fear?
5. What are the lessons you can learn this story?

✍ Record your reflections in your Working Notes.

Confronting our critic

35 minutes

We may have great discussions about 'facing our fears' and we may make a sincere commitment to act with greater courage in the future but sooner or later most of us hear a little voice inside telling us we will never ever really act with the poise and the competence we need to deal with the situations we will inevitably be confronted with.

If we are to get involved with the poise and the competence we need, we have to confront not only our *external circumstances* but also our *internal critics*.[1]

Take a piece of paper and draw a picture of your internal critic—the internalised self-critic whose criticism you fear most. Make the image of your internal critic as clear as you can. Take a little time to characterise it, exaggerate it, caricature it, the best that you can. It may look like a demon, a priest, or a cop, your mum, or your dad, or your partner—or yourself! Whatever it is, once you have thought of it, put the image right in the middle of your piece of paper, leaving lots of space round the edges. In the space around the edges, put in half-a-dozen cartoon speech bubbles coming from the mouth of the internal critic, saying some of the really scary things that your internal critic often says to you.

Like 'You're useless!'

'You'll never get it together!'

'When it comes to the crunch, you're just a scaredy cat!'

'You'll never do any good! (Scaredy cat! scaredy cat!)'

Once you have completed your picture of their internal critic, just spend a little time looking at it. Then say the words out loud your internal critic usually says to you. Repeat what your internal critic says to you out loud—with feeling! As you listen to what your internal critic says to you, reflect on how the words affect you. Pause for a moment.

---

1 Adapted from K. Shields, *In the Tiger's Mouth*, p 19-20

Think about what you'd like to say to your internal critic in defence of yourself. Say what you would like to say in defence of yourself out loud. Then repeat what you would like to say out loud, as honestly and as authentically as you can.

As you listen to what you say to your internal critic, reflect on how your words make you feel. Respond loudly and clearly, to all the criticisms that your internal critic makes.

Note that your internal critics seldom speak 'the truth, the whole truth and nothing but the truth'. The things they say are half-truths or total lies. So by speaking out the truth about yourself as you really are, you can free yourself from the tyranny of these half-truths and total lies.

> 'I am *not* "useless"!'
>
> 'I may have a long way to go, but it's *not* true to say I'll "never get it together".'
>
> 'When it 'comes to the crunch', everyone is a 'scaredy cat'. But a scaredy cat is only a part of who I am—it's the truth, but not the whole truth. Even the biggest 'scaredy cat' has the courage of a wild tiger somewhere deep inside them.'
>
> 'To say I can 'never do any good' is a lie. The truth is that 'I can do a lot of good things. In fact I can think of a lot of helpful things that I have done in the last few days, such as....'

After you have had spoken out against your internal critic, take a little time to reflect on the words that you have spoken.

Write down a couple of phrases you spoke out which encapsulate the core truth at the heart of the responses you made. Write down these phrases in your Working Notes and make them your motto.

Read the following reflection on risk:

Only one who risks is free! [1]

To laugh is to risk appearing the fool.
To weep is to risk appearing sentimental.
To reach out is to risk involvement.
To disclose feelings is to risk disclosing your true self.
To place your dreams before the crowd is to risk their love.
To live is to risk dying.
To hope is to risk despair.
To try is to risk failure.
But the greatest hazard in life is to risk nothing.
The one who risks nothing does nothing and has nothing—and

---

1 A. & W. Howard, *Exploring the Road Less Travelled*, p 80

finally is nothing.
He (or she) may avoid sufferings and sorrow,
but simply cannot learn, feel, change, grow or love.

Conclusion

10 minutes

The follow-up reading for this session is

> 'Prison—The Community's Business', Arlene Morgan, *People Working Together II,* p30-47 (Reading 4)

The set community tasks for this session are

- ☐ Collect as many stories as you can of local incidents where local people have acted courageously and creatively in fearful situations.
- ☐ Meet with your learning partner and at least one other person from the community that you would like to get (more) involved with.
- ☐ Review what you said about what you were going to do in terms of community involvement. Try to identify which parts of what you were *really* going to do you are *actually* most scared about.
- ☐ Share what you learnt in this session about 'facing our fears' and 'confronting our critics', and talk about how you can 'face your fears', 'confront your critics' and discuss how you can still do what you are scared of doing.
- ☐ Then share the stories you collected of local incidents where local people have acted courageously and creatively in fearful situations. And consider how you can live out these storylines in your own life.
- ✎ Record your actions, reflections and conclusions in your Working Notes.

Session 5

Breaking through the Barrier of Futility

Objectives

- To review your understanding of dealing with fear
- To consider how you might overcome a sense of futility.

Review

15 minutes

☐ Review your work from Session 4.
☐ Review the issues raised in course notes in the previous session, particularly how to deal with fear.
☐ Review the reading:
> 'Prison—The Community's Business', Arlene Morgan, *People Working Together II*, p30-47 (Reading 4)

☐ Review the tasks:
  ❖ What was the most important thing you learned while doing the community tasks for last session?
  ❖ You were asked to talk about some of the stories you collected of local incidents. What did you learn from these stories yourself?

☐ Finish with a reflection on how you can do something you know you need to do, that you are scared of doing.

✎ Record your reflections in your Working Notes.

Any anxieties?[1]

5 minutes

- ☐ Articulate any anxieties that have been raised by the course so far. Has anything been said or done that may have left you feeling just a little bit uncomfortable?
- ✎ Record your reflections in your Working Notes.

We are all anxious now and again, especially when we are trying to do something we have never done before, or we are trying to do something we have done before in a way that we have never done it before.

'My biggest anxiety is ... because ...'[2]

15 minutes

- ☐ Brainstorm about 'the anxieties that stop me from having a go at the community work I'd like to do—or at least stop me from having a go as wholeheartedly as I would like'.
- ☐ Draw a picture of a large brick wall on a piece of paper with at least twenty bricks in the wall. Write each anxiety on the paper as the name of a brick in the wall.
- ☐ After you have are named as many bricks in the wall as you can, sit back and look at the bricks in the wall in front of you. Then take up a pen and circle the 'the biggest barrier', and name it by saying out loud 'my biggest anxiety is ... because ...'.

Over the next few weeks, we will try to help you find a way through the wall—or over it, or around it: starting now.

Set up two chairs facing each other. Imagine it is an interview situation, and you are interviewing yourself. Sit in one, facing the other, and ask the following questions, one by one. After you ask a question, go and sit in the hot seat, and answer the question the best you can. Repeat this process with all the questions.

1. Why do you think you have this anxiety?
2. How have you overcome it in the past?
3. What would be the best way to overcome it in future?
4. What help will you need in order to overcome it?
5. Where could you get the help you need?

---

1 Adapted from D. Andrews et al *Building Better Communities*
2 ibid.

Living Community: Session 5

- ✎ After you have finished the "interview" with yourself, don't forget to record details of the conversation in your Working Notes.
- ❏ Then consider the following comments: [1]

Mahatma Gandhi says: *'Almost anything you do will seem insignificant, but it is very important that you do it anyway.'* We must not be put off by the scoffers who say it is impossible. As Lois Brandeus says, *'Most of the things worth doing in the world had been declared impossible before they were done.'* It doesn't matter how small a group we are, nor how big the opposition is. As Margaret Mead says, *'A small group of thoughtful, committed citizens can change the world. Indeed, it's the only thing that ever has!'*

- ✎ Record your reflections on these comments in your *Working Notes*.

Circles of influence and circles of concern

20 minutes

It may be helpful for you to consider Stephen Covey's concept of circles of influence and circles of concern. [2]

- ❏ Draw a large circle on a piece of paper, and call it *'your circle of concern'* (Figure 7).

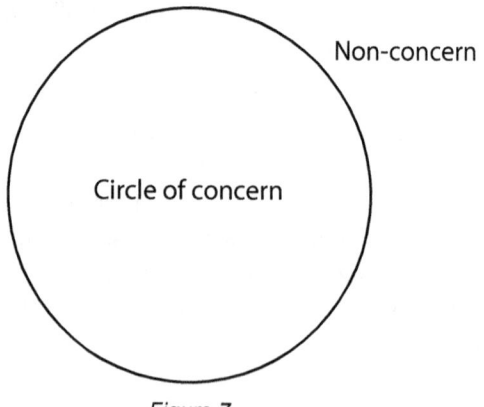

Figure 7

- What are all the things that you would include in your circle of concern? All the things you would like to see changed in your world?

---

1 Adapted from K. Shields, *In the Tiger's Mouth*
2 Adapted from S. Covey, *The Seven Habits of Highly Effective People*

- ☐ Write those things in the big circle – leaving a small space in the middle.
- ☐ Draw a small circle in that small space in the middle, Call it your *'circle of influence'* (Figure 8).

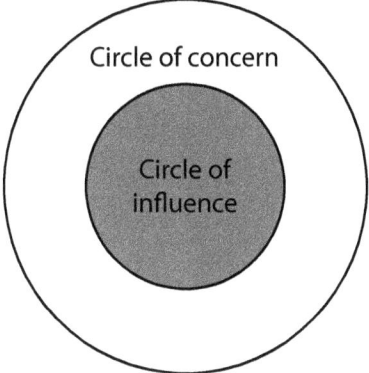

Figure 8

- What are the things you think that you could actually change in the world, that you could include in your circle of influence?

- ☐ ☐Write those things in the small circle.

- What would happen if you concentrated on your circle of concern rather than your circle of influence, and focused on the enormous difference between their size?

That's right: in all likelihood you would probably disempower yourself!

- When was the last time that you did that?
- How did you feel about that?

Hold the feelings. But let's still move on.

- What would happen if you concentrated on your circle of influence rather than your circle of concern, and focused on slowly but surely increasing the size of your circle of influence?

That's right: chances are that you would actually empower yourself!

So the challenge for us is to be *conscious* of our circle of concern, but to *concentrate* on our circle of influence (Figure 9).

Living Community: Session 5

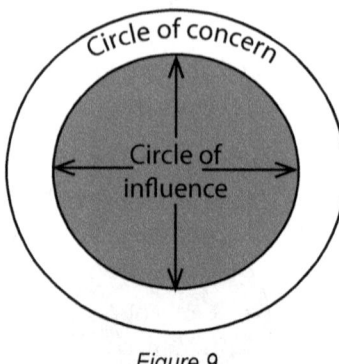

Figure 9

✍ Record your reflections in your Working Notes.

It's a matter of choice [1]

15 minutes

☐ Read the following story of *The Saint in All of Us* by Paulo Coelho:

'Someone must have told you about the meeting between St Savin and Ahab.'

'Of course. The saint came, spent the night, talked to him, and, from that moment on, Ahab abandoned his life of crime and set about transforming the region.'

'That's right. Except that, before going to sleep, the two of them talked together for a while.

'Even though Ahab had begun to sharpen his knife the moment the saint set foot in his house, safe in the knowledge that the world was a reflection of himself, he was determined to challenge the saint and so he asked him:

"If, tonight, the most beautiful prostitute in the village came in here, would you be able to see her as neither beautiful nor seductive?"

"No, but I would be able to control myself," the saint replied.

"And if I offered you a pile of gold coins to leave your cave in the mountain and come and join us, would you be able to look on that gold and see only pebbles?"

"No, but I would be able to control myself."

"And if you were sought by two brothers, one of who hated you, and the other who saw you as a saint, would you be able to feel the same towards them both?"

---

1 Adapted from K. Shields, *In The Tiger's Mouth*, p19-20

> "It would be very hard, but I would be able to control myself sufficiently to treat them both the same."
>
> 'When Ahab realised that Savin was the same as him, he realised too that he was the same as Savin. It was a matter of control. And choice. Nothing more or less.'

- From *The Devil And Miss Prym*

- How do you react to this story?
- In what way are you like Ahab?
- In what way are you like Savin?
- What do you think it means when it says 'when Ahab realised that Savin was the same as him, he realised too that he was the same as Savin'?

✐ Record your reflections in your Working Notes.

The choice is ours [1]

20 minutes

Those of us who feel tempted to think that this talk about choice is a fantasy, not a reality, need to think again in the light of Viktor Frankl's own personal story.

> Frankl was a determinist raised in the tradition of Freudian psychology which postulates that whatever happens to you as a child shapes your personality and basically governs your whole life. The limits ... of your life are set, and basically you can't do much about it.
>
> Frankl was also ... a Jew. He was imprisoned in the death camps of Nazi Germany where he experienced things that were so repugnant to our sense of decency that we shudder to even repeat them. His parents, his brother, and his wife died in the camps or were sent to the gas ovens. Except for his sister, his entire family perished.
>
> Frankl himself suffered torture and innumerable indignities, never knowing from one moment to the next if his path, would lead to the ovens, or if he would be among the 'saved' who would ... shovel out the ashes of those so fated.
>
> One day, naked and alone in a small room, he began to become aware of what he later called 'the last of the human freedoms'—the freedom his Nazi captors could not take away. They could control his entire environment, they could do what they wanted to his body, but Victor Frankl himself was a self-aware being who could look as

---

1 K. Shields, op. cit.

an observer at his very involvement. His basic identity was intact. *He could decide within himself how all of this was going to affect him.* Between what happened to him, or the stimulus, and his response to it, was his freedom, or power to choose his response.

In the midst of his experiences, Frankl would project himself into different circumstances, such as lecturing to his students after his release from the death camps. He would describe himself in the classroom, in his mind's eye, and give his students the lessons he was learning during his very torture.

Through a series of such disciplines—mental, emotional, and moral, principally by using memory and imagination—he exercised his small, embryonic freedom until it grew larger and larger, until he had more freedom than his Nazi captors. They had more *liberty*, more options to choose from in their environment; but he had more *freedom*, more internal power to exercise his options.

He became an inspiration to those around him, even to some of the guards. He helped others find meaning in their suffering and dignity in their prison existence.

In the midst of the most degrading circumstances imaginable, Frankl used the human endowment of self-awareness to discover a fundamental principle about (humanity): *between stimulus and response, (we) have the freedom to choose.* [1]

We all have the ability to choose. We can either be "reactive" or "proactive".

Reactive people are often affected by their physical environment. If the weather is good, they feel good. If it isn't, it affects their performance.

Proactive people can carry their own weather with them. Whether it rains or shines makes no difference to them. They are value driven; and if their value is to produce good quality work, it isn't a function of whether the weather is conducive to it or not.

Reactive people are also affected by their social environment, by the 'social weather'. When people treat them well, they feel well; when people don't, they [don't function well]. Reactive people build their ... lives around the behaviour of others, empowering ... other people to control them. [2]

Proactive people feel the affects of their social environment, take the 'social weather' into account, and decide how they are going to deal with the conditions. Whether people treat them well or not, they do the best they can. Proactive people build their lives around their own behaviour, developing their power over themselves, so as to exercise increasing control over their responses.

---

1 Covey, pp 69-70
2 Covey, pp 69-70

It is only as people become less reactive, and more proactive, they can actually become more responsible. As Covey says, 'Look at the word responsibility—*"response-ability"*—the ability to choose your response. Highly proactive people recognise that responsibility. They do not blame circumstances, conditions, or conditioning for their behaviour. Their behaviour is a product of their own conscious choice, based on values, rather than a product of their conditions, based on (un-thought-through) feelings.' [1]

As people become less reactive, and more proactive, they not only can become more responsible for being who they are, but also can become more responsible for being who they are meant to be. As Covey says, 'I admit this is very hard to accept, especially if we have had years and years of explaining our misery in the name of circumstance ... But until a person can say deeply and honestly, "I am what I am today because of the choices I made yesterday," that person cannot say, "I choose otherwise".' [2]

1. Where does Frankl locate his freedom of choice?
2. What difference did this freedom of choice make?
3. How do reactive people dismiss freedom of choice?
4. Why do proactive people embrace freedom of choice?
5. What would it mean for you to be more 'response-able'?
6. How you could develop a greater degree of control in your life?

✍ Record your reflections in your Working Notes

Empowerment exercise [3]

20 minutes

- ☐ Read the instructions for the whole of this exercise before starting it, then work your way through it as wholeheartedly as you can.
- ☐ Get into a relaxed position. Close your eyes and bring to your mind a time when you were able to say something or do something that made a positive difference to a situation in which you found yourself.

---

1 Covey, p 71
2 Covey, p 72
3 Adapted from K. Shields *In The Tiger's Mouth*

❐ Remember that time. Reconnect with the scene. Play it over and over again in slow motion. Recall the thoughts and the feelings you had at the time. Then ask yourself:

1. What did it feel like, to not feel so powerless?
2. What made you feel so powerful in the situation?
3. How do you feel about those feelings now?

❐ Hold the feelings. And let's turn them into a heartfelt prayer – or wish.

❐ Spend a few moments remembering what it felt like to say something or do something that made a positive difference to a situation in which you found yourself. Pray that you may be able to say something or do something that makes a positive difference more often.
If you believe in a higher power, ask God to help you focus on what you can say or do, rather than what you can't! If you don't believe in a higher power, express your request as a resolution.

✎ Don't forget to record all these reflections in your Working Notes.

Conclusion

10 minutes

The follow-up reading for this session is

> 'A Potent Mixture of Faith, Humour, and Courage', Anthony Kelly, Arlene Morgan and Dierdre Coghlan, *People Working Together III*, pp 129-143.(Reading 5)

The set community tasks for this session are

❐ Meet with your learning partner and at least one other person, from the community you would like to get (more) involved with, who would like to get involved with you.

❐ During this meeting draw a map of 'The Potential within our Group'. Take a large piece of paper and divide it into four. In one quadrant write at the top 'Experiences', in another 'Qualities', in another 'Skills' and in another

'Resources'. Then spend some time filling in the map together.[1]

- ❖ Under 'Experience' put in any experience that you have that could contribute to your community work. (Like living with a family, working as a volunteer etc)
- ❖ Under 'Qualities' put in any qualities that you have that could contribute to your community work. (Like easy going, hard working, etc)
- ❖ Under 'Skills' put in any skills that you have that could contribute to your community work. (Like listening, talking etc)
- ❖ Under 'Resources' put in any resources that you have that could contribute to your community work. (Like a car, a phone etc)
- ❖ Circle the things you'd love to do. Then ask yourselves the question – what does this say about what we as a group have to offer to our community?

✎ Record your actions, reflections and conclusions in your Working Notes.

---

[1] Adapted from K. Shields *In The Tiger's Mouth*

Session 6

Breaking through the Barrier of Selfishness

Objectives

- To review your understanding of dealing with futility
- To consider how you might overcome a sense of selfishness

Review

15 minutes

> ☐ Review your work from Session 5.
> ☐ Review the issues raised in course notes in the previous session, particularly how to deal with futility.
> ☐ Review the reading:
>
> > 'A Potent Mixture of Faith, Humour, and Courage' Anthony Kelly, Arlene Morgan and Dierdre Coghlan, *People Working Together III* pp 129-143.
>
> ☐ Review the tasks:
> > ❖ How was your meeting with your community development support group?
> > ❖ What was the most important thing you learned while doing your community tasks for the last session?

✍ Record your reflections in your *Working Notes*

Values inventory

15 minutes

☐ Read carefully through the following values inventory:
  ❖ Adventure - an exciting life
  ❖ Involvement - a useful life
  ❖ Security - a sheltered life

- ❖ Love - a sacrificial life
- ❖ Prosperity - a comfortable life
- ❖ Pleasure - an enjoyable life
- ❖ Creativity - a productive life
- ❖ Fame - a celebrated life
- ❖ Service - a helpful life
- ❖ Family - a connected life
- ❖ Friends - a sociable life
- ❖ Freedom - an unfettered life
- ❖ Any other

Select your top five life values, and rank them in order of importance to you.

After you have completed selecting and ranking your life values, write your answer to the following three questions in your Working Notes.

1. What three things do you feel you value most in life?
2. Why do you think you value those things most?
3. What evidence do you have that you really value these things so much?

- We'll come back to this a little later on.

The state of play

20 minutes

Consider the significance of *self-interest* and *self-centredness*.

Self-interest is not bad. Self-interest is good, so good that all sages call us 'to love others *as* we love ourselves'. What is bad is not self-interest but self-centredness—our proclivity to 'love ourselves at the expense of others'.

Our culture celebrates selfishness. 'You've got to look after self', we say. 'If you don't look after yourself no one else will!' Our philosophy can be summed up best in the popular slogans doing the rounds of the cocktail party circuit. 'Greed Is Good!' 'If you want it, get it!' 'Buy now, pay later!'

Our political economy is a capitalist economy based on capital as the means of production, and consumption of good and services. Money is the currency required to purchase these goods and services and the market is the mechanism for distributing the goods and services that are purchased.

Those with much money get lots of goods and services. Those with a little money get little goods and services. Those with no money get nothing. We say we believe in charity but we believe 'charity begins at home'. That being so, charity seldom extends much further than our own families.

The older generation—born in the 1920s and 1930s, and brought up with a great sense of responsibility for others apart from themselves through the hardship of depression and war—is declining, and, as that great civic generation is in a decline, so is civic society. [1]

The new generation is a consumer generation, which is much less concerned with non-materialistic values, and is much more preoccupied with materialistic values.

Non-materialistic values include an orientation towards personal acceptance and development, social relationships and responsibilities, and communal connections and contributions. [2] Materialistic values include an orientation towards body image and appearance, private property and finance, public recognition and success. [3]

According to a new study, the little Aussie battler is nothing but a middle-class whinger. Australians have never been richer, it says, yet the majority of middle-income households believe they are doing it tough. At a time of unprecedented abundance, most Australians think they cannot afford to buy everything they need. And most say they spend their entire income on the basic necessities of life.

But the author of the report, Clive Hamilton, director of the Australia Institute, says the problem is not inadequate income, but inflated expectations. 'A large and growing proportion of the population wants to emulate the lifestyles of the rich and famous,' he says. 'Because they can't afford it they constantly feel deprived of the good life.'

A Newspoll survey conducted in September for the study reveals that 62% of Australian households believe they 'cannot afford to buy everything they really need'. Almost half the richest households—with incomes over $70,000—agree. Dr Hamilton said that as incomes rose, perceived needs changed: wealthier people cited items they would like to buy but could not immediately afford, such as a new car, while poorer people thought of a plumber to fix a tap. 'The proportion of the "suffering

---

1 Putnam, p 250, 254, 265
2 Kasser, p 99
3 Kasser, p 12, 15

rich" is even higher than in the USA, a country widely regarded as obsessed with money,' he said.

Australian families enjoyed a real income three times higher than in the 1950s and by any standards the vast majority were comfortably off. However, influenced by television lifestyle programs and the conspicuous consumption of the rich, ordinary Australians aspired to a standard of living well beyond their means. Increasing numbers were in the grip of 'luxury fever'.

In the early 1980s, for example, Australians built barbecues from 150 bricks and a hotplate, the study said. Now super barbecues or 'outdoor kitchens' were on the market for almost $5000. While few bought the top range, their existence served to drive up the level of desire. 'After looking at the Turbo Cosmopolitan ... buyers are more likely to buy the Cordon Bleu for $1299 ... instead of paying $200-$300 for a standard gas model,' Dr Hamilton said.

Homes had become larger though families had become smaller; the amount of space for each occupant in a new house had more than doubled since the 1970s. The extra space was being filled with expensive furnishings, appliances, carpet and curtains. Stoves with turbo grills and six cooking functions adorned new kitchens, along with $2000 refrigerators.

To accommodate all this excess, the self-storage industry has burgeoned. Dr Hamilton says the mortgage stress many Australians feel is the result of borrowing more money than they can comfortably afford to repay. 'In an earlier era, when wealthy people made decisions to live beyond their means, their financial difficulties attracted little public sympathy ... Now they have become a matter of public concern.'

The study, called *Overconsumption in Australia: The rise of the middle-class battler*, says only 5 to 10% of Australians could be considered poor. But politicians ignored their plight in the rush to pander to the imagined hardship of the middle class. Indeed, politicians perpetuated the myth of the Aussie battlers in order to claim to understand their pain and to offer them tax cuts.

Dr Hamilton said over-consumption had serious consequences. Credit card debt had increased fourfold and personal bankruptcies had soared. As well, Australians were working longer hours to finance their purchases, in the process losing the balance between work and family life.

Yet Australians, when asked to reflect on their lives, were uneasy. In response to another Newspoll question, 83% said our society was too materialistic, placing too much emphasis on money and not enough on the things that really mattered. The proportion in agreement with the statement was remarkably consistent across income brackets with the exception of the richest households, where only 69% agreed. 'Most people seem unable to change course,' Dr Hamilton said.

As Tim Kasser shows in *The High Price of Materialism*, more people today are more materialistic, and materialistic people

- are more narcissistic, obsessive, and paranoid [1]
- are more passive-aggressive and over-controlling [2]
- are more unlikely to be self-actualised and satisfied [3]
- are more likely to use/misuse/abuse substances [4]
- are more likely to be abusive (insulting, swearing) [5]
- are more likely to be aggressive (pushing, shoving) [6]
- do not invest in marriages, families and communities [7]
- make hostile choices causing tragedy to the commons [8]
- their relationships are shorter, less positive, more negative [9]
- and more likely to produce a sense of alienation [10]

1. What do you make of the distinction between self-interest and self-centredness?
2. How do you react to Hamilton's analysis of Australian society?
3. How much of Kasser's analysis do you agree with?

✍ Record your reflections in your Working Notes.

The price of salt

10 minutes

☐ Read the following story of 'The Price Of Salt' by Paulo Coelho:

---

1 Kasser, p 17
2 Kasser p 20
3 Kasser p 12
4 Kasser p 62
5 Kasser, p 63
6 Kasser, p 88-90
7 Kasser, p 93
8 Kasser, p 62
9 Kasser, p 63
10 Kasser, p 62

Ahab invited his friends to supper and cooked a succulent piece of meat for them.

Suddenly he realised there was no salt. So Ahab called to his son: 'Go to the village and buy some salt but pay a fair price for it: neither too much nor too little.'

His son was surprised: 'I can understand why I shouldn't pay too much for it, father, but if I can bargain them down why not pay a bit less?'

'That might be the sensible thing to do in a big city, but in a small village like ours it could spell the beginning of the end.' The boy left without asking any further questions.

However, Ahab's guests, who had overheard their conversation wanted to know why they should not buy the salt more cheaply if they could. Ahab replied, 'The only reason anyone would sell salt more cheaply than usual would be because he was desperate for money. And anyone who took advantage of that situation would be showing a lack of respect for the sweat and struggle of the man who laboured to produce it.'

'But such a small thing couldn't possibly destroy a village.'

'In the beginning, there was only a small amount of injustice abroad in the world, but everyone who came afterwards added their portion, always thinking it was very small and unimportant, and look where we have ended up today.'

- From *The Devil and Miss Prym*

- What would you say is the main point of Paulo Coelho's story?
- What evidence is there that 'such small things' destroy community?

✎ Record your reflections in your Working Notes.

Values inventory revisited

15 minutes

☐ Take out your Values Inventory, and in the light of your reflections about self-interest and self-centredness, consider what you have written. [1]

☐ Look again at the answers you wrote in your Working Notes.

---

1 Adapted from J. Staley, *People in Development*, p124

1. What three things do I feel I value most in life?
2. Why do I think I value those three things most?
3. What evidence do I have that I really value these things so much?

☐ Set up two chairs facing each other. Imagine it is an interview situation, and you are interviewing yourself. Sit in one, facing the other, and ask the following questions, one by one. After you ask a question, go and sit in the hot seat, and answer the question the best you can. Repeat this process with all the questions.

- Is what you say you value what you really value—or not?
- Is what you really value self-interest or self-centredness?

✎ After you have finished the interview with yourself, don't forget to record details of the conversation in your Working Notes.

Note that two ways we can test whether our choices are self-interested or self-centred is to ask ourselves the questions:

- Are our choices *with* others or by ourselves?
- Are our choices *for* others or for ourselves?

✎ Record your reflections in your Working Notes.

Leading double lives

15 minutes

We need to deal with the fact that many of us lead **double lives**.[1]

We say 'we love others as we love ourselves'. However, we often actually do not love others as we love ourselves.

Let's consider the dilemmas that are associated with leading double lives—the conflict between what we say we believe in, and how we really live our lives. Focus on times when you are most aware of the conflict of leading a double life.

---

1 Adapted from K. Shields, *In The Tiger's Mouth*

> ☐ Set up two chairs facing each other, as in the 'Values Inventory Revisited' above. Run the interview situation in the same way, with the following questions:
>
> 1. When is the conflict between what you say and what you do most intense?
> 2. What are the core issues involved for you in 'leading a double life'? (a desire for approval? A reluctance to deal with an underlying issue? An addiction? Or something else?)
> 3. How do you feel about these dilemmas?
> 4. What would you like to do about them?

✍ After you have finished the 'interview with yourself', don't forget to record details of the conversation in your Working Notes.

Being our true selves

20 minutes

Stephen Covey says,

- The key to the ability to change is a changeless sense of who [we] are, what [we] value and what [we] are [on] about ... [1]

Parker Palmer says,
- We are not called to 'live according to an ideal'; not asked to 'become an abstract ideal of ourselves', but to 'be our true selves'.
- We should not listen to the call to 'live life like our heroes'. We need to listen to the call to be who we are 'in here, not someone 'out there'.
- Our vocation comes from learning to 'listen to the sound of our own heartbeat'. It is the place where 'our own true self engages the world around us'. [2]

Paulo Coelho says,
- In order to discover our vocation we need to 'listen to the same voices [we] heard as a child—even if adults call it foolishness.'

---

[1] S. Covey, p.108
[2] *Let Your Life Speak*, Jossey-Bass, San Francisco, 2000, p 4,10,11

- Every[one] has a right to doubt [their vocation], and to forsake it from time to time, but what he [or she] must not do is - forget it! [1]

Carl Jung says that, while our call may come to us in our own words, our 'vocation acts like a law of God. It makes demands upon us'. It demands us to be at our best as human beings—'to liberate, to redeem, to transform.' [2]

Ange Andrews has translated her sense of vocation into a set of vows.

- The first vow Ange has taken is a vow of *solidarity*.

This has involved choosing to be open rather than closed to the suffering of those around us. It has meant choosing to see the tears, hear the cries, and open ourselves up to, rather than closing ourselves off from, the agony of our neighbours.

- The second vow Ange has taken is a vow of *simplicity*.

This has involved living, in spite of our comparative wealth, as close as she can to the poverty line. It has meant not only that she has experienced something of the struggle of the poor, but also that she has been able to share her extra time and money with the poor themselves.

- The third vow Ange has taken is a vow of *service*.

This has involved living a life of quiet help and loud protest, with many of the marginalised groups, both rich and poor, that find themselves on the periphery of her locality. It has meant not setting any agendas, but just being available to do anything she can to support them in their struggle for greater opportunity in our society.

Ange is not alone in making these kinds of commitments. 783,000 other Queenslanders volunteer in their communities, while 4.4 million Australians over the age of 18 volunteer each year. [3]

But if we are going to address *all* the issues in our communities, than *all* of us need to be involved.

- What is the difference between being human and being humane?
- What does it mean for you to be your true self as a 'human/e' being?

---

1 *The Fifth Mountain*, Harper Collins, Sydney, 1998, p 23, 53
2 C. Jung, pp 167-187
3 Kasser, p 63

- How can 'true' interest in ourselves be the basis of concern for others? What would you say is your calling as a 'true human/humane' being?
- How would you translate your own vocation into a set of vows?

✎ Record your reflections in your Working Notes.

Conclusion

10 minutes

The follow-up reading for this session is

> 'An Honest Cop' *No Longer Down Under,* Mike Brown, Grosvenor Books, Melbourne 2002 Pages 147-162. (Reading 6)

The set community tasks for this session are

- ☐ Meet with your learning partner and your community development support group.
- ☐ Share what you learnt in the session about 'leading a double life' and about the need to be your 'true self' as a human/humane being.
- ☐ Review your map of the potential within your group that you created in the last session and what this map said about what you had to offer to your community. Then talk about what you are really going to do about it.
- ☐ Review each of the headings of Experience, Qualities, Skills, and Resources. Decide on realistic amounts of each, that you can contribute. Make sure you also review the time you could contribute regularly to your community work.
- ☐ Ask yourselves the question: What are you really going to do? Sit with the question for some time, then as specific ideas come to mind tick off the contributions you *really* want to make. (If you use a red pen, it would help these ideas stand out strongly.)

✎ Record your actions, reflections and conclusions in your Working Notes.

Session 7

Breaking through the Barrier of Spitefulness

Objectives

- To review your understanding of dealing with selfishness
- To consider how you might overcome a sense of spitefulness

Review

15 minutes

- ☐ Review your work from Session 6.
- ☐ Review the issues raised in course notes in the previous session, particularly how to deal with selfishness.
- ☐ Review the reading:

    'An Honest Cop' *No Longer Down Under,* Mike Brown, Grosvenor Books, Melbourne 2002 Pages 147-162. (Reading 6)

- ☐ Review the tasks:
    - How was your meeting with your community development support group?
    - What was the most important thing you learned while doing your community tasks for the last session?

✎ Record your reflections in your Working Notes

'Treat others as you would be treated yourself'[1]

10 minutes

Consider the principle of treating others as you would like to be treated yourself.

---

[1] Adapted from *In-Situ Community Education*, pp 12-13

People of all religions, all over the world, know that there are no short cuts; that there are no quick fixes; and that we cannot hope to develop community unless we 'do to others as we would have them do to us'.

	Hinduism	Buddhism
The Golden Rule	Never do to others what would pain you *Panchatantra 3.104*	Hurt not others with that which hurts yourself *Udana 5.18*
Zoroastrianism Do not to others what is not well for oneself. *Shayast-na-shayast 13.29*	*Jainism* One who neglects existence disregards their own existence *Mahavira*	*Confucianism* Do not impose on others what you do not yourself desire *Analects 12.2*
Taoism Regard your neighbour's loss or gain as your own loss or gain *Tai Shang Kan Ying Pien*	*Baha'i* Desire not for anyone the things you would not desire for yourself *Baha'Ullah 66*	*Judaism* What is hateful to you, do not do to your neighbour *Talmud, Shabbat, 31a*
Christianity Do unto others as you would have them do unto you *Matthew 7.12*	*Islam* Do unto all people as you would they should do to you *Mishkat-el-Masabih*	*Sikhism* Treat others as you would be treated yourself *Adi Granth*

In Taoism the call is *descriptive*. 'Regard your neighbour's loss or gain as our own loss or gain.' In Jainism the call is *instructive*. 'One who neglects existence disregards their own existence'.

In Hinduism, Buddhism, Zoroastrianism, Confucianism, Judaism and Baha'i the call is *imperative* and it is framed *in negative terms*. 'Never do to others what would pain you.' 'Hurt not others with that which hurts yourself.' 'What is hateful to you do not do to your neighbour.' 'Do not impose on others what you do not yourself desire'. 'Desire not for anyone the things you would not desire for yourself.'

While in Christianity, Islam and Sikhism the call is *imperative* and it is framed in *positive terms*. 'Do unto others as you would have them do unto you'. 'Do unto all people as you would they should do to you'. 'Treat others as you would be treated yourself.'

> - What version of the saying can you relate to best?
> - How do you interpret this saying?
> - Why is it important?

✍ Record your reflections in your Working Notes.

'Not as you are treated—but as you would be treated'

10 minutes

Consider the significance of treating others as you would like to be treated, not as you have been treated, or may be treated.

Now, treating others as we would like to be treated is not easy, as we all know. But treating others like this when others have not treated us as **we** would like them to treat us, is excruciatingly difficult to do. Yet 'treating others as we would like to be treated' is at the very heart of effective community work!

Some psychologists like Sigmund Freud would say it is impossible to treat others as we would like them to treat us, when others have not treated us as we would like to be treated.[1] But other psychiatrists, like Viktor Frankl, would say it is not only possible, but it is most imperative where it would seem most impossible.

> 'We who lived in the concentration camps can remember those who walked through the huts comforting others, giving away their last piece of bread. They may have been few in number but they offer sufficient proof that everything can be taken from us but the last of human freedoms—the freedom to choose our spirit in any circumstance.'[2]

While Sigmund Freud tells us to 'love thy neighbour as thy neighbour loves thee', rather than 'love thy neighbour as thyself', Mahatma Gandhi insists that taking 'an eye for an eye' will only end up creating a short-sighted society in which the blind lead the blind.

The Buddha, Siddartha Gautama, gently reminds us, 'Hatred never ceases by hatred, but by love alone is healed. This is the ancient and eternal law of the universe'.[3]

And Martin Luther King, the great 20th century civil rights campaigner, warns us 'never to succumb to the temptation of becoming bitter. As you

---

1 S. Freud, *Civilisation And Its Discontents*
2 J.Kornfield *The Art of Forgiveness, Lovingkindness and Peace*, Rider ,Sydney, 2002 p 7
3 Kornfield, p 5

press for justice, be sure to move with dignity and discipline, using only the instrument of love.'[1]

So the art at the heart of community work is learning to overcome hatred with love.

- What do you think about the idea of 'overcoming hatred with love'?
- How do you feel about using only 'the instrument of love' yourself?

✎ Record your reflections in your Working Notes.

The disciplines of the heart

Overcoming hatred using the instrument of love in the struggle for justice requires learning the disciplines of the heart:[2] **grieving, giving up, forgiving, letting go, and loving.**

The discipline of grieving

15 minutes

If we are to learn to love in the midst of hate—or any other form of perfidy or duplicity—we need to grieve the tragedy of loving without being loved, as we would like, in return.

Grieving is the natural human response to loss. It helps feel the pain of the loss, and in feeling the pain, helps us acknowledge, integrate, and accept the reality of our loss.

If we do not grieve well, we may get stuck in denying the reality, trying to negotiate our way through a situation that was already decided long ago, or raging against our fate. If we get stuck in denying the situation we are in, trying to negotiate our way out, or raging ferociously against our fate, we will not be able to deal well with the reality.

There are many ways to grieve. Some of us prefer to sit with it in silence. Some of us prefer to talk it out. Some of us prefer to sing it through. And others of us prefer just to wail away. Whichever way we prefer to do it, our grief is usually drenched with tears.

---

1 Kornfield, p 82
2 This section is based on J.Kornfield *The Art of Forgiveness, Lovingkindness and Peace.*

A meditation on grieving

- ☐ Create a comfortable atmosphere.
- ☐ If possible set the scene in semidarkness.
- ☐ Sit on your own, or with a friend.
- ☐ Once seated, attend to your breathing.
- ☐ Take one hand and hold it gently to your heart, as if you are holding a precious but fragile human being in their hands. You are—yourself!
- ☐ As you continue breathing, bring to mind a loss you grieve.
- ☐ Let the story of the loss unfold. Allow the feelings associated with it to surface and flow.
- ☐ Let the feelings they have come one by one. Hold them. Name them. And honour them.
- ☐ Touch them tenderly. Treat them kindly. Then let their tears begin to take them away.

> *'When after heavy rain the storm clouds disperse,*
> *is it not that they've wept themselves clear to the end?'* Ghalib [1].

✎ Record your reflections in your *Working Notes*

The discipline of giving up
15 minutes

The idea of giving up is generally repugnant to people working for social change. But in order to work for change well we need to give up many things along the way. Among the many things we need to give up along the way is all hope of a better past.

Maybe things could have been better; maybe they should have been better; but though we might be able to change the future for the better, we simply cannot change the past.

We must not forget the past. We must remember it order to learn from it. But we cannot live in the past any more than we can live in the future. We can only live in the present.

It is only as we give up all hope of creating a better past, and live our lives as faithfully as we can in the present, that we give ourselves a chance of creating a better future.

---

1 Kornfield, p 58

A meditation on giving up

- ☐ Remember a moment of disappointment in the past.
- ☐ Take a piece of paper and write down the event that occurred.
- ☐ Reflect on the event—what happened and what the impact of it was.
- ☐ Then, on a separate piece of paper, write down the main lesson you learned from it.
- ☐ Put the two pieces of paper side by side—the event and the lesson.
- ☐ Give up trying to change the event, but take the lesson to heart.
- ☐ Put the piece of paper on which you wrote about the event to one side; and put the paper on which you wrote the lesson they learned in your Working Notes.
- • It is only as we give up all hope of creating a better past, and live our lives as faithfully as we can in the present, that we give ourselves a chance of creating a better future.
- ✎ Record your reflections in your *Working Notes*

The discipline of forgiving
15 minutes

- ☐ Read the following story, 'The Day of Atonement' by Paulo Coelho:

Ahab instituted a ritual (in Viscos) of his own making—a Day of Atonement.

Once a year, the inhabitants shut themselves up in their houses, made two lists, turned to face the highest mountain and then raised their first list to the heavens.

'Here, Lord, are all the sins I have committed against you,' they said, reading the account of all the sins they had committed: swindles, adulteries, injustices, things of that sort. 'I have sinned and beg forgiveness for offending You so greatly.'

Then—and here lay Ahab's originality—the residents immediately pulled the second list out of their pocket and, still, facing the same mountain, they held that one up to the skies too.

And they said something like: 'And here, Lord, is a list all Your sins against me: You made me work harder than necessary, my daughter fell ill despite all my prayers, I was trying to be honest, I suffered more than was fair.'

Living Community: Session 7

> After reading out the second list, they ended the ritual with 'I have been unjust towards You and You have been unjust towards me. However, since today is the Day of Atonement You will forget my faults and I will forget Yours, and we can carry on together for another year!'
>
> - From *The Devil and Miss Prym*

- What does this story say about the role of forgiving?
- What does this story say about the ritual of forgiving?

✎ Record your reflections in your Working Notes.

We know that we can't change the past. We know that can't undo the pain. However, some of us try to heal the pain we have suffered by inflicting pain on the people who made us suffer, as if their suffering more would somehow result in our suffering less.

But the desire for revenge usually only serves to increase the suffering of the victim. If we do not forgive our tormentors, we will continue to be tortured by our resentment.

Forgiving is not forgetting. We must remember suffering and learn from our suffering. We shouldn't associate with our tormentor, unless we are sure they will not torment us.

Forgiving is not fooling. On the contrary, it's smart. It is a way of maintaining our sanity. As we forgive the unforgivable we release the love that alone can heal the wounds.

A meditation on forgiving

- ☐ Start by visualising the ways you have hurt others.
- ☐ See the pain you have caused others—knowingly or unknowingly.
- ☐ Feel the sorrow, shame, guilt and regret they feel about this.
- ☐ Picture each person that comes to mind, one by one, sense their suffering, and say:

  'I remember many ways I have hurt others. I recognise the pain I have caused. 'I ask for your forgiveness, I ask for you forgiveness, I ask for your forgiveness'.

- ☐ Continue by visualising the ways others have hurt you.
- ☐ See the pain others have caused you—knowingly or unknowingly.
- ☐ Feel the sorrow, anger and resentment you feel about this.

- Picture each person who comes to mind, and, as your heart is ready, say to them:

   'I remember many ways others have hurt me. I have carried this pain in my heart long enough. To the extent that I am ready, I offer those who hurt me forgiveness. I offer you my forgiveness, I offer you my forgiveness, I offer you my forgiveness'.

Forgiving is not a weak reaction, but a strong, courageous, constructive response. As it says in the Bhagavad Gita: 'If you want to see the brave, look for those who can forgive.'[1]

- Record your reflections in your Working Notes.

The discipline of letting go
15 minutes

Letting go is just letting things be as they are: not holding onto anything that would hold us back from moving on and becoming the human/humane person we are called to be. When we learn just to let things be as they are they gradually lose their power over us.

Letting go is not cutting off. It is not cutting ourselves off from ourselves, from our memories or our responsibilities. It is not cutting ourselves off from others, from our families or from our communities. But it is letting go of our disappointment and despair.

A meditation on letting go

- Set the scene with a small candle and a metal bowl.
- Remember some reactions that you feel it is time to let go of.
- Name them (eg sadness, resentment, anxiety, anger, etc).
- Hold these feelings with tenderness in their heart one more time.
- Then, when you are ready to let these feelings go, write them down.
- When the list of feelings you want to let go of is finished, think about the benefits that will come from letting these feelings go - once and for all.
- Take paper on which you have written the list of feelings you want to let go of, then set them on fire with the candle and burn them burn in the metal bowl.

---

1 Kornfield, p 26

- ☐ Then take the paper that you put to one side, on which you had written about the event you wanted to give up on, and burn it to ashes in the bowl.
- ☐ As the smoke rises like incense encourage them to say - 'Let it go. Let it go. Let it go.'

> *If you let go a little, you will have a little happiness.*
> *If you will let go a lot, you will have a lot of happiness.*
>
> Ajahn Chah [1]

✎ Record your reflections in your Working Notes.

The discipline of loving
15 minutes

Loving is treating others, not as we have been treated, but as we would like to be treated. It involves extending the same kind of acceptance and respect and resolute positive regard to others that we would like ourselves. It involves creating the same kind of opportunities for others to participate in community—and realise their potential—as we would like ourselves.

A meditation on loving

- ☐ Start with yourself. Picture yourself and pray for yourself repeatedly: *'May I be filled with loving kindness for myself.'*
- ☐ When you are ready, move on to people you like. Picture them and pray for them repeatedly: *'May I be filled with loving kindness for you.'*
- ☐ If there are any particular feelings of gratitude you feel, just give thanks.
- ☐ When you are ready, move on to people who you don't like. Picture them and pray for them repeatedly: *'May I be filled with loving kindness for you'.*
- ☐ If there are any particular feelings of irritation you feel, hold them gently.

> *'Like a caring mother holding the life of her only child*
> *so with a heart of loving kindness hold all beings*
> *as your beloved children.'*
>
> Buddha [2]

✎ Record your reflections in your Working Notes.

---

1 Kornfield, p 54
2 Kornfield, p 70

- **Note:** Practice makes perfect. You will need to go through this meditation repeatedly.

On the wall of the home for the dying in Calcutta Mother Teresa had a liturgy for loving.

Any way

People can be unreasonable, illogical and self-centred.
Love them anyway.
If you do good, people will accuse you of selfish motives.
Do good anyway.
The good you do today will be forgotten tomorrow.
Do good anyway.
People really need help but may attack you if you help them.
Help people anyway.
If you are successful, you win false friends and true enemies.
Succeed anyway.
What you spend years building may be destroyed overnight.
Build anyway.
Give the world the best you've got; it may never be enough;
But give the world the best you've got anyway.

Anonymous

Conclusion

10 minutes

The follow-up reading for this session is

'King Of The Wharfies' *No Longer Down Under*, Mike Brown, Grosvenor Books Melbourne 2002, pp 130–144 (Reading 7)

The set community tasks for this session are

- ☐ Talk to people in your community who have a reputation for always being respectful. Ask them how they do it—especially under pressure.
- ☐ Meet with your learning partner and your community development support group.
- ☐ Share what you learnt in the session about treating others as you would like to be treated, rather than treating others as they (might or might not) treat you. Also share what you learnt in class about grieving, giving up, forgiving, letting

go, and loving. And share what you learnt from talking to some of the respectful people in your community.

✎ Record your actions, reflections, and conclusions in your Working Notes.

Session 8

Building Bridges to People

Objectives

- To review your understanding of dealing with spitefulness
- To introduce the art of building community networks; to consider the times, levels, and phases of building bridges to people.

Review

15 minutes

- ☐ Review your work from Session 7.
- ☐ Review the issues raised in course notes in the previous session, particularly how to deal with spitefulness.
- ☐ Review the reading:
   'King Of The Wharfies' *No Longer Down Under*, Mike Brown Grosvenor Books Melbourne 2002, pages 130–144 (Reading 7)
- ☐ Review the tasks:
   ❖ How did you find talking to people in your community who have a reputation for being respectful?
   ❖ What was the most important thing you learned while doing your community tasks for the last session?

✎ Record your reflections in your Working Notes.

The art of networking

10 minutes

The art of networking is the art of developing networks of reciprocal relationships that are at the foundation of all community development.

Bonding and Bridging

In order to develop these networks in a community we need to move from simply *bonding* with a few people to *bridging* to a whole spectrum of people.

Bonds are strong inward-looking connections, like marriage, that of necessity are exclusive. Bonds produce deep, 'thick' trust, and are essential for nurturing and supporting one another, for 'getting by'. Families usually do bonding pretty well.

Bridges are weak outward-looking connections, like the civil rights movement, that of necessity are inclusive. Bridges produce broad, 'thin' trust, and are crucial for co-operating and campaigning with others, for 'getting on'. Friends, with a suspicion of others who are not friends, do not do bridging very well.

We need to continue to do our bonding in our friendship circles, but not at the expense of building bridges to people in our communities who are outside our circles of friends.

❒ Answer the following questions:

> - What is the difference between bonding and bridging behaviour?
> - How are you going with the work of building bridges to people in your locality?

✍ Record your reflections in your Working Notes

Schmoozing and maching

There are two traditional ways of building bridges to people in the community that Jews refer to in Yiddish as *schmoozing* and *maching*. [1]

Schmoozers take an informal approach to bridging. Schmoozers like to visit family, drop in on friends, invite newcomers over for a barbecue, or take old-timers out on a picnic. Machers tend to take a more formal approach to bridging. are more likely to attend a workshop on community, start a community group, and implement a community project.

Interestingly, the distinction between schmoozers and machers often reflects the different stages in the life cycle. As Putnam says,

> Schmoozing peaks among young adults, enters a long decline as family and community obligations press in, then rises again with retirement;

---

[1] Adapted from Putnam, p 92-94

while maching is relatively modest early in life, peaks in late middle age, and declines with retirement.

The two types of involvement overlap. Schmoozers can be machers, and machers can be schmoozers. Most of the time we tend to be mainly one or the other.

- What do you think you are?
- What do you think most of the people you know are?

✎ Record your reflections in your Working Notes.

However, to mix well, we need to be a bit of both. We need to take an informal approach to bridging:
- Visiting family, dropping in on friends
- Inviting new-comers over for a picnic
- Taking old-timers out on a barbecue

And we need to take a formal approach to mixing:
- Attending seminars on community
- Starting a community organisation
- Implementing a community project

Remember we don't all have to do it the same way. Different people will play different roles at different times. However, whatever we choose to do will be but a beginning in the long, slow process of mixing that will slowly but surely ferment change in the community: *developing the relationships that will raise the quality of life.*

❒ Answer the following questions.

- How do 'schmoozers' mix with people in their circles?
- How do 'machers' mix with people in their circles?
- What are you already doing that could be called 'schmoozing'?
- What are you already doing that could be called 'maching'?
- How could you do more 'schmoozing' in your circles?
- How could you do more 'maching' in your circles?

✎ Record your reflections in your Working Notes.

Networking in our community

10 minutes

Effective networking involves more than establishing a credible local identity *as* a neighbour. It means *being* a neighbour. That takes a lot of time—time many of us never seem to have. We always seem to be too busy to be neighbourly. We have to make the time. It is a constant struggle to make sure we're not too busy to be neighbourly.

If we want to relate to people in our community, we need to *be* in our community: not just for a short while, but over the long haul. People who move a lot are less likely to get involved—and others are much less likely to get involved with them. If we want to get more involved, we need to stay around.

If we want to relate to people in our church community, we need to spend less time at work and more time in our church community. Part-time work is more likely to increase our involvement in the church community. If we want to relate to people in our local community, we need to spend less time at church and more time in our local community. However, we need to make sure we still spend enough time at church. Three meetings a week is a manageable amount: one large celebratory gathering, one small nurture group, and one small mission group. Then we will still have time for involvement in our local community.

Remember that if we want to relate to people in our community, we need to spend less time *commuting* and more time *communicating*. Every ten minutes not spent in commuting increases the possibility of community involvement by 10%.

Remember too, if we want to spend more time communicating we need to stop watching *Neighbours* and start relating to neighbours. Each extra hour a day of watching TV reduces community involvement by 10%. So the easiest way for us to make more time for our community is to chuck out, or at least turn off the TV!

- How could you make time for networking next week?
- How could you make more time for networking next month?
- How could you make more time for networking next year?

✎ Record your reflections in your Working Notes.

Opportune moments in community networking
30 minutes

There are two kinds of time that we can use for building bridges to people in our community — *scheduled time* and *casual time*. [1]

- Scheduled time involves planned meetings, dominated by the clock, and are usually formal.
- Casual time involves opportune moments orientated to the event, and are usually informal.

Both kinds of contact are essential for building bridges in the community.

Formal contacts are a way of connecting us with representatives of groups we may not normally have access to and may give us access to the resources of the group that they represent. Informal contacts are a way we can turn our connections into friendships where we can relate to one another, not in terms of our respective roles, but as real people.

In practice, many formal meetings build barriers rather than bridges. The very formality of proceedings often keeps people apart. People relate to each other on the basis of their official roles, not as relatives in the human family. If formal meetings are to build bridges between people as people, the formality of the proceedings needs to be interspersed with informality so people can relate to each other authentically as brothers and sisters.

We may live in a modern society characterised by formal meetings, rather than a traditional society characterised by informal gatherings, but all of us are aware that it is in our *informal* encounters that the real business of relationship building takes place.

Tragically, many of us in community organisations are often so preoccupied with our programs that we cannot respond to opportunities to develop community as they arise with the ebb and flow of daily life. We need to make sure we are not so preoccupied with scheduled time that we miss the 'opportune moments' when people are more open than closed, and we have the opportunity to develop significant relationships with one another.

These opportune moments often pass as quickly as they come. So it is important that we grasp these moments when they come our way—or risk losing the opportunities they present forever. In order to grasp these moments, we must either make time for these events in our schedules—or throw out our schedules altogether!

Significant opportune moments include *changes, cycles, conflicts, celebrations and chance* encounters. These are the times when even the most

---
1 Kornfield, p 82

closed people in our society are open to relationships; and they represent our best opportunity to build bridges to people in the community who would usually be suspicious of anyone approaching them.

Opportune moment 1: A time of change

When there is a change, people are suspicious; but they are also curious. More often than not, at least for a little while, their curiosity overcomes their suspicion. That moment—when their curiosity overcomes their suspicion—presents us with a window of opportunity to introduce ourselves to people. This window of opportunity may last a day to a week; but once a person becomes used to the change, their interest subsides. They tend to close off again and the moment of openness passes.

- What are examples of times of change that are opportune moments?
- How could you make the most of these moments to connect?

✎ Record your reflections in your Working Notes.

Opportune moment 2: A stage in the life cycle

The stages in the life cycle also bring with them the opportunity for new or renewed relationships. At significant stages of the life cycle—birth, marriage, and death—we are reminded of our common humanity, and we remember the similarities that transcend our differences.

Everyone loves to show off a new baby. You can stop a total stranger in church and chat with them about their toddler. When the kids first start school, it's not hard to make contact with the other parents dropping off their children at the gate. When they finally leave school, it's easy to talk to other parents about their concerns for the future of their kids. Weddings provide plenty of opportunities to get acquainted or reacquainted with people we have not had contact with. Funerals can bring people together who have not even seen or even spoken to one another for many years.

- How could you make the most of these moments to connect?

✎ Record your reflections in your Working Notes.

Opportune moment 3: Open crowd conflicts

In community there is a phenomenon known as an 'open crowd'. It's an event in which people get together in a way that naturally draws other people in. It's the complete opposite of a closed meeting—it's an open gathering. The indicators of an open crowd are colour, movement—and noise, lots of noise. If the colour and movement doesn't attract the crowd, then the noise usually will.

Conflicts are often open crowds. There is nothing like a fight in the church, in the factory, or in the office, to bring people together. Ironically, conflicts can often break down the walls of alienation. Having to resolve a conflict can build bridges between people who never had to relate to each other before, as long as those who join in relate to people respectfully.

- How do you usually respond to conflict? How could you respond differently to turn conflict into an opportune moment?

✍ Record your reflections in your Working Notes.

Opportune moment 4: Open crowd celebrations

We noted above the characteristics of an open crowd. Celebrations can be open crowds, as well as conflicts. At celebrations, people are often as happy to talk to a new person as to talk to an old friend. A potluck dinner, where everybody is invited to bring a plate of (hopefully their best home-cooked) food and share it with everybody else, is a classic example of a celebration that is an open crowd with great opportunities to connect with one another. Christmas and Easter celebrations can also open up the crowd for others.

However there is probably no better way to get to know an Aussie neighbour than to invite them over for a barbecue on Australia Day.

- Think of a celebration you attended recently. Were you able to make the most of this moment to connect? How might you make more of an opportunity next time?

✍ Record your reflections in your Working Notes.

Opportune moment 5: Chance encounters

Some people will never respond to an invitation, no matter how many times we may try to invite them. The only way we may ever meet them is by chance.

Some people only feel safe to relate to others if they meet by accident. It's the only way they can be sure that they are not being set up. An accidental meeting is by definition unpremeditated.

It may be that we come late to a meeting and the only seat left is next to somebody we have never met before. It may be we are scheduled on to a cleaning roster working with a team of people we have only just met before we got to work. On the other hand, it may be on the way out of the parking lot, we have a minor collision with another car driven by a stranger. We need to re-adjust our perspective, so that we are ready to turn any of these accidental encounters into opportunities to connect!

> ☐ Be on the look-out today for a chance encounter that becomes an opportunity to connect.

✎ Use your Working Notes to record how you used the opportunity.

Critical levels in community networking

20 minutes

There are four levels at which we can build bridges to people [1].

Critical Level One: at the level of our feet
Where we stand – in our locality
As *compatriots*, with a sense of *shared history*

Critical Level Two: at the level of our hands
What we do – in our activity
As *colleagues*, with a sense of *shared industry*

Critical Level Three: at the level of our heads
How we think – in our ideology
As *comrades*, with a sense of *shared solidarity*

Critical Level Four: at the level of our hearts
How we feel in our personality
As *companions*, with a sense of *shared intimacy*

---

1 Adapted from D. Andrews et al, *Building Better Communities*

1. Who do you think are, or could be, your compatriots?
2. Who do you think are, or could be, your colleagues?
3. Who do you think are, or could be, your comrades?
4. Who do you think is, or could be, your companion?

✍ Record your responses in your Working Notes.

We need to recognise these four different levels of relationships and relate to people accordingly.

- We can expect *acceptance* from level-one compatriots.
- We can expect *help* from our level-two colleagues.
- We can expect *support* from our level-three comrades.
- We can expect *sympathy* from our level-four companion(s).

Problems come from expecting too little or too much from people. We will probably be able to build bridges with hundreds of people at level one, scores of people at level two, a dozen people at level three and one person at level four. This means that at best we can expect some degree of acceptance from hundreds of people, some degree of support from scores of people, some degree of help from a dozen or so people, and some degree of sympathy from one or two along the way.

But for most of us that should be enough to start our own DIY community revolution.

1. Why is it unreasonable to expect intimacy with everybody?
2. What are the dangers of expecting sympathy from everybody?
3. What is it reasonable to expect from your compatriots?
4. What is it reasonable to expect from your colleagues?
5. What is it reasonable to expect from your comrades?
6. What is it reasonable to expect from your companion?

✍ Record your reflections in your Working Notes.

Crucial phases in community networking

25 minutes

Most groups involved in this long, slow process of community networking, will discover four very distinct phases in the process.

Not every group will go through these phases in exactly the same way. Your group may skip one or two phases entirely, or go forward a couple of steps and then go back before making any progress. However, the following phases are typical of the experience of most people who try to mix with their communities.

Crucial Phase 1: the Angel Phase

The Angel Phase involves such *superficial connection* with people that everyone seems like an absolute angel. People reach out to one another, but keep one another at arm's length. They are very pleasant, very polite, and very superficial. As long as this phase lasts, therefore, the dream of real connectedness remains unrealised.

This phase lasts for as long as people can suppress their real thoughts and feelings. Once our deeply held thoughts and feelings erupt, we move to the next phase.

Crucial Phase 2: the Devil Phase

The Devil Phase usually involves a *critical disconnection* from people when the ones who acted like angels start to act like devils. People are no longer so superficial. They act from deep within, and the reality emerges, or rather, erupts. Discussions turn into disputes and arguments turn into fights. The cosy dream of connectedness becomes a scary nightmare.

This phase lasts as long as people can cope with the crisis that has erupted. Once we decide we can't cope with the crisis any longer, we can either try to deal with it by imposing law and order on the situation, or try to deal with it by exploring the issues in terms of love and understanding.

If we opt to impose law and order on the situation to deal with the chaos, chances are the relationships we have built will move back to the previous phase of superficial, but comfortable, connection. If we opt to explore love and understanding of the situation as a way to deal with the chaos, we can move on to the next phase.

Crucial Phase 3: the Human Phase

The Human Phase usually involves a *careful reconnection* with one another as people realise that others are not angels, or devils, but humans with good points and bad points, just like themselves. Therefore, they no longer keep one another at a distance but embrace one another, sharing their hopes and their despair, including the despair they share about not being able to make their dreams of real human connectedness come true.

This phase lasts as long as we can cope with the discomfort associated with affirming the people with whom we have unresolved conflict, without resolving the conflict. Once we decide we can't cope with the discomfort any longer, we will either resume or resolve the conflict. If we decide to resume the conflict, people will either give up and go home, or move back to superficial but comfortable connection. If we decide to resolve the conflict, we can move on to the next phase.

Crucial Phase 4: the Family Phase

The Family Phase involves a meaningful connection with people in the light of the realization that they are family! People realise that regardless of whether they are friends or enemies, they are beautiful, but fallible, brothers and sisters who need one another and need to resolve their conflicts with one another in order to meet one another's needs. Only then can their dreams of real human connectedness come true.

In the light of this perspective, it's not surprising many people end up with superficial connections rather than meaningful connections. Few are willing to endure the chaos and extend the care that is required to develop meaningful mutual connections with people.

If we are to create meaningful, rather than superficial connections, then we need to encourage one another to endure the chaos and extend the care that is required. For there is no other way that we can ever hope to make our dream of community come true.

1. What are the four crucial phases in building bridges to people?
2. Which phase do you think you are at in your community now?
3. What is the evidence that you are in a particular phase?
4. If you are not in the final phase, how can you progress towards it? If you are in this final phase, how can you strengthen it?

✍ Record your reflections in your Working Notes.

Conclusion

10 minutes

The follow-up reading for this session is

> 'Beginnings' from Kris Saunders and Teresa Scott, *People Working Together II*, Boolarong, Brisbane 1986, p 5-17 (Reading 8).

The set community tasks for this session are

- ❒ Meet with your learning partner and your community development support group.

- ❒ Discuss how each person in your group can connect with two other people in the community you want to be involved with. Share what you learnt in class about 'the art of networking', 'networking in our community', 'the opportune moments', 'the critical levels' and 'the crucial phases'. Plan how you can put it into practice in your community.

- ❒ Each person in your group should have a go at making a connection with two other people in your community. Afterwards, meet again as a group to discuss how you all went. Talk about what worked best and what you would need to do in order to network better in your community.

- ✍ Record your actions, reflections and conclusions in your Working Notes.

Session 9

Building Bridges on Relationships

Objectives

- To review your understanding of the art of building community networks including the times, levels, and phases you will encounter in building community networks
- To consider the 'protocols' on which relationships are built.

Review

15 minutes

- ❐ Review your work from Session 8.
- ❐ Review the issues raised in course notes in the previous session, particularly how to build community networks, taking the 'times', levels', and 'phases' for building community networks into account.
- ❐ Review the reading:

  'Beginnings' from Kris Saunders and Teresa Scott, *People Working Together II*, Boolarong, Brisbane 1986, p 5-17 (Reading 8)

- ❐ Review the tasks:
  - ❖ How was your meeting with your learning partner and your community development support group?
  - ❖ What was the most important thing you learned while doing your community tasks for the last session?

✍ Record your reflections in your Working Notes.

Beyond game playing

10 minutes

By and large our society operates on superficial relationships. We ostensibly build bridges of friendship to one another, but want little or no involvement. Instead we play games with one another. We all know the rules: keep the conversation shallow but pretend it is deep; talk about yourself but tune out when others talk about themselves; use meaningful jargon but avoid a genuine meeting of souls.

Religious people have their own variations on these games. As a friend who has stopped going to his local church says, 'Religious people love to play a game called 'church'. We all dress up and go through our paces in the service together and whoever look the most religious wins. The prize for the winners is approval. No one gives a damn about really being involved in one another's lives.'

After church the people go home, convinced they have had meaningful contact with one another and shown significant concern for this person. After all, they did pass the peace to him as part of the liturgy. He feels, even though he made an effort to meet people, the encounters that he had with them were totally superficial. The banal chatter bore no relevance to the loneliness of his single room in a boarding house.

The object of a 'piety game' is to convince ourselves and others of our virtue. The piety game is characterised by judging people on the basis of petty issues. It is not concerned about meeting people at their point of need. It is about using their needs to make them look 'bad', and make us look 'good' by comparison. The piety game prevents a genuine encounter in which we can come to terms with our common needs together.

The object of the 'proselytisation game' is to convince as many people as possible to join our cause. In the proselytisation game we treat people as faceless commodities—potential trophies for us to win. We do not treat people as people. If we meet people's needs, it is not so much to help them win, but to help us win them over. The proselytisation game may promote encounters with people, but subverts the possibility of developing relationships of mutual acceptance and respect.

Many of us, realising the destructiveness of the piety and proselytisation games, give up playing religious games. But few of us give up playing games altogether; we take up secular games instead! One of the secular games people play is the 'welfare game'. The object of the welfare game is to appear as if you are involved with the needs of the community, without actually getting too involved. If you play the game well, you can get a lot of credit without paying the price of costly involvement. The game begins when a group is challenged about being involved in their community. The group can't say 'no', because they would be denying the voice of their conscience. Nevertheless, they find it hard to say 'yes', because of the cost. To resolve the dilemma, a committee is appointed to do the job for them. Moreover, the committee appoints a professional to do the job on their behalf. The welfare game is played with a number of variations but the aim is always the same: to get the credit for being involved in the needs of others without actually getting involved.

- What is the definition of a game?
- Which of these games, if any, do you identify with?
- What aspects of the welfare game do you see being played out in your community?

✎ Record your reflections in your Working Notes.

Playing it straight

20 minutes

According to activist comedian Fran Peavey, it is absolutely imperative that those of us working for social change stop playing games, and learn to play it straight.

> Those of us working for social change tend to view our adversaries as enemies, to consider them unreliable, suspect, and generally of lower moral character. Saul Alinsky, a brilliant community organizer, explained the rationale for polarization this way:
>
> "One acts decisively only in the conviction that all the angels are on one side and all the devils are on the other.
>
> "A leader may struggle toward a decision and weigh the merits and demerits of a situation which is 52 percent positive and 48 percent negative, but once a decision is reached he must assume that his cause is 100 percent positive and the opposition 100 percent negative…"
>
> But demonising one's adversaries has great costs. It is a strategy that tacitly accepts and helps perpetuate our dangerous enemy mentality.
>
> Instead of focusing on the 52 percent 'devil' in my adversary, I choose to look at the other 48 percent. To start from the premise that within each adversary I have an ally. That ally may be silent, faltering, or just hidden from my view. It may be only the person's sense of ambivalence about morally questionable parts of his or her job.
>
> When I was working to stop the Vietnam War, I'd feel uneasy seeing people in military uniform. I'd get furious inside when I imagined the horrible things [they]'d probably done in the war.

Several years after the end of the war, a small group of Vietnam veterans wanted to hold a retreat at our farm in Watsonville, I consented, although I felt ambivalent about hosting them.

That weekend, I had a chance to listen to a dozen men and women who had served in Vietnam. Having returned home only to face ostracism for their involvement in the war, they were struggling to terms with their experiences.

They spoke of some of the awful things they'd done, as well as some things they were proud of. They told why they had enlisted in the army or cooperated with the draft: their love for (their country), their eagerness to serve, their wish to be brave and heroic ... Now some questioned their own manhood or womanhood, and even their basic humanity. They wondered whether they had been a positive force or a negative one overall ... Their anguish disarmed me, and I could not view them as simply perpetrators of evil.

How had I come to view military people as my enemy? Did vilifying soldiers serve to get me off the hook and allow me to divorce myself from responsibility for what my country was doing in Vietnam? Did my own anger and righteousness keep me from seeing the situation in its full complexity?

When my youngest sister and her husband, a young career military man, visited me several years ago, I was again challenged to see the human being within the soldier.

I learned that as a farm boy, he'd been recruited to be a sniper.

One night toward the end of their visit, we got talking about his work. Though he had also been trained as a medical corpsman, he could still be called on at any time to work as a sniper. He couldn't tell me much about this part of his career: he'd been sworn to secrecy. I'm not sure he would have wanted to tell me even if he could.

But he did say that a sniper's work involved going abroad, bumping off a leader, and disappearing into a crowd. When you're given an order, he said, you're not supposed to think about it. You feel alone and helpless. Rather than take on the army, and maybe the whole country himself, he chose not to consider the possibility that certain orders shouldn't be carried out. I could see that feeling isolated can make it seem impossible to follow one's own moral standards and disobey an order.

I leaned toward him and said, 'If you're ever ordered to do something that you know you shouldn't do, call me immediately and I'll find a way to help. I know a lot of people would support your stand. You're not alone.'

He and my sister looked at each other and their eyes filled with tears.[1]

There haven't been too many divisions deeper in the psyche of our society in recent times than our conflict over that war in Vietnam. But Fran

---

1 F. Peavey, *Heart Politics*, pp 142-147

Peavey's story shows that when we refuse to play games, with care, even a pacifist and a sniper can find some common ground, in their humanity, in which they can flourish together, as a family.

> 1. What is the difference between Saul Alinsky's 'game playing' and Fran Peavey's 'non-game playing' approach to relationships with people?
> 2. How is Fran Peavey's 'non-game playing' approach illustrated in the story?
> 3. If you are to relate to people in a non-game playing way, what do you need to ensure you practise in your approach?

✎ Record your reflections in your Working Notes.

We must approach relationships not only with great sincerity, but also with great sensitivity because, as Stephen Covey says, 'to touch the soul of another ... is to walk on holy ground.'

The practice of civility

20 minutes

We should practise a sequence of protocols that can help us relate to other people as reverentially as we can.

The initial protocol we should practise is *civility to others*. Civility is more than politeness. It involves acting appropriately with people in a relationship. It includes honesty and integrity, acceptance and respect, modesty and commitment, humility and confession.

All relationships with people depend on the practice of *honesty* and *integrity*. Honesty is saying what we mean. Integrity is meaning what we say. If we practise honesty and integrity in our dealings with people, all people, without exception, all the time, then the people we are relating to will have reason to trust us because they can trust our word. They will know that our word is our bond.

All relationships with people depend on the practice of *acceptance* and *respect*. Acceptance means recognising people just as they are. Respect means regarding people just as they are. If we practise acceptance and respect, it doesn't mean we will always agree with what people say or how people act. However, it does mean we will always express our recognition and our regard for them as people, consistently, publicly and privately, whether we agree with them or not. Our trust may need to be conditional, but our love should be unconditional.

All relationships with people depend on the practice *of modesty* and *commitment*. Modesty is the opposite of extravagance. It involves promising people only what we are sure we can deliver. Commitment means delivering whatever we promise. If we practise modesty and commitment, people may not be excited about us, but they will be able to count on us.

All relationships with people depend on the practice of *humility* and *confession*. Humility is the opposite of arrogance. It means owning responsibility for any instance where we over-promise and under-deliver. Confession means owning up, and making up, for any promises we break, by under-promising and over-delivering in future. If we practise humility and confession, we will create a context for people to count on us even when we make mistakes, and in so doing open up the potential for developing the relationship.

- ❏ Write down a list of the eight qualities that contribute to the practice of civility on a piece of paper.

    1. Honesty
    2. Integrity
    3. Acceptance
    4. Respect
    5. Modesty
    6. Commitment
    7. Humility
    8. Confession

- ❏ Go through the list, thinking particularly of specific examples of each of them.
- ❏ Then take your list and write your name on the top of the paper in a column beside the list of qualities that contribute to the practice of civility, and then rate yourself on a scale from one to three, with 1 being "I always practise this" 2 being "I sometimes practise this", and 3 "I never, or rarely, practise this".
- ❏ Finish by answering the following questions:
    ❖ What is one area of civility I do well?
    ❖ What is one area of civility I need to work on?.
- ✎ Record your reflections in your Working Notes.

The practice of compassion

20 minutes

The second protocol we should practice in building bridges to people, is *compassion for others*.

Compassion is more than civility. It's more than sympathy. It's more than empathy. It is actually interacting with people in such a way as to be able to transact their pain. It includes attending and reflecting, listening and speaking, grieving and forgiving, singing and dancing.

All relationships with people where we can transact our pain depend on the practice of *attending and reflecting*. Attending means not pretending, but truly concentrating on the other. Reflecting means not only understanding, but also communicating that understanding of the other in terms they can understand. If we practise attending and reflecting, we will be able to create a space that is safe for listening and speaking.

All relationships with people where we can transact our pain depend on the practice of *listening* and *speaking*. Listening means hearing not superficially, but deeply, the pain of the other. Speaking means not only talking about the pain of the other, but also, after talking about their pain, talking about our own pain too, in so far as it relates to the pain of the other. If we practise listening and speaking, we will be able create a period that is free for grieving and forgiving.

All relationships with people where we can transact our pain depend on the practice of *grieving* and *forgiving*. Grieving means not struggling with our anguish alone, but working through the agony of the pain together. Forgiving means not holding on to the rage, but letting go of the resentment, and starting all over again, in spite of the pain. If we practise grieving and forgiving, we will be able to create the possibility for singing and dancing once more.

> ❏ Write down a list of the eight qualities that contribute to the practice of compassion on a piece of paper.
>
> 1. Attending
> 2. Reflecting
> 3. Listening
> 4. Speaking
> 5. Grieving
> 6. Forgiving
> 7. Singing
> 8. Dancing

☐ Go through the list, making sure that you understand each quality by thinking of specific examples.

☐ Then take your list and rate yourself on a scale from 1 to 3, with 1 being 'I always practise this', 2 being 'I sometimes practise this', and 3 'I never, or rarely, practise this'.

☐ When you have rated your own practice, think of how another person might rate your practice of compassion. Think of someone close to you who would not be afraid to tell you the truth about who you really are, and imagine how they would rate you in terms of your practice of compassion.

☐ Cover your own ratings with a piece of paper, and write down how you imagine they would rate you from 1 to 3, with 1 being 'I always practise this', 2 being 'I sometimes practise this', and 3 'I never, or rarely, practise this'.

☐ Then compare the ratings you gave yourself and what you imagine they would give you.

1. How similar or different are the ratings?
2. What are the similarities?
3. What are the differences?
4. What do the similarities in ratings signify?
5. What do the differences in ratings signify?

☐ Finish by answering the question:
   ❖ What is one area of compassion I do well?
   ❖ What is one area of compassion I need to work on?

✎ Record your reflections in your Working Notes.

The practice of cooperation

25 minutes

The final protocol we should practise is *cooperation with others*.

Cooperation is more than compassion, more than coincidence, more than concurrence. It is actually interacting with people in such a way as to be able to transact their hopes. It includes communication and collaboration, trusting and risking, giving and receiving, and if not consensus, at least consent.

All relationships with people, where we can transact our hopes, depend on the practice of *communication* and *collaboration*. Communication is a dialogue in which all the people concerned can speak, and all the people concerned can be heard. Collaboration implies some sort of ongoing negotiation that takes into account the hopes of all the people concerned. If we practise communication and collaboration, it is possible to start to transact our aspirations.

All relationships with people where we can transact our hopes depend on the practice of *trusting* and *risking*. Trusting means believing there is a chance to do something about our hopes together. And risking means taking the chance to do something about our hopes together when it comes up. We all know there are great dangers associated with trusting and risking. We should never trust any one more than we have reason to. And we should never risk any thing more than we are prepared to lose, in the short term, for a long-term gain. But the dangers associated with *not* trusting and *not* risking are even greater than the dangers associated with trusting and risking. It is only as we practise trusting and risking that we are free to explore our aspirations together.

All relationships with people where we can transact our hopes depend on the practice of *giving* and *receiving*. Giving means sharing something of ourselves in order to do something about our hopes together. And receiving means welcoming something of others, in order to do something about our hopes together. We all know that is better to give than to receive, but if we only ever give, without ever receiving, it doesn't do anyone any good because we never give anyone else the chance to give. Receiving without giving constitutes exploitation. Giving without receiving constitutes manipulation. Both experiences are dehumanising. It is only as we practise giving and receiving that we are free to explore our aspirations together as fully functioning human beings.

All relationships with people where we can transact our hopes depend on the practice of at least *consent*, if not *consensus*. Consensus means finding a way forward together, on which we can all agree with without any underlying reservations. Consent means finding a way forward together, in spite of our reservations, that is consistent with our aspirations. Consent constitutes a group decision (which some members may not feel is the best decision, but which they can all live with and commit themselves not to undermine). This decision is reached without voting, through a process whereby the issues are fully aired, all members feel they have been adequately heard. Everyone has equal power and responsibility. Different degrees of influence, by virtue of individual stubbornness or charisma, are avoided so that all are satisfied with the decision-making process.

Living Community: Session 9

The process requires the members to be emotionally present and engaged; frank in a loving, mutually respectful manner; sensitive to each other; selfless, dispassionate, and capable of emptying themselves. Group members must also possess a paradoxical awareness of the preciousness of both people and time (including knowing when the solution is satisfactory and that it is time to stop and not reopen the discussion until such time as the group determines a need for revision).[1]

- ☐ Write down a list of the eight qualities that are key to the practice of cooperation on a piece of paper.

    1. Communication
    2. Collaboration
    3. Trusting
    4. Risking
    5. Giving
    6. Receiving
    7. Consensus
    8. Consent

- ☐ Go through the list and make sure you understand the qualities of cooperation by thinking of examples of each.
- ☐ When you have made sure you understand each quality, take your list and rate the practice of your community development support group, as a group, so far, on a rating from 1 to 3 in terms of the practice of these qualities, with 1 being 'I always practise this', 2 being 'I sometimes practise this', and 3 'I never, or rarely, practise this'.
- ☐ When you have rated the group's practice, give your learning partner a phone call, and ask them how they would rate your group in terms of cooperation.
- ☐ Then discuss your ratings.

1. How similar or different are the ratings?
2. What are the similarities?
3. What are the differences?
4. What do the similarities in ratings signify?
5. What do the differences in ratings signify?

---

1 S. Peck, *A World Waiting To Be Born*, pp 290-291

Before concluding the conversation, try to come to some agreement—consent, if not consensus—in answering the following questions:

1. What are we already doing really well?
2. How can we celebrate that in the group?
3. What do we need to work on most?
4. How can we address that in the group?

☐ Finish by answering the question:

- How cooperative were you in the conversation with your learning partner?

✍ Don't forget to record your reflections in your Working Notes.

Conclusion

10 minutes

The follow-up reading for this session is

> Pages 214-226 of *Building A Better World,* Albatross, Sutherland, 1996. (Reading 9)

The set community tasks for this session are

☐ Meet with your learning partner and your community development support group.

☐ Discuss how it went for each person in your group last week as they connected with two other people in the community.

☐ Share what you learned in the session about the principles of getting beyond game playing, playing it straight, extending civility to others, expressing compassion for others, and developing cooperation with others.

☐ Talk about what you already do really well and celebrate it. Then talk about what you need to work on most, and how you can address that in your relationships inside the group, and also outside the group - especially with the two other people each one of you has connected with.

- ☐ Encourage each person in the group to connect again with the two other people in the community they connected with last week, but with a greater degree of civility, compassion, and cooperation this time round. And agree that you will discuss how this went at the next meeting.
- ✎ Record your actions, reflections, and conclusions in your Working Notes.

Session 10

Building Bridges through Groups

Objectives

- To review your understanding of the 'protocols' on which relationships are built
- To introduce the important part played by groups, both existing groups, and starting groups, in community development.

Review

15 minutes

☐ Review your work from Session 9.
☐ Review the issues raised in the previous session, particularly the 'protocols' on which relationships are built—civility to others, compassion for others and cooperation with others
☐ Review the reading:
   Pages 214-226 of ***Building A Better World,*** Albatross, Sutherland, 1996 (Reading 9).
☐ Review the tasks:
   ❖ What did you learn from meeting with your learning partner and your community development support group?
   ❖ What was the most important thing you learned while doing your community tasks for the last session?

✐ Record your reflections in your Working Notes.

Existing Groups

Surveying Groups
10 minutes

If we want to work in our community, then we need to begin with the groups that are already established in our community, and find those that we might be able to work with.

There are many different kinds of groups in a community:-

- Government agencies
- Non-government agencies
- Large formal organisations
- Small non-formal groups
- Neighbourhood centres
- Community associations
- Church denominations
- Local clusters of people

☐ With some pens and a large piece of paper, draw a Group Map of all the formal groups that you know of in your community.

☐ Add any informal groups associated with your community that you are personally involved with, or potentially could get involved with.

> 1. Are there any other groups?
> 2. What group(s), if any, are you in?
> 3. What group(s), if any, would you like to be in? Why?

✎ Record your observations in your Working Notes.

Selecting Groups
10 minutes

The best groups for us to start with are dynamic groups, characterised by:

1. An orientation towards the present rather than the past
2. An awareness of problems
3. An acceptance of the importance of problem-solving
4. An appreciation of change

5. A perception of change as positive rather than negative
6. An understanding of the pace of change
7. A concern for people rather than programs
8. A commitment to nurture rather than to maintenance
9. A consideration of accountability not just accounts
10. A comprehension of the whole rather than the parts
11. A capacity to provide a wide range of knowledge and skills.[1]

- Which of these criteria are most important to you for your community work?
- What group(s) do you know of that meet this criteria?
- What else do you need in a group to help you with your community work?
- What group(s), if any, do you think could help you?

✐ Record your reflections in your Working Notes.

Joining groups
15 minutes

If we find the kind of group that we are looking for—a group that is, for example, concerned for people rather than programs, and has the capacity to provide a wide range of knowledge and skills that we would need in our community work—then we need to think about joining this existing group rather than starting our own.

There are a number of important steps that we need to take very carefully if we want to join an existing group successfully.

1. The first step is to *accept the guidelines of the group* and abide by their requirements as much as we can. If we go along with the group, we have a better chance of getting on with the group.
2. The second step is to *seek a sponsor in the group* who sympathises with the work that we want to do and who is willing to give us some space to do it through the group. It doesn't have to be a lot of space. Even a little space can make a lot of difference. It can give us the room we need.

---
[1] *Building A Better World*, p 145-146

Living Community: Session 10

3. The third step is to try to *find some supporters in the group* who share our passion for the work we want to do and who are willing to work cooperatively with us through the group. It doesn't have to be a lot of help. Even a little help can make a lot of difference. It can give us the resources we need.

> 1. If you have already joined a group, did you take any of these steps?
> 2. If not, why not? If so, how did you go?
> 3. If you are planning to join a group, would you take any of these steps?
> 4. If not, why not? If so, how would you go about it?
> 5. Do you think it is possible to succeed in a group without taking these steps?

✎ Record your reflections in your Working Notes.

Initiating Groups
20 minutes

Sometimes we can find an existing group in our local community that is interested in the community development work that we want to do. It is just a matter of joining the group and getting on with the job. But often we cannot find a suitable group. There is no existing group that is engaged in community work. In that case we may need to start our own group.

Respected community development worker Alan Twelvetrees says: 'It is probably more difficult to re-orientate an existing group to take up [new] objectives than to work with a new group to that end.'[1] Initiating groups can be surprisingly easy and infuriatingly difficult. It can be as easy as getting together with two or three people who share a common concern. However, at times the search for people with a common concern can be extremely difficult and frustrating. Search as we may, we just can't seem to find someone whose heart beats in harmony with ours. These are times of quiet desperation that call for quiet determination.

We need to look among people we already know, who may be interested. We should talk to these people about our concerns. On the one hand, they may think we are crazy. But on the other hand, they may share our concerns. We should also look at existing groups that may be

---
1 A. Twelvetrees, *Community Work*, p.58

engaging in activities related to those we are interested in. When we find two other people, and the three of us decide to work together, then a group has formed.

You are already involved in new groups—the community development support group with your learning partner and at least one other person from the community. And on top of this, you may need to initiate another new group, including other people.

- Do you think you need to start another group to help with your work?
- If so, why? What are the reasons? How valid are those reasons?

To initiate a new a group is essentially a political process that needs to be handled diplomatically. So you shouldn't set up a new group unless it is absolutely necessary.

- Why is initiating a new group a political process?
- Why does it need to be handled diplomatically?

✍ Record your reflections in your Working Notes.

Setting up new groups can be perceived as a criticism of existing ones. There are two strategies we can use to initiate a new group diplomatically: a *formal* strategy, and an *informal* strategy.

We can initiate a new group formally by consulting the leaders of the church and asking for their permission to set up a new group. Or we can initiate a new group informally by simply setting up a new group with a few of our friends with no official recognition.

- Would you set up a new group formally? If so, why?
- Would you set up a new group informally? If so, why?

✍ Record your reflections in your Working Notes.

A simple rule of thumb for selecting your strategy that many workers use is:

> If you think the leaders will give you permission,
> ask for it, and set the new group up *formally*.

> If you think the leaders will not give you permission,
> don't ask for it, and set the new group up *informally*.

> • How would you go about the task of setting up a new group?

✍ Record your reflections in your Working Notes.

Maintaining Groups
20 minutes

Setting up a new group can be difficult, but initiating a group is never as difficult as the task of maintaining the group.

Understanding the development phases that all groups pass through can be helpful to facilitators. The commonly recognised phases are forming, storming, reforming and performing.

- **Forming** is when a group gathers round a common concern.
- **Storming** is when the group manages some stormy disputes.
- **Reforming** is when the group develops a plan as a way forward.
- **Performing** is when the group carries through an agreed plan.

☐ Give examples of these phases from your own experience in groups.

> 1. Can you think of a group that is forming? What characterises this group as one that is forming?
> 2. Can you think of a group that is storming? What characterises this group as one that is storming?
> 3. Can you think of a group that is reforming? What characterises this group as one that is reforming?
> 4. Can you think of a group that is performing? What characterises this group as one that is performing?

✍ Record your reflections in your Working Notes.

All groups pass through these phases; any dynamic, growing group will pass through these phases again and again. The role of a facilitator is to help the groups deal with these phases:

- *Initiating* when the group is forming;
- *Conciliating* when the group is storming;
- *Consolidating* when the group is reforming;

- *Co-ordinating* when the group is performing.
- ❏ Consider one of the groups that you are involved in when answering the following questions.

1. What phase is your group in at the moment?
2. What does it feel like to be in that phase?
3. What role should a facilitator play right now?
4. What would that role look like in your group?
5. What can you do to help at the moment?

✎ Record your reflections in your Working Notes.

Facilitating Groups
20 minutes

Groups must be developed with a lot of care if they are genuinely going to help people grow. They must be *open*, not closed; *inclusive*, not exclusive; *co-operative*, not competitive; *big* enough to have a critical mass and creative mix of people; *small* enough for all the people to be able to participate meaningfully; and *dynamic* enough for everyone in the group to be active, not passive members of the group.

The facilitator is not an expert, but an encourager who creates opportunities for everyone in the group to participate, and helps the group to wrestle with the issues it is confronted with as a group.

The facilitator doesn't try to answer all the questions. Instead the facilitator asks probing questions, helping the group to come up with their own answers. The facilitator doesn't try to solve all the problems. Instead the facilitator brings a range of points of view to bear that can help the group manage their many problems more responsibly.

Wherever possible a facilitator will include others in the facilitation of the group—rotating the role, and broadening and deepening the role to include co-facilitating. In this way, the group will develop a sense of ownership of its identity and its development.

The facilitator of a group needs to constantly monitor and manage two quite separate but equally important dynamics through every phase of the group:

- The *content* of the group, for example the aims and activities of the group. What do we want this group to do?
- The *process* of the group: for example the affinity and interaction in the group. How do we want to be in this group?

The facilitator of a group needs to learn to
- sit silently
- talk cautiously
- listen attentively
- reflect faithfully
- clarify carefully
- summarise clearly
- re-frame creatively
- act enthusiastically
- shift focus subtly when necessary
- use verbal and non-verbal signals

1. What is a facilitator?
2. What does a facilitator need to monitor in a group?
3. How can a facilitator manage the content in a group?
4. How can a facilitator manage the process in a group?
5. What are the skills a group facilitator needs to learn?
6. Which of these skills have we already learnt?
7. Which of these skills do we need to learn?

✐ Record your reflections in your Working Notes.

❒ Think of the last time your community development support group met.

1. Who acted as the facilitator(s) in the group?
2. What did the facilitator do to manage the content of the group?
3. What did the facilitator do to manage the process of the group?
4. What did the facilitator do well? What do you need to work on a bit more?

✐ Record your reflections in your Working Notes.

Conclusion
10 minutes

The follow-up reading for this session is:

> 'Journey Into The Acting Community' David Thomas, *Group Work: Learning And Practice,* ed. Nano McCaughan, George Allen & Unwin, Sydney, 1978, pp 167-181 (Reading 10).

The set community tasks for this session are:

- ☐ Meet with your learning partner and your community development support group.
- ☐ Share what you learnt in the session about 'initiating', 'maintaining' and 'facilitating' a group and talk how you operate as a group.
- ☐ Then talk about the other groups in your community and whether, with the community work you have in mind, you should operate through an existing group or whether you need to start a new group of your own.
- ☐ Either way, make plans as to how you can work through a group.
- ✍ Record your actions, reflections and conclusion in your Working Notes.

Session 11

Building Bridges for Cooperation

Objectives

- To review your understanding of the important part groups play in the process of community development.
- To consider the importance of cooperation between groups.

Review

15 minutes

> ☐ Review your work from Session 10.
> ☐ Review the issues raised in course notes in the previous session, particularly the important part groups play in the process of community development.
> ☐ Review the reading:
>
> 'Journey Into The Acting Community' David Thomas, *Group Work: Learning And Practice,* ed. Nano McCaughan, George Allen & Unwin, Sydney, 1978, pp 167-181 (Reading 10).
>
> ☐ Review the tasks:
> ❖ How did your meeting with your learning partner and your community development support group go?
> ❖ What was the most important thing you learned while doing your community tasks for the last session?

✎ Record your reflections in your Working Notes.

The possibility of cooperation

35 minutes

☐ Try to remember your first experience of cooperation, good, bad or indifferent. How and when and where did it occur?

✎ Record your reflections in your Working Notes.

We can discover the possibility of cooperation in a variety of ways. We may have grown up traditionally cooperating; grow into cooperating circumstantially or incidentally; or we may grow towards cooperating intentionally.

Traditional cooperation

Cooperation may be a reality we have grown up in as a tradition all our lives. Dave Andrews tells us the following story:

> My wife, Ange, grew up in a traditional Greek Australian migrant community. When they migrated to Australia from Greece, Ange's family sponsored the settlement of as many relatives from *Rihia* as they could. So Highgate Hill is often affectionately called 'little Greece' and dotted all over with *Rihiates*.
>
> Many of the next generation didn't appreciate the significance of the traditional community they grew up in and couldn't wait to get out of the neighbourhood. Now they are getting older, they are beginning to appreciate what the older generation have going for them. Like those friendships, which not only endure the years, but also make the years endurable.
>
> So they come back to the old neighbourhood in the hope of being able to experience the traditions of the communities that made them strong—like the ritual cup of coffee that my father-in-law still has every morning, at the break of day, with friends he used to herd goats with on a hillside over seventy years ago, and the accompaniment, personal support and mutual help those conversations over coffee together provide.
>
> For some of us who have grown up in traditional communities, discovering cooperation might be a matter of just waking up to ourselves and realising the significance of the heritage we may have taken for granted.

- What experience, if any, have you had of this kind of traditional cooperation?

✐ Record your reflections in your Working Notes.

Circumstantial cooperation

Cooperation may be a reality we have grown into gradually as a result of our circumstances. Because it happens slowly, in the ordinary course of our everyday lives, we've not realised it. Let's hear Dave Andrews again.

Ange and I chose to live in our neighbourhood to be near her family. Her mother and father live down the road and her sister lives round the corner. She has one cousin that lives at one end of the street, and another cousin that lives at the other end of the street.

Now, when we chose where to live, we were able to choose our neighbourhood, but we weren't able to choose our neighbours. They came with the territory. It was a bit like taking potluck at an office party.

However, over time, we got to know Len and Marie pretty well. We didn't stop at sharing a fence. We started to share over the fence borrowing tools, lending condiments, and swapping juicy bits of local knowledge. Therefore, it wasn't long before we became good friends.

My brother Phil, and his wife Karen, moved into their house without knowing a soul in their street. However, they hadn't been there long before their neighbour, Al, invited them over for a drink.

From then on they were in one another's houses all the time. Al adopted Phil and Karen as his own kids. He would do anything he could for them. Nothing was too much.

Phil and Karen adopted Al as an honorary granddad to their kids. Adrian, their son, brought Al a lot of joy. Moreover, when they named Alina, their daughter, after him, Al was on top of the world. They had become family.

For some of us, who have grown into community gradually, through circumstances in the ordinary course of our lives, discovering cooperation may be a matter of becoming more aware of the significance of our situation.

- What experience, if any, have you had of this kind of circumstantial cooperation?

✍ Record your reflections in your Working Notes.

Incidental cooperation

Cooperation may be a reality we have grown into quickly. Because it happened so dramatically, changing the ordinary course of our lives, we are acutely conscious of it.

Twenty years ago Brisbane suffered its worst natural disaster. The Australia Day Floods of 1974 claimed 14 lives, washed away 56 houses, and damaged another 8,500 in the deluge.

'Such disasters always produce their heroes.' says David Fagan. 'In Brisbane two men are often cited as the heroes of the 1974 flood.'

'Leo Hartas skippered the launch that caught runaway barges before they could run into the oil tanker, Robert Miller, which had broken its moorings in the city reach of the river.'

'Mathew Carrell was the first mate of the Cape Morton lighthouse tender who dangled a metre above the flood waters to free his ship's anchor from a thirty-five thousand volt submarine power line.'

'But such heroics are only a part of a bigger picture. Hundreds of volunteers quietly saved the day in 1974. Most of the flood victims were on the receiving end of a huge community effort.'

As a result of that 'huge community effort', in response to the flood, many local people experienced community as never before.

For some of us who have grown into cooperation quickly, through dramatic incidents that have changed the ordinary course of our lives, there is, at least for a while, a consciousness of the life-and-death significance of community.

- What experience, if any, have you had of this kind of incidental cooperation?

✎ Record your reflections in your Working Notes.

Intentional cooperation

The reality of incidental cooperation that comes with a crisis like the Brisbane floods, usually ends as the crisis passes, unless we choose to make that incidental cooperation an intentional cooperation.

Whether we grow up in community traditionally; or grow into community slowly, circumstantially; or are thrown into community quickly, incidentally; a continuing sense of community depends on developing a sense of cooperation intentionally.

It is one thing to get people to cooperate with one another intentionally in a group, but quite another to get a group to cooperate intentionally with other groups. Miscommunication, suspicion and competition ensure that most groups move in their own circles and keep a safe distance from one another.

- What experience, if any, have you had of this kind of intentional cooperation?

✎ Record your reflections in your Working Notes.

The difficulties in cooperating
20 minutes

As we all know, there are many difficulties in trying to cooperate.

- ❐ Take out a piece of paper and write a list of as many of these as you can think of in sixty seconds.

A list of difficulties in cooperating may include:

- A little suspicion
- Habits of isolation
- Fear of co-option
- Mistrust of motivation
- Proneness to competition
- Experience of polarization
- Disagreeable personalities
- Differences in language and style
- Conflicts over religion and politics

- ❐ Add any of these to the list you wrote. Think about which of them would be the greatest difficulties for you and your group, in trying to cooperate with others.
- ❐ Choose one of the difficulties that you nominated, and spend the next ten minutes thinking about how you would go about trying to overcome it.
- ✎ Don't forget to record your reflections in your Working Notes.

Some of the ways people try to overcome difficulties in cooperating include:

- Making phone calls
- Meeting one another
- Sharing information
- Consulting one another
- Swapping some ideas
- Affirming one another
- Encouraging mutual respect
- Apologising for past mistakes
- Resolving present problems

- Organising visits to the group
- Doing a personnel exchange
- Running joint training programs
- Co-hosting a specific one-off event
- Developing guidelines for cooperation

A great way to overcome the difficulties of cooperating between groups is by creating opportunities for people in those groups to meet together to chat or to work on a small manageable joint project. That way people can get to know one another in a more personal way, and deal at a personal level with the difficulties they have in cooperating.

It is often helpful to have one person from each group to act as a contact person to help liaise with the other group(s), to look for opportunities to develop the relationship(s), and to watch out for any problems that may arise.

The benefits in cooperating

20 minutes

There are obviously many benefits in cooperating.

❐ Take out a piece of paper and write a list of as many of these as you can think of in sixty seconds.

A list of benefits in cooperating may include:

- Not being alone
- Knowing others
- Widening contacts
- Deepening connections
- Broadening perspectives
- Reducing competition
- Increasing collaboration
- Sharing personnel and resources
- Developing integrated joint strategies.

The practice of cooperating between groups as well as in groups unleashes the potential in the whole 'body' that is greater than the sum of the parts. Social scientists refer to the hidden dynamics of this explosion of potential as *synergy* and *serendipity*.

Consent, as we have seen, involves finding a way forward together, in spite of our conflicts, that we can all affirm is in harmony with the hopes we have. Synergy means finding a way to make our differences work for us rather than against us. Serendipity means that what works out could be far greater than any of us imagine.

A group may consent to cooperating with another group. The decision may be one which some members may not feel is the best decision, but which they can all live with and commit themselves to support the best that they can.

Such consent releases latent synergy. Synergy is the essence. It catalyses, unifies and unleashes the greatest powers within people. Simply defined, it means that the whole is greater than the sum of its parts. It means that the relationship that the parts have to each other is a part in and of itself. It is not only a part but the most catalytic, the most unifying, the most empowering, and the most exciting part.

Synergy is everywhere in nature. If you plant two plants close together, for example beans and onions, the roots co-mingle and improve the quality of the soil so that both plants will grow better than if they were separated. The challenge is to apply to our social interactions the principles of creative cooperation that we learn from nature.

Family life provides many opportunities to observe and practise synergy. The very way that a man and a woman bring a child into the world is synergistic. The essence of synergy is to value differences, to respect them, to build on strengths, and to compensate for weaknesses.

We obviously value the physical differences between men and women. But what about the social, mental, and emotional differences? Could these differences not also be sources of creating new, exciting forms of life, creating an environment that is truly fulfilling for each person, that nurtures the self-esteem and self-worth of each, that creates opportunities for each to mature into independence and then gradually into interdependence?[1]

Serendipity is latent in synergy. You don't know exactly what's going to happen or where it is going to lead. Synergy is almost as if a group collectively agrees to scrap old scripts to write a new one. It is to start all over again.

> Could synergy not create a new script for the next generation—one that is more geared to service and is less selfish; one that is more open and is less protective; one that is more loving and is less judgmental?[2]

With synergy and serendipity you just don't know. Anything is possible.

---

1 Covey, p 262-3
2 Covey, p 263

- Can you think of any examples of synergy and serendipity?

✎ Record your reflections in your Working Notes.

The opportunities for cooperating

20 minutes

George Lovell reminds us

> 'community development means working for the growth of each individual, group and organisation, *and for the establishment of healthy inter-dependent relationships between them* [italics added].'[1]

1. What are some of the groups in your community which are more open to developing healthy interdependent relationships with other groups?
2. How could your group encourage cooperation between the groups?

✎ Record your observations in your Working Notes.

Conclusion

10 minutes

The follow-up reading for this session is

> 'The Settlement House: Mediator for the Poor' Buford Farris, Gilbert Murillo, and William Hale, in *The Practice of Group Work*, William Schwartz and Serapio Zalba, Columbia UP, New York, 1971, pp 73-95 (Reading 11).

The set community tasks for this week are:

- ☐ Meet with your learning partner and your community development support group.
- ☐ Share what you learnt in the session about cooperating with other groups in the local community.

---

[1] Lovell p 52

- ❏ Make a map of all the groups in your local community that might be interested in the community work that you want to do.
- ❏ Nominate the groups that you need to cooperate with, and arrange to visit them to explore the possibilities for collaboration.
- ✍ Record your actions, reflections and conclusions in your Working Notes.

Session 12

Bringing About Personal Hope

Objectives

- To review your understanding of the importance of cooperation between groups in the local community.
- To consider the importance of imparting hope

Review

15 minutes

- ☐ Review your work from Session 11.
- ☐ Review the issues raised in course notes in the previous session, particularly your understanding of the importance of cooperation between groups in the local community.
- ☐ Review the reading:

    'The Settlement House: Mediator for the Poor', Buford Farris, Gilbert Murillo, and William Hale, in *The Practice of Group Work*, William Schwartz and Serapio Zalba, Columbia UP, New York, 1971, pp 73-95 (Reading 11).

- ☐ Review the tasks:
    - ❖ How was your meeting with your learning partner and your community development support group?
    - ❖ What was the most important thing you learned while doing your community tasks for the last session?

✎ Record your reflections in your Working Notes

The importance of hope

10 minutes

If we want to try to facilitate transformation in our community, then sooner or later, we are sure to be confronted by the hopelessness that completely incapacitates most people in most communities.

We teach courses on transformation in many communities. At first glance most of the people who come to these courses seem hopeful enough; but when we begin to talk about the possibility of individual and collective transformation, it doesn't take very long for the discussions to bog down in despair; and those who seem to know the most about themselves and their society seem to be those most stuck in despair.

Without hope, there is no motivation for growth or change. It doesn't matter how many courses people go to, how many skills they acquire, how many certificates they accumulate. It is absolutely crucial that for any personal growth or social change to occur, people can experience hope in the midst of their hopelessness.

But how? How do you impart hope to the woman contemplating suicide because the man she loves is having an affair with a younger woman? How do you impart hope to a man who as a child was abused by his father and now finds himself doing the same to his own children? How do you impart hope to grieving parents whose only son has been killed by a runaway truck? How do you impart hope to a whole community of people whose homes are to be demolished to make way for a freeway?

There are many ways to impart hope. 'Hope is natural. We all possess it. It needs only to be *un*covered, not *dis*covered,'[1] says counsellor Maurice Lamm. He suggests the best way for us to impart hope is by encouraging people

- Not to trust statistics—the ones you see quoted may not apply to you
- Not to waste energy denying there is a problem—use it to find a solution
- Not to look for approval of absolutely everything you do—you won't get it
- To see yourself as others see you—your strengths as well as weaknesses
- To learn from the past, set your sights on the future, but live in the present
- Not look at the world around for answers—but look inside yourself instead.
- To link up with God through prayer and put love where fear used to be.[2]

---

1 M. Lamm. *The Power of Hope*, Rawson Associates, New York 1995, p 23
2 Lamm, p 65, 141

- Do you agree or disagree with the idea of uncovering hope?
- Which of the strategies suggested has worked best for you?

✍ Record your reflections in your Working Notes.

The example of Grow

20 minutes

Quite a few of our friends are involved in a group called 'Grow'.[1] Grow is a self-help, peer-support group which seeks to enable people to struggle more effectively together with issues that tend to cause mental and emotional trauma in our society.

Grow began in Sydney in 1957, when a group of psychiatric survivors decided to use a twelve-step program as a method for their own rehabilitation. As they say:

1. 'We admitted we were inadequate or maladjusted to life.
2. We co-operated with help.
3. We surrendered to the healing power of God.
4. We made a personal inventory and accepted our selves.
5. We made a moral inventory and cleaned out our hearts.
6. We endured until cured.
7. We took care and control of our bodies.
8. We learned to think by reason rather than by feelings.
9. We trained our wills to govern our feelings.
10. We took our responsible and caring place in society.
11. We grew daily closer to maturity.
12. We carried the Grow message to others in need.'

Since they started, more than 500 Grow groups have been set up round Australia, helping people who have had breakdowns put the pieces of their lives back together again, and develop, maintain and sustain a healthy way of life by showing them how to avoid unnecessary pitfalls in future.

Grow is both anonymous and inclusive, and open to all people, regardless of colour, class or creed, who respect the group and would like to participate in the group in order to enhance the mental and emotional health of our society.

---

[1] *The Program for Personal Growth*, Grow International, Canberra A.C.T. p5

Our friends in Grow believe individual problems require individual solutions, collective problems require collective solutions, and a sick society like ours desperately needs 'therapeutic community'.

> Beyond the whole humanity of the person and [their] close relationships, the developing adult cannot but be concerned with the wholeness of [their] human community. For, to the extent that [they] do not participate in the building of a community of persons, the progressively de-personalised social body which [they] go along with will tend to undermine and deform [their] personal life and [their] choicest relationships. There can be nothing static or neutral in the life of society any more than in the life of an individual.
>
> In other words, there can be no such thing as free and whole persons outside of free and wholesome relationships; nor can there be either of these profoundly healthy human realities, for any length of time, outside of a vigorously growing free and whole community, however small to begin with ... It starts with you and me caring about each other, doing things with each other, and sharing the striving of our hearts, giving each other constructive leadership. The more deeply we are affected by the loving acceptance and support we experienced from our earliest attendance at [the] group, the more unshakably we believe in the importance of sharing with others and nurturing them through the painful early stages of their growth with the group ...
>
> [O]utreach is the indispensable starting point with each new person who comes ... for help, no matter how slightly troubled or how severely disfigured by ... suffering he or she is. This elementary meeting of human beings contains implicitly the offer of, and invitation to, friendship ... We don't limit our outreach only to those ... who easily appeal to us and with whom we feel an affinity. The more truly we love our fellow human beings, the more likely we are to be affected by a sense of their immense worth when we see them most scarred by their background environment or experience. So much the more generously, then, will we be led to reach out to them and to bring to light the treasure buried and obscured within them. For we all have a treasure within us, and we're more able to realise it when we ourselves are on the receiving end of a genuine manifestation of love. Once touched to life by love that we have experienced, our vision enlarges to include many whom we would never have related to before, and, potentially, all suffering people ...
>
> In treasuring our friends we reveal their best selves to themselves, summoning them forth, bidding them to live, inviting them to grow ...
>
> This, in my opinion, is what real love is all about. For 'love is the consistent active concern for the whole welfare of another human being as equally important to one's own'.
>
> How many of us can say with feeling that we've been 'loved back to health'?

That is not to deny that we've had to do a great deal of work on our thinking, and our actions as well. [But] how many, once tormented and shattered, do you know who will tell you that they were motivated to struggle and grow only because some one significant person, or the group, dared to be generous with their love, their time and patien[ce] in between the weekly meetings? To the extent that we have grown to a certain maturity through the experience of friendship ourselves, and the example of other friendships round about us, we are able to give of ourselves with like generosity to help so many other lost ones who still have to find themselves.

The seeking and finding of ourselves only comes about through a sharing with another person who is prepared to cherish us as another self. For we are all other selves to each other.

I like to recall often a beautiful thought I heard years ago, attributed to Rabbi Brasch. Commenting on the commandment 'Love thy neighbour as thyself', he explained that in the original Hebrew the precise meaning was: 'Love thy neighbour for s/he is thy self' ...

Mary came to [the community] after years of struggle in rearing two children on her own. She was then a bitter woman, a mainlining drug addict with a long way to go ...

She made no secret of the drastic disorders she was battling with or what she had to do to change. Within two or three years she quit [shooting up] and from then on never looked back. She became a living example of God's healing work amongst us, and a personal link with many people to hope ...

When I first met Mary I found her very strong personality, difficult to cope with, for I was also very sick then. But, strange to say, Mary and I soon forged bonds of easy affection and became firm friends. From those earliest years we grew out of maladjustment together ...

She was often like a stiff dose of shock treatment to me. I remember when, to my tormented mind, everyone was watching me, talking about me, hating me ... However, Mary broke through to me bluntly: 'Gawd, just who do you think you are that other people would want to be talking about you all the time!'

I needed this devastatingly strong message. From then on I stopped saying those things, and eventually stopped thinking them.

Community ... can bring the best out of us all.[1]

> *May the spirit of friendship*
> *make us free and whole persons,*
> *and gentle builders*
> *of a free and whole community.'* [2]

---

1 Keogh,C.(ed.) 'Mary' and 'The Caring and Sharing Community' *Grow Comes of Age*, Grow Sydney 1979, pp 40, 118-120

2 *The Program of Growth to Maturity*, Grow ACT 1957, p 79

Living Community: Session 12

- What parts of the Grow story can you relate to most easily?
- What parts of the Grow story are more difficult for you to relate to?
- Do you know any other stories of people who have been helped by the process of surrendering to God or to their 'Higher Power'?

✎ Record your reflections in your Working Notes.

Prayer

45 minutes

The process of prayer

Dave and Ange Andrews lived for many years in a multifaith community known as Aashiana, a small group of some 20 to 30 young people from various religious backgrounds, who had got together to discern what it might mean to practise the compassion of God, exemplified in the life of Jesus of Nazareth, in New Delhi.

At the heart of their sprituality was prayer. In Aashiana, prayer was the process of developing an awareness of, and availability to, the Other.

- How would your definition of prayer compare with this definition?

✎ Record your reflections in your Working Notes.

The place of prayer

Prayer had an important place in the life the people of Aashiana shared together. It was considered to be the centre of the community and the catalyst for community development. They emphasised the importance of prayer because they believed that community begins and ends with the Other, and, in prayer, they could meet the Other who is the beginning and the end of the community development process.

It was in encounter with the Other that they believed that all that is good could be defined and affirmed, and all that is evil could be exposed and opposed, and our task for the future outlined.

It was in encounter with the Other that they believed a vision of justice could be revealed and an infusion of grace could be realised.

- Which of these statements best reflects your own perspective? Why?

✎ Record your reflections in your Working Notes.

The inspiration of prayer

It was in prayer that a vision for justice emerged:

*A vision of equality,
in which all the resources of the earth
would be shared equally between all the people on earth
regardless of nationality, colour, caste, class or creed.
A vision of equity,
in which even the most disadvantaged people
would be able to meet their basic needs
with dignity and joy.
A vision of a great society of small communities
interdependently cooperating
to practise political, socio-economic
and personal righteousness and peace
in every locality.*

Dave and Ange knew that there were many who pray but do not act and many who act but do not pray. However, it seemed to them that such people had misunderstood the meaning of both prayer and action. Prayer, for them, was the inspiration for action.

Through prayer, they developed contact with the Kanjars, the so-called "Unclean Ones", who lived across the road.

> The Kanjars were a tribe of a thousand people who migrated to the city in search of food during a time of famine, and ended up eking out an existence ever since in one of the city's slums.
>
> It was a very precarious existence. They lived in 200 little huts with thatch roofs, supported by bamboo poles, that that consistently failed to keep out inclement weather - the cold in winter, the heat in summer, or the rain in monsoon.
>
> Each hut housed a family of five, or more, a grandparent, a couple of parents, and two or three children in the space of a tent fit for two in a tight squeeze. Around the huts the dusty ground was covered with bits of trash, different kinds of refuse and faeces. Pigs rooted through the rubbish, searching for tit bits of excrement to snaffle.
>
> The only water was a smelly, stagnant pool nearby that bred mosquitoes carrying malaria round the settlement. There wasn't a

single tap or pump that supplied any drinking water. If people wanted a drink, they had to beg for it.

They tried to survive on a diet of rotten fruit and vegetables that they scavenged from the waste bins in the neighbourhood. Disease was rampant. Death stalked the encampment. It seemed like someone died in the slum every week.

They lived with tremendous dignity. But behind the smiles, there were always tears. The joke was always on them. They were outcaste, illiterate, illegal squatters, always being hassled by the public, and harassed by the police. We were determined to join them in their struggle for justice.

- Does prayer work for you like this? If it does, why? If it does not, why not?

✑ Record your reflections in your Working Notes.

The power of prayer

Hope of justice, for people without any hope of justice, like the Kanjars, could not possibly develop on the basis of their experience. Their experience, characterised by a continual litany of one injustice after another makes hope imperative, but it also makes it impossible.

We all knew there was no quick fix for the Kanjars. The only hope they had was in the construction of an alternative future that would be in total contrast to their present situation and a total contradiction of their past history. The only hope for the Kanjars depended on their capacity to access a power beyond themselves.

We were aware that there was a power that could be released in prayer that could be explained in terms of psychology and sociology. 'A self-therapy takes place', Jacques Ellul explains. 'There is the giving up of anger and aggressiveness, a validation through responsibility and meditation, a recovery of balance through the rearranging of facts on successive levels as seen from a fresh outlook.'

But we were also aware that there was a power that could be released in prayer that was beyond the capacity of contemporary psychology and sociology to explain. Ellul calls it 'the effectual, immediate presence of the wholly Other, the Transcendent, the Living One'.

We knew that if we were to access enough power to break the bondage of our conditioning ... we not only needed as much 'self-therapy' as we could get, but we also needed something altogether 'Other' than anything we had ever tried before.

It was in the early days of our involvement with the Kanjars when it happened ... The people were still quite nervous about any innovations. But, more out of desperation than anything else, they had decided to go ahead with a primary health program. They built a hut for a clinic, and a medical student volunteered to help the people with sanitation, nutrition and basic health care.

For a while it seemed as if the program might not only empower the community to deal with their dysentery, but also with their despair. But at a critical stage in the development of this program, a child fell seriously ill. She was brought to the clinic for help. But there was nothing that either the medical student or the other doctors she consulted could do to help.

The diagnosis was: 'tetanus'. The prognosis was: 'death'.

We sensed that if this child were to die, with it would die, not only the hopes of the parents, but also the hopes of all the other parents, who had hoped against hope that, at long last, their lives might be different. So we did the only 'Other' thing we could do at the time - we called the community together for prayer.

Even though we all prayed for the child to live, I think all of us expected it to die. But it didn't. And that made all the difference. Because it proved beyond doubt that things could be different.

And that belief, that things could be different, unleashed the latent confidence in people, that they could be different in spite of their conditioning. That confidence ... became the foundation of all the work that the Kanjars have done to develop the community since then.

I remember talking to Ramu, a Kanjar leader, before I left India. I asked him what he thought were the most significant changes that had taken place in the Kanjar community ...

He said: 'We have changed in many ways, Daud bhai.

'We believe God is for us. Not against us. Though we are little people, we are no longer afraid of big people. We are prepared to stand up for what is right. ... We work things out better now in the community council. We do not have as many fights. Remember the fights we used to have, when we used to throw those big bricks at one another? These days we men spend less time taking drugs and getting stoned.

'We work in the garbage recycling co-op we have set up. We are able to bring in enough money—two or three times more than we used to get before—to meet more needs at home. Our wives are happier. Our children are healthier. And not so many of us die so young any more.

'Not everything is good. Many things are still bad. But it's a whole lot better than it was before.'[1]

---

1 A. Twelvetrees, *Community Work*, p 58

> - What is an example of 'self-therapy' that can occur through prayer?
> - What is an example of something 'wholly Other' occurring through prayer?

✍ Record your reflections in your Working Notes.

We cannot predict what will happen when we pray. All we can say is that something will surely happen. Sometimes something will happen that is 'wholly Other'. There are two kinds of wholly Other things that can happen. Either our problems will be solved; or, though our problems may not be solved, we will be given power to cope with our ongoing problems. We tend to see only the first thing, and not the second, as a miracle. But both are miracles—and may make all the difference in the world.

The practice of prayer
20 minutes

May we suggest a few ways of praying, that many people in our community have found very helpful—and our community is not particularly 'religious'.

Be glad to be alive

We need to make sure we get enough sleep each night, so we wake up every morning, not groggy, not grumpy, but glad to be alive. As we wake we can be more aware of the love of God in us and around us and so we give ourselves over to the joy of living more fully and more freely.

Let the grudges go

In order to prepare ourselves for the day, we can take a bit of time just to sense the tensions in our bodies that signal things we are uptight about. Often these are grievances, real or perceived, of ways that people thwart our plans. We can note the issues they raise that we need to address. Then let them go.

Let the love flow

Once we let our grievances go we can begin to let the love flow. We can try to do this by bringing to mind all the people that we are connected to in our community, then one by one, picture their face, speak their name, and pronounce a blessing upon each and every one of them, friend and foe alike.

Deliberate on the locality

We can often be in a hurry, on the move from morning to night. At regular intervals throughout the day we can always take the time to stop, to look, and to listen to deliberate on the activities, conversations, and undercurrents in our community.

Meditate on the community

Every now and again we can try to get a bit of distance from our community and put it into a bit of perspective. We can meditate on our community, both as it is, and as it might be. Imagining all the things we could do to bring people in the locality together more.

Contemplate responsibility

Because there are so many things we *could* do, it's very difficult to figure out exactly what we *should* do. We are often confused. We can seek clarity by listening to the still small voice inside us. We can listen until we hear a word that is right for us. Then we can take that word to heart.

Discern a direction

We can take it to heart but not go for it on our own. We can run it by a group of people whose opinions we trust and together decide on what we are going to do about it. Discern the direction that we ought to take on the basis of consensus and consent.

Reflect on actions

Even if we get the direction right, doesn't mean we get the action right. We may actually get it wrong far more often than we'd like to admit. It's really important to be a part of a group that can help us monitor our progress by reflecting on our actions.

Celebrate an achievement

When we reflect on our actions, we are brought face to face with our failures, as well as our successes. If we're not careful we can let our failures discount our successes. So it's important to be a part of a group that can help us not only evaluate our progress but validate our progress.

- Which of these disciplines do you practise?
- Are they helpful? If so, why so? If not, why not?
- Which of these disciplines would you like to practise?

- How would you expect the practice to help you?
- Which of these disciplines would you like people you work with to practise?
- How would you expect the practice to help the people you work with?

✎ Record your reflections in your Working Notes.

☐ Finish this time of reflection with a prayer by Michael Leunig.

Michael Leunig, Australia's foremost cartoonist, writes prayers for the *Sunday Age* as his contribution to what he calls 'this wonderful, free-form, do-it-yourself ritual of connection and transformation'. Here is an excerpt from *A Common Prayer*.

> *God help us to change.*
> *To change ourselves,*
> *and to change our world.*
> *To know the need for it.*
> *To deal with the pain of it.*
> *To feel the joy of it.*
> *To undertake the journey*
> *without understanding the destination.*
> *The art of gentle revolution.* [1]

Conclusion

10 minutes

The follow-up reading for this session is

'The Spirituality of Community' *Building A Better World*, Albatross, Sutherland, 1996, p 335-356 (Reading 12)

The set community tasks for this session are

☐ Meet with your learning partner and your community development support group.

☐ Share what you learnt in the session about hope, and imparting hope through the practice of prayer in the process of community development.

---

1 Michael Leunig, *A Common Prayer*, Collins Dove, North Melbourne, 1990

❏ Encourage your community development support group to discuss their answers to the following questions about prayer:

- Which of these disciplines do you practise?
- Are they helpful? If so, why so? If not, why not?
- Which of these disciplines would you like to practise?
- How would you expect the practice to help you?
- Which of these disciplines would you like people you work with to practise?
- How would you expect the practice to help the people you work with?
- What will you do in the coming week to incorporate this practice into the way that you work with the people in your community?

✍ Record your actions, reflections and conclusions in your Working Notes.

Session 13

Bringing About Social Empowerment

Objectives

- To review your understanding of the importance of imparting hope, and the role of prayer in promoting hope.
- To consider the importance of promoting empowerment, and the role that articulating, communicating, demonstrating, cultivating, and celebrating our dreams can play in realising our power.

Review

15 minutes

- ☐ Review your work from Session 12.
- ☐ Review the issues raised in course notes in the previous session, particularly your understanding of the importance of imparting hope - and the role that prayer can play in promoting hope.
- ☐ Review the reading:

    'The Spirituality of Community' *Building A Better World,* Albatross, Sutherland, 1996, p 335-356 (Reading 12)
- ☐ Review the tasks:
    - ❖ How was your meeting with your learning partner and your community development support group?
    - ❖ What was the most important thing you learned while doing your community tasks for the last session?

'Those who lose their dreaming are lost'

20 minutes

Powerlessness

Hope alone cannot bring transformation. Hand in hand with hope must come empowerment. Hope is a fragile quality that is quickly destroyed by any feelings of powerlessness. Unless our feelings of powerlessness are dealt with, the hope infused today will be gone tomorrow.

Most of us are paralysed to some extent by a sense of powerlessness. Ironically, it is those of us who have tried hardest to transform the community who feel the most powerless. We know only too well how much the system is stacked against anyone who wants to work for transformation. If we are going to promote personal growth or social change, it is crucial for us to deal with our underlying sense of powerlessness.

Mordja amari boradja

For over 40,000 years, the indigenous people of Australia have struggled for survival in this often quite inhospitable continent, battling everything from flood and drought to genocide. They have a saying about survival:

> *Mordja amari boradja.*
> **Those who lose their dreaming are lost.**

- What, if anything, does this ancient saying say to you?

✍ Record your reflections in your Working Notes.

Unless we seek the dream of who we are meant to be, we will never find out what we are really meant to do. Unless we seek the dream of what we are meant to do, we will never find out who we are really meant to be.

The Story of the Willy Wagtail

Maureen Watson, a respected aboriginal elder, tells a dreamtime story that illustrates this point[1]. It's the story of the willy wagtail, a very common and cheeky little Aussie bird:

> The willy wagtail and the hawk lived by this big wide river and willy wagtail used to look across the river and try to fathom out what was going on on the other side.

---

1 Black, L. *To See the Storyteller*, Network News, Queensland Community Arts, Brisbane, 1st ed. 1995, p 8-9

But whenever she talked about crossing, flying across the wide river for a visit, hawk would clip her wings so she couldn't make the journey.

So she'd spend her time planning and waiting for her wing feathers to grow so she could make the journey. But every time she started to fly she'd get her wings clipped again.

So she laid her eggs and she hatched them out. Taught the babies how to fly. Showed them from the tops of the high branches the big wide world around them and the world across the water.

And she waited for them to grow so their wings would be wide and strong and they could all fly across the river. And time went by and she waited and there were more eggs and more babies and more times when she got her wings clipped.

One day, a pelican, who used to live on the river stopped by and said I often see you looking over the river.

She said 'I'd love to fly over there.'

And the pelican said 'Well you can.'

She said 'No, whenever my wings grow long and strong enough they get clipped and I couldn't make the journey.'

Then the pelican said 'You can do anything you want to do. If you want to do it bad enough then you will find a way.'

And she said 'Well, that's very nice of you to tell me that but' she said, 'I haven't been able to find a way.'

And pelican said 'You will.'

Sometime later pelican stopped by again and said: 'Are you still wanting to cross the river?'

And she said 'Yes, I do. '

He opened up his beak and said 'Well there is enough room for you and your babies to hop in and hide.'

The willy wagtail gathered up her babies and they settled themselves comfortably in the pelican's roomy beak and they flew away. And over the other side with all the adventuring and the wonderment of new discoveries, her wings grew big and strong and to this day nobody has ever clipped her wings again.

Most people can relate to this story. Like the willy wagtail, they want to be themselves, realise their potential, and in spite of the opposition they may face, they long to grow big and strong, stretch their wings, and fly as far as they can into the adventure of life together.

However, they can't do it without the help of a few pelicans!

- If you feel like a willy wagtail, what kind of pelican would you look to for help?
- If you feel like a pelican, how would you help a 'willy wagtail' in your community?

✍ Record your reflections in your Working Notes.

Finding ourselves again

Power [1]
15 minutes

- Do you know anyone who is powerful?
- What do you think makes them powerful?

✍ Record reflections in your Working Notes.

Typically, there are two kinds of power: *access* and *influence*. Access is the ability to develop connections, make calls, write letters, talk to people, and actually get invitations to meetings. Influence is the ability not only to get to the table, but to also get our issues on the table, not only to speak, but also to be heard. Influence can be applied through sanctions, bargains, or persuasion.

Sanctions

The use of punishments, threats, or the 'stick' to influence an outcome. This is coercive power—getting people to do what you want them to do, with an implied penalty if they don't do it.

1. When are we most tempted to be coercive?
2. What fears provoke this reaction?
3. What fears do we invoke in others?
4. What are the outcomes we achieve that cause us to continue?
5. What are the dangers associated with continuing to be coercive?

✍ Record reflections in your Working Notes.

Bargains

The use of inducements or rewards, the 'carrot' to influence an outcome. This is collaborative power—getting people to do what you want them to do, with an implied reward for them if they do it for you.

---

1 Adapted from B. Lee *The Power Principle*

1. What do we offer to people in exchange for doing us a favour?
2. How can we improve our bargaining power in negotiations?
3. What are some of the limits to our bargaining power?
4. What are some of the limits to bargaining per se?

✎ Record reflections in your Working Notes.

Persuasion

The use of the simple dignity, integrity, and credibility of the truth to influence an outcome. This is cooperative power—getting people to do what needs to be done, the best they can, by working things out with each other.

- ☐ Think of a person who has influenced you for the better, not because of any threats they made, or rewards they offered, but because of the inspiring example that they set for you.
- ☐ Reflect on their influence on your life and consider how you might become more like them by answering the following questions.

1. Who has influenced you for the better, not because of any threats they made, or rewards they offered - but because of the inspiring example they set?
2. How do you think you might be able to become more like them?

✎ Record reflections in your Working Notes.

Empowerment

Empowerment is about the development of power. But developing strong but gentle power does not involve sanctions or bargains exercised over others, but persuasive power that we exercise over ourselves.

Traditionally, power has been understood as the ability to control other people. This dominant notion of power emphasises the possibility of bringing about change through coercion and/or collaboration—an approach that tries to make others change according to our agendas.

Alternatively, a strong but gentle notion of power is best understood as the ability to take control of our lives, not by taking control of others, but by taking control of ourselves. This alternative notion emphasises bringing change by persuasion and conversion—an approach that does not try to make others change, but advocates change, individually and collectively, in the light of a glorious agenda for justice. It breaks the control that others have over us, and liberates us from our desire to control others.

The dominant notion of power is popular because it often brings quick, dramatic results. However, it brings short-term gains for some, and long-term losses for everyone else. Every violent revolution has sooner or later betrayed the people in whose name it fought its bloody war of liberation. The alternative notion of power is unpopular because it is usually a slow, unspectacular process. But it is the only way for groups to transcend their selfishness, resolve their conflicts, and manage their affairs in a way that does justice to everyone.

The essential problem in any situation of injustice, is that one human being is exploiting and exercising control over others. The solution to the problem is not simply to reverse roles, in the hope that the manipulation will discontinue. The solution is for people to stop trying to control each other. All of us, to one degree or another, exploit the opportunity if we have control over another person's life. Common sense therefore dictates that the solution to the problem of exploitation cannot be through the dominant approach to power with its emphasis on controlling others. The solution is in the alternative, the strong but gentle approach, which emphasises controlling ourselves, individually and collectively, through self-managed processes and structures.

☐ Answer the following questions:

1. What is the dominant approach to power?
2. What is the alternative strong, but gentle approach to power?
3. How do you develop power *with people* - rather than power *over people*?
4. How can you encourage people to change without trying to control them?
5. How can we encourage people to learn to take control of their own lives?

✎ Record your reflections in your Working Notes.

Helping people realise the power within

We need to remember that strong but gentle power essentially comes from within a person or within a group of persons.

We can help people realise the power we have within by articulating, communicating, demonstrating, cultivating, and celebrating our dreams in our own local community.

Step 1 – Articulate our vision ourselves
10 minutes

Dave Andrews writes:

> Some time back I felt the need to write out my vision. At the time I felt a bit embarrassed about putting down my vision alongside the visions that others had put up.
>
> Nevertheless, I knew I needed to articulate my own vision regardless of how it compared or contrasted with others.

> *I dream of a world*
> *in which all the resources of the earth*
> *will be shared equally*
> *between all the people of the earth,*
> *so that even the most disadvantaged*
> *will be able to meet their basic needs*
> *with dignity and joy.*
> *I dream of a great society of small communities*
> *co-operating to practise*
> *personal, social, economic, cultural and political*
> *integrity and harmony.*
> *I dream of vibrant neighbourhoods*
> *where people relate to one another*
> *genuinely as good neighbours.*
> *I dream of people developing*
> *networks of friendship*
> *in which the private pain*
> *they carry deep down*
> *is allowed to surface,*
> *and is shared*
> *in an atmosphere*
> *of mutual acceptance and respect.*
> *I dream of people*
> *understanding the difficulties they have in common,*
> *discerning the problems, discovering the solutions,*

*and working together for personal growth and social change
according to a visionary agenda of Jesus of Nazareth.
And I dream of every church in every locality
acting as a catalyst to make this dream come true.*

My vision statement has since become my mission statement. This is a vision that I share with groups of people who want to build a better world. In addition, it seems every time I share it, it strikes a chord that puts people in touch with the beat in their own heart.[1]

- What is your dream? (Take 5 minutes to write out a rough first draft.)

✍ Write your draft in your Working Notes.

Step 2 – Communicate our vision through stories
10 minutes

We can communicate our vision best through stories.

Stories are inclusive. They can be apprehended intellectually and emotionally—at different levels by different people. Stories are also inspirational: they can put soul into the body, and flesh on the bones of our dreams.

- What is a story about community that you feel would communicate your vision of community most clearly and most cogently to other people?

✍ Write a one-page story in your Working Notes.

Step 3 – Demonstrate our vision in our own lives
10 minutes

Change doesn't begin with others but with *ourselves*. The changes we advocate, need to be demonstrated first and foremost in our own lives. It is only as we demonstrate those changes in our own lives, that we can prove they are possible to live out in our own context.

---

[1] D. Andrews, *Can You Hear The Heartbeat?* Hodder and Stoughton, London, 1989. p. xiii (edited)

> • What is an initiative that we can take that will demonstrate the possibility of community development in the context of our own community?

✏ In your Working Notes, write two or three initiatives you can take.

Step 4 – Cultivate our vision in the lives of others
10 minutes

When it comes to working for change in our community, while it's true that we alone can do it, it's also true that we cannot do it alone! Change may start with us, but if it stops with us, it will stop totally. We need to make changes that encourage others to make changes.

> • What is a change you can make that will encourage others in your community to make some changes in terms of community development?

✏ In your Working Notes, write down a few ideas you can discuss with your community development support group.

Step 5 – Evaluate our progress in development
10 minutes

We need to remember that anything that's good enough to do is worth doing badly to begin with, but if we want to do good, then each time we have a go at something, we should try to do it better than we did before. And if we are going to try to do something better than we did before, we need to develop the capacity to critically evaluate our progress.

> • How can you help other people evaluate their progress in community development both critically and constructively?

✏ Make a plan you can discuss with your community development support group. Record your plan in your Working Notes.

Step 6 – Celebrate our progress in development
10 minutes

We need to encourage people to continue to work for community development in their community even when they are discouraged. Each person who feels inadequate needs to be helped to realise their capacity to act. Each person who feels afraid needs to be helped to realise their courage to act. Each person who feels impotent needs to be helped to recognise the potential of their actions. And each person who feels insignificant needs to be helped to recognise the consequences of their actions.

Even when people are discouraged, we can encourage them to continue to work for community development in their community:

- by commemorating every act of truth as a victory over lies, and every act of love as a victory over hatred
- consecrating every act of justice as a victory over brutality, and every act of peace as a victory over bloodshed
- celebrating every risk a person takes to make a stand—no matter how big or small—as a victory in the battle for the light of the world against the forces of darkness.

- How can you help other people celebrate their progress in community development happily - in private, and also in public?

✎ Make a note to yourself in your Working Notes to brainstorm the idea with your community development support group.

'A small group of citizens can change the world'
5 minutes

We mustn't let the people we work with get discouraged by those who say it's impossible to make our dreams for our community come true. For as Louis Brandeis said, 'Most of the things worth doing in the world had been declared impossible before they were done!'[1]

It doesn't matter how small a group they may be, nor how great the odds they may be up against. Anthropologist Margaret Mead would say to them: 'A small group of thoughtful, committed citizens can change the world. Indeed, it's the only thing that ever has!'[2]

---

1 Shields, p 24
2 ibid.

Robert Putnam says there are three specific reasons for people to believe that they can actually reverse the current trends, and reweave the fabric of our community:-

- People want real community networks, not just 'virtual' networks. Gen X'ers say flesh-and-blood friends are 20 times more important than cyber-friends. [1]
- People are exploring the development of 'real' community networks through participation in small groups. Currently 40% of the population is involved in the 'quiet revolution' going on in small groups. [2]
- Contrary to the previous downward trend 'volunteering' is up again. In 1998, 74% of high school students were involved in volunteering in the community, as compared with 62% in 1989. And, in 1998, 42% of first year university students were involved in volunteering regularly in the community, as compared with 27% in 1987. [3]

✏ Record your reflections in your Working Notes.

Conclusion

10 minutes

The follow-up reading for this session is

> 'Making our Place in the Sun', Anthony Kelly, Arlene Morgan and Dierdre Coghlan, *People Working Together III*, Boolarong, Brisbane, 1997, p 7-34 (Reading 13)

The set community tasks for this week are

- ☐ Meet with your learning partner and your community development support group.
- ☐ Encourage your community support group to answer the questions:

1. What is your own personal dream of community?
2. What are some good stories that illustrate your vision?
3. What can you do to demonstrate your ideal in your reality?

---

[1] Putnam, p 275
[2] Putnam, p 248-9
[3] Putnam, p 265

4. What can you do to cultivate those values in the lives of others?
5. What can you do to help others reflect constructively on their actions?
6. What can you do to celebrate any small progress the people you are working with may make towards realising their dream of community development?

- ☐ Don't forget to share your own ideas - and surprise them with your own effort to celebrate their progress so far at the end of the meeting!
- ☐ Look for opportunities to put these ideas into action with other people in the community over the next week.
- ✐ Record your actions, reflections, and conclusions in your Working Notes.

Session 14

Bringing About Problem Resolution

Objectives

- To review your understanding of the importance of promoting empowerment—helping people realise the power within
- To consider the importance of problem-solving in community development and the way to promote problem-solving by 'creating a problem-solving culture' and 'using the problem-solving cycle'.

Review

15 minutes

- ❏ Review your work from Session 13
- ❏ Review the issues raised in course notes in the previous session, particularly of the importance of promoting empowerment—helping people realise the power within
- ❏ Review the reading:

    'Making our Place in the Sun', Anthony Kelly, Arlene Morgan and Dierdre Coghlan, *People Working Together III*, Boolarong, Brisbane, 1997, p 7-34 (Reading 13)

- ❏ Review the tasks:
    - ❖ How was your meeting with your learning partner and your community development support group?
    - ❖ What was the most important thing you learned while doing your community tasks for the last session?

✐ Record your reflections in your Working Notes.

Problems and problem-solving

5 minutes

Even after hope has been infused and people feel empowered to take control of their own lives, there is the nitty-gritty business of getting down to resolving problems. A mechanical problem can be solved once and for all. Problems in human relationships are never solved once and for all—they must be resolved over and over again by the people involved.

A community that is transformed is **not** one that no longer has problems; it is one that has developed a process for resolving problems. In fact, a community is transformed only to the degree that everybody in the community can participate freely and fairly in resolving their problems together. The essence of transformation is in creative problem resolution.

1. How do you react to the idea that 'human problems are never solved once and for all—but must be resolved again and again by the people involved'?
2. How do you respond to the idea that 'a community that is transformed is not one that no longer has problems; it is one that has developed a process for resolving problems'?

✍ Record your reflections in your Working Notes.

The possibilities for problem-solving

30 minutes

Consider the circumstances for problem-solving

There are some circumstances in which problem-solving **is** possible, and some circumstances in which it **is not** possible. Problem-solving is only possible where all the parties in dispute are willing to move towards dialogue.

When we are faced with a dispute between people, we are faced with five possibilities:
1. No-one is interested in intracting with us or with the issues, and there is nothing that we can do.
    ❖ All we can do is give up on our goals and our relationships
    ❖ The only option is Total Avoidance.

2. People are interested in interacting with us, but not with the issues we are concerned with; so we can do something about the interactions but nothing about the issues.
   - ❖ All we can do is let go of our goals and hold onto our relationships
   - ❖ The only option is **general accommodation**.
3. The opposite to 2: People are not interested in interacting with us, but are interested in the issues; so we can do some work on the issues, but can do nothing about the interaction.
   - ❖ We can hold onto our goals and let go of our relationships
   - ❖ The only option is **unilateral action**.
4. To a certain extent, people are interested in interacting with us and with the issues we are concerned with; so we can do something to improve our interaction, and progress our issues quite substantially.
   - ❖ We can hold on to some of our goals and hold onto our relationships.
   - ❖ **Modest negotiation** becomes an option.
5. People are interested in interacting in an open-ended way, with us and with the issues we represent; so we can do several things to improve our interaction, and progress our issues a long way.
   - ❖ We can hold onto our goals and hold onto our relationships.
   - ❖ **Meaningful dialogue** is now an option as well.

- In which of these circumstances is problem-solving a real possibility?

✍ Record your reflections in your Working Notes.

Note: Problem-solving is possible where there is modest negotiation, but preferable where there is the chance of meaningful dialogue.

- What are indicators of modest negotiation or meaningful dialogue?

✎ Record your reflections in your Working Notes.

Note that one indicator is a willingness to actually get together. Another is a willingness to try to resolve the problem. See Figure 10.

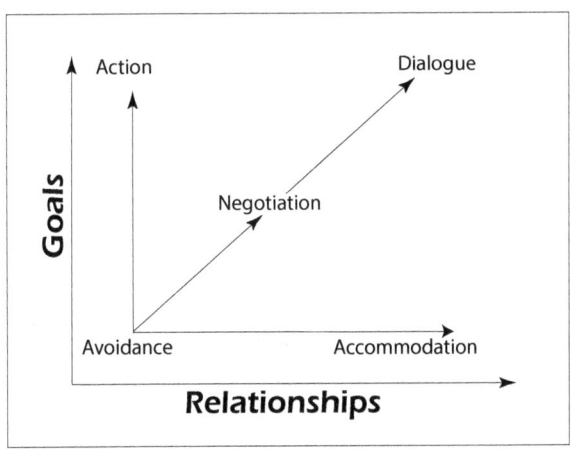

Figure 10: Possibilities for Dialogue [1]

☐ Identify a problem you are currently facing. Assess which possibility is a realistic option for you take in the situation and outline a way forward.

✎ Record your reflections in your Working Notes.

A problem-solving atmosphere

10 minutes

☐ Consider the characteristics of a problem-solving culture.

- What kind of culture makes it hard to discuss issues?
- What kind of culture makes it easy to discuss matters?
- How could we create culture that makes it easy to solve problems?

✎ Record your reflections in your Working Notes.

---
1 S. Fisher et al., *Working with Conflict*, Zed Books, St. Martin's Press, New York, 2000.

Living Community: Session 14

If we want to solve problems, we need to develop a problem-solving culture that is

- positive—even about negatives.
- accepting—of problems that exist.
- respectful—of the parties in dispute.
- aware—of the fears and desires behind the dispute.
- ready—to take some risks to try to resolve the problem.

> - What are some specific things you could do to promote a healthy problem-solving culture?

✎ Record your reflections in your Working Notes.

A problem-solving approach

30 minutes

If we are going to get involved in helping individuals or groups solve their problems, it will be helpful if we understand the five stages in a simple, straightforward problem-solving cycle (Figure 11):

- *Defining* the problem;
- *Identifying* all possible options for solutions;
- *Selecting* an option as a solution to the problem;
- *Implementing* the option selected as a solution;
- *Reflecting* on the results of our effort to solve the problem.

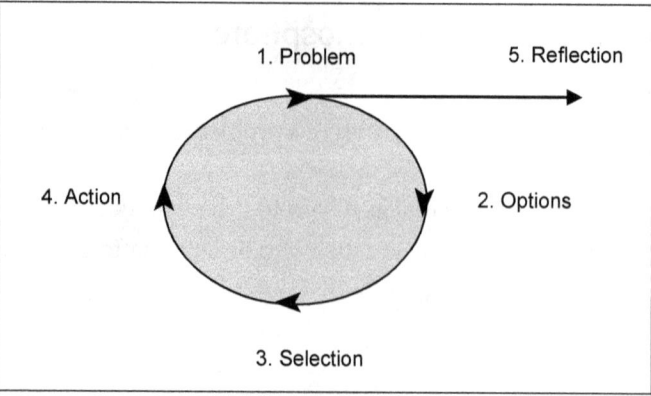

Figure 11. Problem-solving cycle process

At each stage of the cycle we need to encourage people to answer a strategic question:

1. **What is the real problem we are facing?**

This is often the most difficult stage in problem-solving. People confuse the symptoms with the cause. Often the problem is overlaid with unresolved past conflicts.

As witnesses, we must help those with the problem to get beyond a superficial view to a deeper understanding of the problem.

If people cannot agree on what the problem is, then they have no chance of agreeing on a possible solution.

2. **What are all the possible solutions to this problem we are facing?**

At this stage it is a good idea to have a 'brainstorm' of possible solutions. Each person thinks of as many possible solutions as possible and these are listed—no matter how wacky or crazy they seem. Accept all the ideas uncritically at this stage, so that people do not feel inhibited in bringing forward their suggestions.

After the list is completed, it is time to look over each solution more critically. This can be done by trying the idea out in our imagination.

- What would the possible results be if it were implemented?
- What are its weaknesses? What are its strengths?
- Is there some way it can be modified?

There should be lots of discussion about each of the possible solutions. Disagreement will be healthy at this stage.

3. **Which solution will we opt for and implement?**

Those implicated in the problem must now agree on what they consider to be the best solution. The solution must be acceptable to everyone, and everyone must be convinced that it has a fair chance of solving the problem.

4. **Who is going to do what by when?**

Once the solution has been chosen, the implementation has to be discussed. It is a good idea to write down all the tasks that need to be done, and beside each task the name of the person responsible and the deadline they have agreed to.

5. **How is our problem-solving plan working out?**

Reflection must take place both during and after the implementation of the solution. During the implementation, people need to get together regularly and report on how they are going with their allocated tasks. Those involved need to discuss whether the program is actually solving the problem, or whether there needs to be some modification to the program. Sometimes the whole program will need to be scrapped and the whole process started again.

Before starting again it will be important to discuss what was learnt from the previous effort.

- Why did it fail?
- Were we treating the symptoms or the cause?
- Did it fail because the solution was wrong, or because we failed to implement it properly?

Experience shows that often people must be willing to 'try, try, try again' before they eventually succeed.

When the solution has been fully implemented, it is important to discuss the results. Each person should have the opportunity to say whether they feel the problem has been adequately solved. Each person should share what they have learned from the experience.

Our role as catalyst in this problem-solving process is to help those involved work through the cycle sensibly and to be sensitive to the needs of everyone involved.

- ☐ Pick an issue you are concerned about, and spend twenty minutes working through the issue using the problem-solving cycle as a guide.
- ✍ Record your reflections in your Working Notes.

A problem-solving anecdote

20 minutes

Consider Dave Andrews' story of 'The Big Bad Backyard Feud.'

> Ange and I had one set of neighbours who wouldn't even acknowledge one another, and there was nothing we could do about it that seemed to make a blind bit of difference.
>
> The problem was, you see, that the bloke we'll call Barry had some banana trees growing in his backyard, which cast a shadow across his neighbour's prize vegetable patch; and the bloke we'll call Bill used to mow his lawn at seven o'clock on a Sunday morning when his neighbour was trying to sleep off his hangover from a bout of serious heavy drinking the night before.
>
> As a result of this conflict Barry and Bill hadn't talked to each other for ten years ... [They] wouldn't even give one another the time of day.

We talked to them about resolving the conflict many times but neither of them would budge.

Till one day, we heard the sounds of fighting—some swearing, pushing and shoving—that ended ominously in with a loud thump. Then, after a few moments pause, someone screamed 'Bill's killed Barry!'

By the time we got there it was all over. Bill was hanging over the fence, breathlessly, staring at Barry. And Barry was laying, sprawled, in a heap on the ground.

We ran to Barry to see if he was still alive. He was knocked out cold, but would live to fight another day ... When he eventually came round, I said to him, 'Listen mate, you could have been killed today, all because you don't want to shift your banana trees . . . You've got to sort it out ... Be at my place tomorrow at three for a cup of tea.' And he nodded.

Then we jumped the fence, and went into Bill's place. He was sitting at the kitchen table with his wife who was chastising him in no uncertain terms. When she'd finished with him I asked if I could say something ...

I said to him, 'Bill, you could have killed someone today all because you want to mow the lawn at seven o'clock on a Sunday morning . . . You've got to sort it out. ... Be at my place tomorrow at three for a cup of tea.' And he nodded.

The next day at three, bang on time, Barry and Bill turned up. I invited them in, and they sat down, looking about rather shamefacedly.

As I gave them cups of tea, I caught their eye, and said, 'Well, what are we going to do?'

They said nothing. Just shrugged their shoulders and sat there staring back at me.

'Well,' I said. 'It seems to me that we've got to try to end this dispute before it's the end of us ... What do you think you can do about it, Barry?'

'I could cut down my banana trees after the next bunches ripen, and replant them, further away from the fence.'

'What do you think of that, Bill?'

'That's all I want,' said Bill.

'What do you think you can do in return, Bill?' I asked.

'I guess I could mow the lawn a bit later.'

'How much later?' I asked.

'Two hours later.'

'What do you think of that, Barry?'

'That'll do me,' said Barry.

'Well I reckon we might be pretty close to a deal here. What do you reckon?'

'Sure thing!' they replied, looking pretty pleased with themselves.

'Then I've just got two final questions ... First question is, what are you going to do next time one or other of you comes home drunk?'

Barry said, 'We don't have to hang over the fence and abuse each other. We can go to bed and sleep it off—as long as people let us sleep it off, that is.'

'What do you think of that, Bill?'

'Fine by me,' he said.

'So you're both happy with that?'

They nodded.

'Second question is, what if something comes up—what if you get into a bit of a scrap—what are you going to do then?'

Bill said, 'No worries! We'll just come over here, have a cup of tea and sort it out!"

'What do you think of that, Barry?'

'Fine by me,' he said.

From then on, they did exactly what they said they'd do. There were no more fights. After they bore the next bunch, the banana trees were cut down. The lawn still got mown regularly on a Sunday, but later, much later, in the day. In fact, the only sound I ever heard from then on, early on a Sunday morning, was the sound of Barry and Bill swapping handy hints with one another about their gardens, as they went about their work side by side.

1. What did you like about this story?
2. What does it say about creating a problem-solving culture?
3. What does it say to you about using the problem-solving cycle?

✍ Record your reflections in your Working Notes.

Conclusion

10 minutes

The follow-up reading for this session is:

> 'The Hotham Hill Neighbourhood Association'. John Goff, *People Working Together*, UQ Press, Brisbane, 1969. p 123-131 (Reading 14)

The set community tasks for this session are:

☐ Meet with your learning partner and your community development support group.

- ☐ Share what you learnt in the session about problem solving by creating a 'problem-solving culture' and using the 'problem-solving cycle'.
- ☐ Then out of all the problematic situations you face in your community, pick one where there is both a willingness to meet and a willingness to try to deal with the problem, and do what you can to help solve it.
- ✎ Record your actions, reflections and conclusions in your Working Notes.

Session 15

Bringing About Real Transformation

Objectives

- To review your understanding of the importance and methods of problem-solving in community development, by creating a problem-solving culture and by using the problem-solving cycle.
- To consider the importance of problem-solving that is not just 'spinning our wheels' but making some progress, by using a soul-centred problem-solving process.

Review

15 minutes

- ❐ Review your work from Session 14.
- ❐ Review the issues raised in course notes in the previous session, particularly your understanding of the importance of problem-solving in community development and the way to promote problem-solving by 'creating a problem-solving culture' and by 'using the problem-solving cycle'.
- ❐ Review the reading:
    > 'The Hotham Hill Neighbourhood Association' John Goff, *People Working Together*, UQ Press, Brisbane, 1969. p 123-131 (Reading 14)
- ❐ Review the tasks:
    - ❖ 1. How was your meeting with your learning partner and your community development support group?
    - ❖ 2. What was the most important thing you learned while doing your community tasks for the last session?

✎ Record your reflections in your Working Notes.

Real transformation

30 minutes

The problems with problem-solving

We have already noted that imparting hope is not enough to bring about genuine transformation in a community. People need to be empowered to take control of their own lives. But empowerment alone is not sufficient if people still don't understand how to use that power to resolve their problems.

However, even helping people solve their own problems is not enough. They may resolve the problem in such a way that does not contribute to the long-term development of themselves or their community. In fact, the problem may be resolved in a way that yields short-term gains but long-term losses. If genuine transformation is to occur, it is absolutely essential that people discover how to resolve their problems together in a way that yields long-term gains for everyone, even if it means short-term losses in the meantime.

- What is the problem with problem-solving that yields short-term gains but long-term losses?
- Why is it important to promote problem-solving that yields long-term gains, even if it means short-term losses in the meantime?

✍ Record your reflections in your Working Notes.

The importance of prophetic input in problem-solving

In order for people to settle disputes, creatively and constructively, we need to enable people to solve problems together in the light of a prophetic soulful perspective.

Throughout history, there have always been prophets, both secular and religious, who have spoken with soulfulness. These prophets courageously speak to us, with passion for love and justice. They call on us to grow and to change by solving problems in the context of a radical spirituality of compassion, and to develop a world in which all the resources will be shared equally between all the people, so that even the most disadvantaged among us will be able to meet their basic needs with dignity, integrity and joy.

Sadly, history has so often been the story of the silencing of the voice of the prophet and hence the silencing of the voice of the soul. In rejecting the voice of the soul, history has become a tale of paradise lost, revolutions betrayed, and lives wasted.

If genuine, sustainable transformation is to occur, we need to enable people to solve problems in a way that takes into account the soulful insights of the prophetic tradition.

It is impossible to create a more loving and just society unless we take into account the agenda of love and justice advocated by secular and religious sages through the ages.

1. What is a prophet?
2. What does a prophet do?
3. What are the consequences of ignoring or rejecting the prophetic voice?

✍ Record your reflections in your Working Notes.

Consider the example of Fred Hollows

We need to solve our problems in a way that takes into account the insights of the prophetic tradition. 'What is a prophet?' asks Paulo Coelho. 'Someone who goes on listening to the same voices he heard as a child—even if adults call it foolishness.'[1]

A prophet is in touch with the soul, and speaks to us with a passion for love and for justice which seems naïve, but calls us to live out the wisdom we hide in our hearts.

One of our great modern secular prophets in the twentieth century was Fred Hollows. Dr. Fred Hollows was among the most well-known and well-loved of all the advocates of human rights in Australia. The irrepressible and irascible 'wild colonial boy of Australian surgery', as Tom Keneally once called him, set a pace that it would be very difficult for the rest of us to keep up with, but he set a lead along a path of practical, personal social justice that we would only refuse to follow at our own peril. We would do well to consider his far-sighted example in trying to solve the problems we are facing. Fred's story goes like this:

> 'Some years ago, a friend sent me a card with a snatch of verse attributed to Ralph Waldo Emerson on it. I put it on my office wall. It goes:

---

1 Paulo Coelho, *The Fifth Mountain*, Harper Collins, Sydney 1998, p 23

To laugh often and much.
To win the respect of intelligent people
and the affection of children,
To earn the appreciation of honest critics
And to endure the betrayal of false friends.

To appreciate beauty.
To find the best in others,
To leave the world a bit better,
Whether by
a healthy child,
a garden patch
Or a redeemed social condition,

To know even one life has breathed easier
Because you lived—
This is to have succeeded.

... When the Gurindji committee told me they were taking Donald and Vincent back to the Northern Territory and there were some seats on the planes for a few doctors who were willing to make themselves useful, I jumped at the chance to go. Barry Pascoe, who was an endocrinologist and general physician and Ferry Grundseit, a pediatrician, were interested, so we flew up to the Gurindji camp. It took us three days to get there.

Just before we turned in, Vincent asked me what I wanted to do in the morning and I said I wanted to see all the grown men in the camp. We slept the first night under a tarpaulin, all in together, pilots, a nurse, the lot, and it was mayhem. This was the Watti Creek camp. The bloody dogs fought all night and ran over us and I'd had hardly any sleep when Vincent woke me up with a gentle shake on the shoulder.

'Fred,' he says, 'the men are ready.'

About twenty or thirty men were sitting quietly under a shelter waiting. I got my magnifiers on and went over and had a look at them. Every man who'd been a stockman for any length of time had Labrador keratopathy. It was cattle camp country and the stockmen worked long hours in the daylight. Their hats didn't protect them from this scatter of reflected light from the ground. It wasn't a blinding condition but it impaired sight. As well, there were cataracts that were blinding them, and signs of advanced trachoma ...

The next day I saw all the women. The day after that all the children. They were free of the hazy cornea condition, because they weren't obliged to work in the sun all day, but the women had a lot of cataract and trachoma, and there were signs of the juvenile forms of trachoma in most of the children.

Corneal blindness from prolonged trachoma is the end of the road. Trachoma has two stages—follicular, indicated by the presence of small white or creamy objects (collections of white blood cells) found inside the conjunctiva, and cicatricial, referring to the scarring and other damage to the eyelids and eye. When trachoma reaches its vision-threatening stage—characterised by in-turned upper eyelashes and ulceration—it is a very painful condition.

It was a shock to me. I'd been working at the hospital and in my private practice and seeing a parade of eye disorders, but nothing like this. I thought I'd seen every sick eye condition there was to be seen, but I was wrong. It was like something out of the medical history books—eye diseases of a kind and degree that hadn't been seen in western society for generations! The neglect this implied, the suffering and wasted quality of human life were appalling.

I went wild, walked over to Wave Hill station and virtually commandeered the radio. I got on to Darwin and demanded that they send a doctor down to look at this situation ... Not long after I'd been quoted in the press as saying that the discrepancy between rural and metropolitan health care in Australia was a scandal, Ross McKenna from the French Department of the University of New South Wales began sending me notes inviting me to attend a meeting of the Redfern Aboriginal Legal Service. I knew that the university had helped to set up a sort of shopfront legal centre for blacks in Redfern (along the lines of some of the services set up by the Black Panthers and others in the States), but legal matters bore me to tears so I hadn't taken any particular interest. However, Ross was very persistent; his notes pursued me all over the university and the hospital and one Friday night, after a bit of a drinking session at the pub, I decided to go along and see what it was all about.

After some to'ing and fro'ing, Redfern was unfamiliar territory to me then, I got to the meeting. I took a seat and prepared to be bored for a while. It was a small group—two or three whites, three or four Aborigines—and to my surprise they were talking about medical matters. There were no doctors, maybe a nurse in the group, I was the only medico present and it was impossible not to be interested in what they were saying in general and in particular.

In general, the legal service was getting swamped by people with a whole range of social and medical problems. In particular, they were talking about a case in which a sick Aborigine had died in the back of Gordon Briscoe's car. Gordon Briscoe was a field officer with the legal service. He is an Aborigine from the Centre and not many people have had a more profound influence on my life than him. At that time he was one of the very few Aborigines in Sydney who had a car—an old Volkswagen.

Briscoe was at the meeting along with Shirley Smith, 'Mumshirl', who's done a lot for Aborigines over more than thirty years, and Gary Foley, and they asked me if I could help them set up a medical service for blacks. I said that whatever lawyers could do doctors could do, and I agreed to talk to a few people.

Next Friday there was another meeting, better attended. The Aborigines started to outline the case for a medical service and they were utterly convincing: blacks weren't welcome in doctors' surgeries, they got pushed to the back of the line in Casualty wards and public hospital clinics and so on. Paul Beaumont stood up and he said, 'You only need six things to start a medical service. Doctors, Fred and I can get the doctors' premises, Len Russells can organise that; Aboriginal receptionists and managers, Shirley Smith can find them; publicity in the pubs and shops, Ross McKenna can do that; and transport, Eddie Newrnan can handle that.'

Everyone there saw that he was right and they got very excited. Someone said, 'When can we start?'. Someone else said, 'Monday night.' I said, 'Whoa, it might take a bit longer than that.'

But in fact we opened just ten days later. One of the first things I did was to check out the one doctor in the area who the Aborigines had any time for. I had to make sure that our service wasn't going to bugger up something that was already in existence. I went to see this doctor, who said that he paid calls on Aborigines and collected the tiny fee the government paid GPs for services to 'indigent persons'. It was next to nothing. He admitted that he didn't see blacks in his surgery because if he did the whites wouldn't come and the practice would go broke. He said that a medical service for blacks would be the best thing possible.

So we went ahead. We plundered the Prince of Wales Hospital for equipment—stethoscopes, thermometers, scales, all the accoutrements of a medical practice, we shamelessly stole. And we learnt as we went along. I remember seeing a man, early in the piece, deciding what he needed and writing out a script.

He said, 'What's this, doc?'

'Take it to a chemist and you'll get the medicine.'

He shook his head. 'No money, doc.'

We backed a truck up to the pharmacy at the hospital and loaded it half full—tens of thousands of dollars worth of pharmaceuticals.

It wasn't always a matter of clandestine raids, there were some sympathetic people around. Pretty soon we had more doctors, GPs, specialists, professors of this and that, volunteering their services than we could handle. The medical service was a great success and there are more than sixty of them now Australia-wide, in the cities and in country towns, all owing something to that original model and the principles on which it was based.

One of the most important of those principles was that the Aborigines staffed and managed it to the fullest extent possible.[1]

---

1 Adapted from B. Lee, *The Power Principle*

Living Community: Session 15

1. What was Fred's response to 'appalling neglect'?
2. What does he mean when he says: 'I went wild'?
3. What did he do about the health problems?
4. How did he try to solve these problems?
5. How did Fred's attitude to 'blacks' contrast to the attitude of 'white' society?
6. What is it about Fred's response that is a prophetic challenge to all of us?

✎ Record your reflections in your Working Notes.

Real, genuine, sustainable transformation can only be brought about by enabling people in the community to solve their problems in the light of this prophetic tradition.

Soul-centred problem-solving

15 minutes

Peter Westoby, a community work consultant with the Community Praxis Co-op, writes:

> Community development has become the latest *technique* that [governments have decided to take on in order to try to] solve the problems of society.
>
> Governments for so long have been called upon to fix things: they have tried all sorts of techniques, right, left, and centre—[and] they have failed.
>
> ... There has been a mighty shift in focus. As part of that shift in focus there is a stronger rhetoric advocating 'the community must take responsibility'—the community must solve the problem.
>
> [But] community development is much less about [a problem-solving] *technique* and more about *soul*. Community development practitioners cannot simply 'move in' [using the latest problem-solving technique] and quickly 'mobilise' a community to solve their problems. They can only participate, along with others, in invoking the 'soul of community' without which no community problems will ever be successfully resolved.
>
> It is my thesis that the problems are not the problems; that the fundamental problem is a lack of soul and our community problems are simply symptoms that act as voices calling us back to soul. We have to look with depth beneath the forms of problems as they manifest themselves to us. This deeper look into ourselves will lead us to soul.

Soul itself is not the solution, it is a dimension of experiencing life in a way that adds relatedness and value. Our answer (to our questions) lies in the relatedness and value.

Thomas Moore puts it well: *'civility and community are not—as some would say—a humanistic achievement: they are the work of the genius of things, the soul of culture'* (italics added) [1].

But what—asks the average Aussie man or woman—is the soul of our culture? Michael Leunig, the Australian cartoonist, depicts the soul of our culture as a duck—and depicts the rediscovery of the soul of our culture as a man kneeling before a duck (see Figure 12). He says:

I have drawn a simple picture of a person kneeling before a duck to symbolise my ideas.

The duck in the picture symbolises one thing and many things: instinct, innocence, the primal and the mysterious; qualities we can easily attribute to a duck and which coincidentally and remarkably, we can easily attribute to ... the soul.

The act of kneeling in the picture symbolises humility. The kneeling man knows that a proud and upright man cannot talk to a duck. The man kneels. He humbles himself. He comes closer to the duck. Because it improves his chances of communicating with it. This picture can be seen as a symbol of the human spirit ... searching for soul.

The man wants a robust relationship with it, he wants to trust it, he wants its advice and the vitality it provides. Its important to him. The more he come(s) to terms with his soul, the more the spirit leads to love and a better world, for him and those around him. This personal act is also a political act because it affects so many people ...'

Figure 12

---

1 P. Westoby 'Soulful Community Development', *Praxis* Vol.I, Community Praxis Co-op Brisbane 2001, p 7-17

'But how do we search for our soul?' he asks. 'How do we connect with this transforming power?' Answering his own question, he says: 'It seems as difficult as talking to a bird.' He goes on to say, 'there are many ways, all of them involving great struggle, and each person must find his or her own way. But an important, perhaps essential part, of this process seems to be an ongoing humble acknowledgement of the soul's existence.'

Michael Leunig says:

> It is timely that we give thanks for the lives of all prophets, teachers, healers, and revolutionaries, acclaimed or obscure, who have rebelled worked and suffered for the cause of love and joy; [and] celebrate that part of us, that part within ourselves which has rebelled, worked, and suffered for the cause of love and joy.
>
> Let us search for these places in the world—where all creatures may find acceptance—within ourselves and others. Let us restore them. Let us strengthen them. Let us create them. May we mend this outer world according to the truth of our inner life—[our] soul.[1]

1. What would you say is the soul—or the essence—of what Fred calls Ralph Waldo Emerson's 'pretty good summary of what life is all about'?
2. Why is a deep appreciation of this dimension of life so important for us if we are to solve the problems that we face every day in our communities?

✎ Record your reflections in your Working Notes

Using a soul-centred problem-solving cycle

10 minutes

We need to find a way to facilitate this process of transformation by enabling people to solve their problems together, in the light of what Fred calls 'what life is all about'.

With those who acknowledge the significance of soul to some degree or other, it is reasonably straightforward. See Figure 13.

---

1 Michael Leunig, *A Common Prayer*, Collins Dove North Blackburn 1990

Bringing About Real Transformation

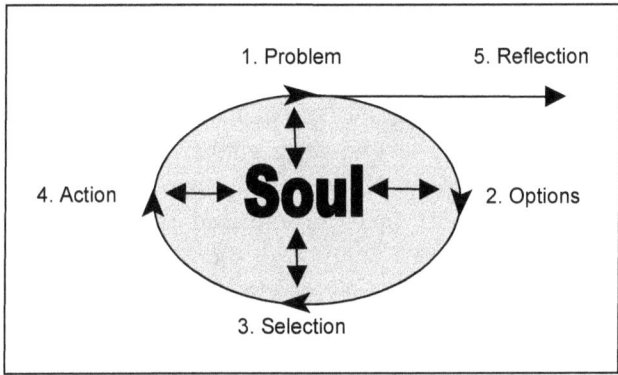

Figure 13: Soul-Centred Problem-solving Cycle

When we meet together, we encourage each other to share our problems and to help each other resolve these problems in the light of the spirit of radical compassion advocated in the prophetic tradition. We acknowledge the problems we are trying to solve. We discuss the issues with the people who share the problems we are trying to solve. Then we search our soul in order to come up with some inspiration to help us try to resolve the problem in terms of our deep commitment to love and justice.

- Pick an issue you are concerned about in your community and spend twenty minutes working through the issue using a soul-centred problem-solving cycle as a guide. Try to understand the problem and deal with the problem in terms of your community soul.

- Remember, as Peter Westoby says, 'we can either see our role as being that of an exterminator attempting to eradicate problems, or we can develop a soulful approach that give what is problematic back to the community in a way that uncovers its values and invites people to give it attention. Attention, astute attention, attention requiring deep listening, is critical. Our answers [to our community questions] lie in this depth.'[1]

- Record your reflections in your Working Notes.

---

1 Westoby, p 12

Using a soul-centred cycle with sceptics

20 minutes

The real challenge is being able to facilitate the same kind of process with the majority of people who, for a whole range of reasons, might be sceptical of a soul-centred problem-solving approach.

Soul is at the heart of every situation that we encounter in a community. The effective resolution of the problems inherent in each situation depends on people being able to feel something of that radical spirit of compassion for themselves and for others; being able to be free to transcend their anger and guilt and inadequacy; and being able to act in a beautiful, free, self-aware, other-orientated, soulful manner.

However, most of the people we work with initially come across as being very sceptical of 'all this soul brother-soul sister nonsense'. So the challenge is to introduce them to the importance of soul in community work, in the very context of community work.

We do this by using a simple centred problem-solving process, as we introduced in the previous chapter. See Figure 14.

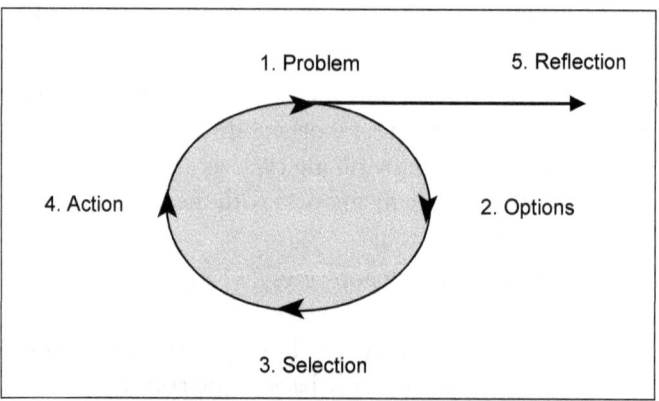

Figure 14: Centred Problem-Solving Cycle

We agree to work with people struggling with the issues that are important to them on the basis of *common sense* and *consensus*.

Because we believe soul is at the heart of every situation we encounter in a community, we find that soul is often expressed in the common sense that people often express in community meetings without their even knowing it.

We dialogue with people about their problems, about possible solutions to their problems, and try to decide on a particular course of action that we can take together on the basis of consensus.

Quite often, to the embarrassment of believers who claim to have exclusive rights to the truth, it is those without claims to a corner on the market of truth, who seem to be more intuitively in touch with the reality of their problems and of possible solutions.

We only decide on taking a particular course of action if we are convinced that it will move us in a direction that is true to the vision at the heart of a healthy community. The vision at the heart of a healthy community, as we have talked about, is:

- a safe space,
- a place where people are accepted as people,
- a place where both similarities and differences are respected,
- a place where everyone is important, and no-one is expendable,
- a place where people can participate in decisions that impact them,
- a place where people seek to do justice to the most disadvantaged—not only those inside the group, but also those outside the group.

Usually, if not invariably, we can come to consensus with the way that sensible people want to go about solving their community problems. Because—whether they know it or not—there is no fundamental conflict between a 'sensible' approach, and a 'soulful' approach, to solving our problems. Neither want to take any unethical quick-fix shortcuts. Both want genuine, loving, just, long-term, sustainable solutions.

Sometimes this connection—between the 'sensible' approach and the 'soulful' approach in the way we go about solving problems—is best left as *implicit* (Figure 15).

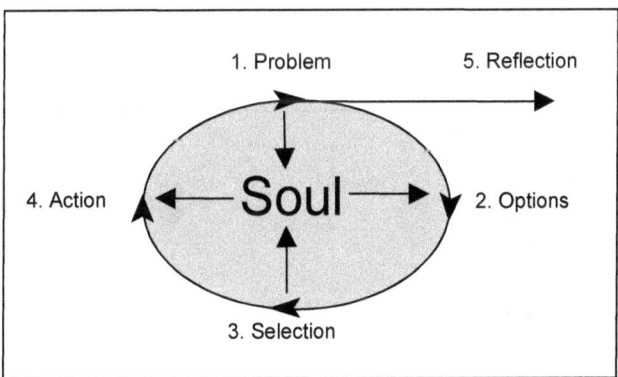

Figure 15: Implicit Soul-Centred Problem-solving Cycle

But wherever possible it is best to make this connection *explicit*. The best time to do this is when people are celebrating a successful resolution of a problem. It's a good opportunity to tell them that their success is a result of their having taken a 'soulful' approach without knowing it. And regardless of their attitude to soul, they cannot deny the successful resolution of the problem or disregard the value of 'soulful' approach they have taken. See Figure 16.

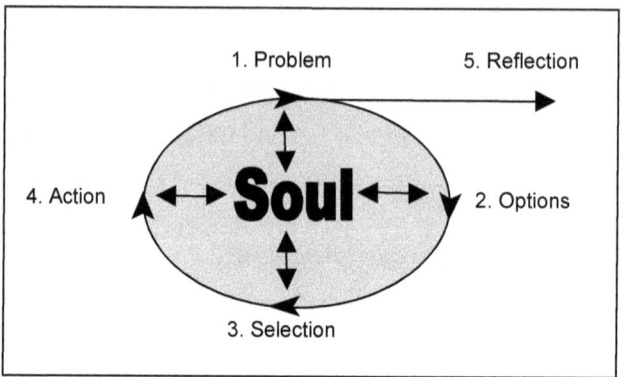

Figuree 16: Explicit Soul-Centred Cycle

As a result, the soulful approach becomes a significant point of view. Some see it as one point of view among many. However, some start to see it as the most important point of view by which community issues can be judged. Thus the soulful approach may graduate from one point of view, to become a significant point of reference. If people adopt the soulful approach as the point of reference for decision-making in their everyday lives, then they dramatically increase the chance of real transformation taking place in the community (Figure 17).

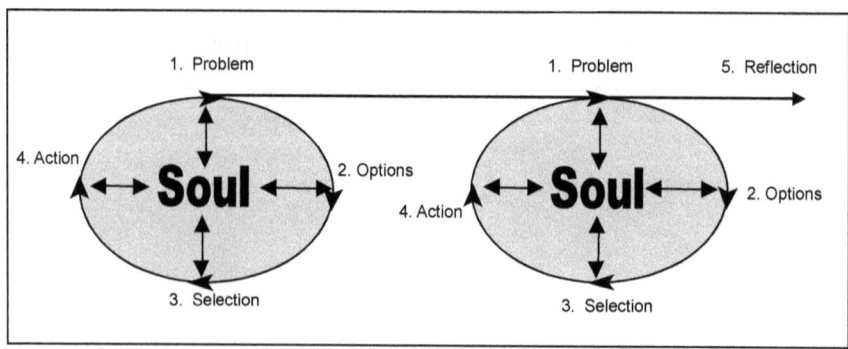

Figure 17: Soul as Central Reference Point in Ongoing Problem Solving Process

1. Why do we need to work with people on the basis of common sense and consensus?
2. What is an implicit soul-centred problem-solving cycle? How does it work?
3. What is an explicit soul-centred problem-solving cycle?
4. How can we move from an implicit to an explicit cycle?

✎ Record your reflections in your Working Notes.

The case study of the Cabramatta Gardens
20 minutes

Read the story of The Cabramatta Gardens as a case study of a 'soulful' approach to problem-solving.

> Peter and his wife Adrienne wanted to go to work in Vietnam. But, as often happens, things didn't work out the way they had hoped they would. So, instead of moving to Hanoi, this Kiwi couple decided that they would move to Sydney and work with the Vietnamese community in Cabramatta.
>
> Through Urban Concern, Peter and Adrienne were introduced to Cabramatta and got to know not only the Vietnamese, but also the Cambodians and refugees from Former Yugoslavia as well. The whole world was on their doorstep!
>
> In late 1999 Peter and his friends began to discuss the idea of 'doing something together' in the community. By January 2000 this idea had resolved itself into the idea of 'a community garden'. In February the Hughes Street Playground had been identified as the preferred site, and in April a formal proposal was submitted to lease a portion of the Playground for the community garden.
>
> Now the Hughes Street Playground was a notorious place. It had been taken over by the 'smack squad' a long time ago. But Peter and his friend Jeremy thought it was the perfect place for local people to begin to take back some of their space and put it to good sustainable community use.
>
> They not only got permission to use Hughes Street, but also a grant from the Fairfield City Council of $10,000 to fund the initial set-up of the garden.
>
> They got together with a group of local representatives over a twelve-month period to work out the details as to how to proceed with the project. The group came up the idea of having an 'Open Day', to share the dream of the garden with the community, and to invite people

of various ethnic backgrounds, especially those people on the 'margins', to join in and work on the project together.

Invitations were given out in seven different languages through community radio and a letter-box drop, and about 200 people turned up for the Open Day in March 2001. 90 people filled in forms with their suggestions.

In June there was an excursion to other community gardens round town. In August there was a training day on organic gardening. And in October there was the first on-site work-day. So by December 2001 the first eight plots were planted, and by January 2002 the first crops were harvested. By July 2002 all 23 plots had been completed and allocated.

The construction of the garden has been dependent on the people in the project who are prepared to work for benefit of the whole garden, not just their own patch. A committee of three people has been elected from each of the three language groups represented to manage the project.

The garden has been a great success on a number of significant levels. It has restored the park. The play area that had fallen into disuse is now being used again by families. The plots are fully subscribed and well maintained and people can gather fresh herbs and vegetables on a daily basis.

Moreover, the garden provides a productive therapeutic occupation for a group of retired, unemployed or underemployed Cabramatta migrants and refugees. It also provides a safe place for people to forge reciprocal relationships of acceptance and respect across the cross-cultural divide—a symbol of what some people believe is a little bit of 'heaven on earth'.

1. How would you summarise the story of the gardens?
2. What struck you as really significant about the story?
3. Where do you think the soul is in this story?
4. What lessons can you learn for your community work from this case study?

✍ Record your reflections in your Working Notes.

Conclusion
10 minutes

The follow-up reading for this session is

> 'A Civilisation which is still to be created', *Building a Better World,* Dave Andrews, Albatross, Sutherland, 1996. pp 297-311 (Reading 15)

The set community tasks for this session are

- ☐ Meet with your learning partner and your community development support group.
- ☐ If the other people in your group are open to it, discuss a problem that you all are trying to resolve from an explicitly soulful perspective.
- ☐ If the people in your group are not open to an explicitly 'soulful' discussion, just talk about a current problem from an implicitly soulful perspective.
- ✍ Record your actions, reflections and conclusions in your Working Notes.

Part Two

Community Work Practices

Session 16

Working within a Vocational Framework

Objectives

- To review your understanding of the importance of soul-centred problem-solving for real transformation in community development.
- To consider the importance of working within a vocational framework.

Review
15 minutes

- ☐ Review your work from Session 15.
- ☐ Review the issues raised in course notes in the previous session, particularly your understanding of the importance of 'soul-centred problem-solving' for real transformation in community development.
- ☐ Review the reading:

    'A Civilisation Which is Still to be Created' *Building A Better World,* Dave Andrews, Albatross, Sutherland, 1996. pp 297-311 (Reading 15)

- ☐ Review the tasks:
    - ❖ How did your meeting with your learning partner and your community development support group go?
    - ❖ What was the most important thing you learned while doing your community tasks for the last session?

✎ Record your reflections in your Working Notes.

The trend towards professionalisation

10 minutes

All of us know that most community work is still being done as it always has been done, not by professionals, but by volunteers. But as we look around, we see a significant trend in community work towards increasing professionalisation.

Many of us have agreed with the sociologist Harold Wilensky as he has witnessed the successive stages of professionalisation. At first, people who wanted to be involved in community work just went ahead and got involved. Then, various parties pressed for more adequate training in community work. Then those with more adequate training pressed for a professional association. Then those in the professional association pressed for the support of the system to impose certification requirements on the practice of community work.

So now we have a situation where voluntary community work goes largely unrecognised, unless it is under the auspices of professional community work.[1]

- What would be the reasons for this trend towards professionalisation?

✍ Record your reflections in your Working Notes.

There are of course many explanations of this trend. Some say it is due to an increasing sense of *responsibility* among community workers. It is simply a matter of community workers accepting responsibility for our area of work and assuming the responsibility to make sure that everything done by everyone in our area of work is done well. After all 'every other profession has carefully defined boundaries to its domains.'[2]

Others say the increasing trend towards professionalisation is due to an increasing sense of *desperation* among community workers. It's not merely a matter of mapping out our area of work. It's also a matter of staking out our claim to our territory of work and standing up against anyone who would dare to encroach upon our rights to exclusive control of our territory. 'It's a matter of self-preservation for practitioners in all fields of public service to draw their own circles within which no outsider may enter.'[3]

---

1 Wilensky, H. 'The Professionalization of Everyone' *American Journal of Sociology* 70, 1964, p 137
2 Richans, C. & Mendelson, A. *Social Work: The Unloved Profession,* 1973, p 12
3 Meyer, C. H. *Social Work Practice,* Free Press, Toronto, 1970, p 12

Still others say the increasing trend towards professionalisation is due less to the need for preservation, and more to the desire for *prestige* among community workers. It's actually a matter of getting some recognition for the type of work we do and gaining a bit of respect into the bargain. As a matter of fact, 'most (community) workers want professional status.'[1]

Kay Laursen, speaking of the social work profession of which she is a part, is quite scathing about the increasing trend towards professionalisation.

> It is my thesis that professionalism is primarily a quest for power: and that the individuals feel they can achieve greater personal prestige, financial remuneration, and even political power by becoming members of a profession.[2]

Whether Laursen is correct or not, there is no doubt that professionals are an emerging power in community work circles. Ernest Greenwood, who wrote a classic paper on professionalism in 1965, noted that professionals have become a class apart from volunteers when it comes to systematic knowledge, ascribed authority, official sanctions, careful transactions, and an associated professional subculture.[3]

It is true that there has been some doubt over the years as to whether community work professionals are fully-developed professionals in this sense.[4] But most community workers within our networks do indeed display all the essential characteristics of fully-developed professionals.

- **Which of these reasons do you think are most significant?**

✍ Record your reflections in your Working Notes.

The disabling effects of professionalisation

25 minutes

John McKnight is worried that much of our professional work we do, far from enabling communities, actually disables them. He sets out his case in a classic paper called *Professionalised Services and Disabling Help.*[5]

He says that service is the biggest business in modern society. To stay in business, professional community workers must convince the

---

1 Timms, N. & R., *Perspectives in Social Work*, Routledge Kegan Paul, London 1970, p 129
2 Laursen, K. in author's notes (1975)
3 Greenwood in Tripodi, T. *Social Workers at Work*, Peacock, Itasca, 1974
4 Toren, N., *Social Work: the Case of the Semi-Profession* Sage, Beverley Hills, 1972 p 40
5 McKnight, J. (1977)

client communities they work for, that their services are indispensable. Professionals' convince these clients by trying to communicate several propositions, which distort the truth, but serve the purpose of disabling client communities, and making the disabled client communities dependent on their professional community workers.[1]

The first proposition is: *You are deficient!*

Communities may have needs, but not all needs are deficiencies that must be filled by a professional service. Some needs may be illusions that people ought to give up. Some may be obligations that people ought to take up themselves. Some may be rights that people ought to struggle for against even expert opinion. And some may be unresolvable problems that people should just accept responsibly, if not happily, as unalterable facts of life.

The second proposition is: *You are the problem!*

McKnight remarks that even where communities may be deficient, it is not good to give people the impression that the problem is simply a deficiency. They may well be deficient in some area. Most of us are deficient in one area or another of our lives. But sometimes people's problems aren't caused so much by deficiencies themselves, as by an emphasis on their deficiencies that prevents people recognising their capacity to function effectively.

The third proposition is: *You haven't just got a single problem, you have an entire collection of problems!*

It may be better to consider people as having problems, rather than being problems, but it still doesn't do people much good to give them the impression that they are simply a bundle of dysfunctional bits and pieces. They may well have a lot of problems. In fact most people have a lot of problems. But most people also have the potential to solve a lot of their problems themselves.

The fourth proposition is: *We are the solution to your problem!*

The people themselves are not the answer to the question their problems pose. Their peers are not the answer to the question their problems pose. The only answer to the question the client asks, is the professional. It is not a bilateral process. It is a unilateral process. It is essentially a dictatorial process, under the control of the professional, to which the client submits.

---

1 ibid p 89

The fifth proposition is: *We know your situation!*

There is no greater power than the power to question. For from the power to question flows the power to find answers. If a professional can take control of the definition of a person's difficulties, the professional can take control of a person's life. From then on autonomy ceases to exist. The citizen becomes a client. The professional assumes the prerogative to decide a person's fate. Communities no longer exercise the right to decide matters for themselves.

The sixth proposition is: *You can't understand the problem or the solution.*

The language of the professional mystifies both the problem and the solution so the ordinary person cannot evaluate the process for themselves. The ordinary person thus becomes totally dependent on the professional, with the result that communities can no longer choose whether to be a client or not. They can only choose whose client they will be.

The seventh proposition is: *Only we can decide whether the solution has dealt with your problem!*

The person has already been reduced from a citizen with inalienable rights to a client with limited rights. Now the person is being reduced further, to become a consumer, with no rights at all, except the right to consume uncritically. The professional is everything. The client is nothing. Communities, as such, cease to exist.

To many self-respecting professionals McKnight's perspective on the disabling effect of professionalisation might seem preposterous. He argues that though many professionals seek a democratic understanding of their role, the evidence seems to indicate that, in spite of community-orientated rhetoric, the way they usually work is not only undemocratic but actually anti-democratic and detrimental, if not destructive, to community.[1]

Kay Laursen, surveying the Australian social work scene, agrees with McKnight.

> It is my contention that professionalism is primarily characterised by self-interest, expressed in a quest for power, economic, social, personal, and political; that professionalism by its very nature makes little difference to the underlying causes of client's problems (it does not, nor does it intend to, change the social structure in any radical way such that the more fundamental causes of problems are dealt with); that when it comes to the crunch, to a choice between "the

---

1 McKnight, p 90

powers that be" and the welfare of their clients, professionals opt for the former, while simultaneously trying to convince their erstwhile clients that this betrayal is in their best interests; and finally, that professionalism militates against a genuine service to clients because it alienates professionals from their own humanity, and naturally from the common humanity they could share with their client.

Thus! I question professionalism itself, in social work as elsewhere, because as a social institution, it seeks only greater power for its members, while offering very little in the form of a genuine human service to people, in return. [1]

No wonder Richard Titmuss, quoting George Bernard Shaw, once stated that 'professions are conspiracies against the laity.' [2]

- ☐ Draw a line down the centre of a piece of paper dividing it into two equal parts. On the left hand side write all the reasons you can think of in support of McKnight's ideas about the disabling effects of professionalisation. On the right hand side write all the reasons you can think of in opposition to McKnight's ideas about the disabling effects of professionalisation.

- How do you react to the idea that professions often act as conspiracies against ordinary people—manipulating and exploiting them?

✍ Record your reflections in your Working Notes.

A vocation for a new generation of professionals

10 minutes

Henri Nouwen says that 'when we go back to the original meaning of the word "profession" (we) realise that it refers to "professing" one's own deepest conviction.' [3]

We desperately need to rediscover our vocation, and deconstruct and reconstruct our professions in terms of our vocation. According to the existential psychiatrist, Viktor Frankl, 'Everyone has their own specific

---

1 Laursen (author's notes)
2 ibid p 6
3 Nouwen,H., *Our Greatest Gift*, Hodder and Stoughton, London, 1994 p 66

vocation'.[1] Carl Jung says, 'To have a vocation is to be addressed by a voice. We hear a voice. We are called.'[2]

While our call may well come to us in our own voice, a still small voice from somewhere deep inside us, 'our vocation acts like a law of God. It makes demands upon us It demands our best, and,at times, even better than our best. To liberate. To redeem. To transform.'[3]

If this is our vocation, then, anyone who would aspire to be a 'vocational professional', would need to be a professional who, in the words of Henri Nouwen, 'dares to claim ... a vocation that allows him or her to enter into deep solidarity with the anguish underlying all the glitter.'[4]

This, of course, is not easy. John McKnight considers the notion of a vocational professional a complete contradiction in terms, and insists that while his analysis is an argument **for** the importance of reform, it is also an argument **against** any possibility of real transformation. He asserts that 'the disabling effects of professionalisation are intrinsic (not extrinsic) to modern professionalised services, and so cannot be ameliorated' under any circumstances.[5]

However, William Doherty, the Director of the Family Therapy Programme at the University of Minnesota, argues that though transformation may be difficult, it is not only theoretically possible; it is actually happening right now. In his bestselling book, *Soul Searching*, Doherty tells of an exciting new movement in which professionals are getting together to encourage one another to intentionally pursue a more personally and socially responsible approach to their practice.[6]

Jean Vanier, who works with people who are profoundly disabled, says that the only way that any one of us can become a vocational professional is by listening to the cry of the suffering as it echoes in our own soul. He says that

> if we listen intently, we will quickly learn that people have suffered a great deal at the hands of the powerful—doctors, psychologists, sociologists, social workers, and others. They have suffered so much from broken promises, from people wanting to learn from experiments, or to write a thesis, and then having gained what they wanted—recognition, an impressive book, article [or report]—going away and never coming back. [That] they are waiting for someone who really cares, who sees

---

1 Frankl, V., *Man's Search for Meaning*, Simon & Schuster, New York, 1959
2 Jung, C., *Collected Works*, Princeton University Press, Princeton, Vol 17, pp 167-187
3 ibid.
4 Nouwen,H., *In the Name of Jesus*, Darton, Longman and Todd, London 1989, p 27
5 McKnight, p 91
6 Doherty, W., *Soul Searching*, Basic Books, New York, 1995

them in the light of love, who recognises their gifts [not just their deficits], who accepts their need for change, but who will accept them just as they are, with no preconceived ideas [of] change.[1]

The purpose of the process of re-professionalisation is not to discount the importance of professional competence, but to develop our competence in the context of authentic compassion.

We must make sure that that we don't serve our professions to the detriment of the people our professions purport to serve, and that we don't impose our ideology or explicate our mythology at the expense of people.

We must make sure that we don't allow our specialisations to fragment reality, or to separate us from people whose fragment of reality we do not specialise in, and that we don't develop a mystique about our procedures, or the secrets of our trade, that could be shared so as to empower people.

We must make sure that that we don't manufacture a sense of need in order to secure a contract to meet it, and that we don't abuse our power in the performance of our duties, or avoid our responsibility to the people in whose name we perform those duties.

- What are the arguments for de-professionalisation?
- What are the arguments for re-professionalisation?
- What are the core issues that would need to be taken into account and addressed in any meaningful attempt to transform a profession?

✍ Record your reflections in your Working Notes.

Amateur, radical and revolutionary professionals

If we are to transform our profession, and become vocational professionals, we need to become **amateur, radical, and revolutionary professionals.**

Amateur professionals
10 minutes

A vocational professional is an amateur professional.

This is not the contradiction that it might appear to be. Because the opposite of amateur is not professional: it is mercenary. The vocational professional is not a mercenary, but an amateur, at heart. As David Augsberger says, the notion of an 'amateur' comes from the Latin word

---
1 Vanier, J., *The Broken Body*, St Paul, Homebush, 1988, p 78-79

'amator', which in English means 'lover', or in this context, 'someone who does something for the love of it.'[1] Hence, anyone who serves others for the love of it, is an amateur at heart.

Paul Mercer is an excellent example of an amateur professional. He is a general practitioner, who treats his patients as people and treats people with respect. He takes a lot more time with people than he is supposed to. He gives people not only his attention but also himself. He enters into their struggle, and in the context of their struggle he seeks to serve them, minimising their pain, maximising their opportunities and enabling them to cope with the difficulties they face. He loves the people he works with in the community and, not surprisingly, the people love him.

The medieval medical dictum that Kadushin cites is a motto which Paul Mercer lives out in his community, and each of our communities would be much better off if every community worker tried, like Paul: 'To cure sometimes, to relieve often, to comfort always.'[2]

- **What is an amateur community work professional?**

✍ Record your reflections in your Working Notes.

Radical Professionals

10 minutes

A vocational professional is a radical professional.

Martin Rein suggests that if we are going to begin to do justice to the people we work with we should develop 'a radical profession.' A radical profession, according to Rein, is not a profession made up of people who are single-issue activists, but a profession whose single most important issue is the people that they work with.[3]

Jack Rothman says there are three types of professional role orientation that he has observed:

1. a professional role orientation, which 'implies a high degree of concern with professional values and standards'
2. a bureaucratic orientation, which 'refers to a preoccupation with policies and terms of the employing agency'

---

1 Augsberger, D (1982) in Kraybill, D et al
2 Kadushin, A., *Child Welfare Services*, Macmillan, New York, 1980
3 Rein, M., 'Social Work in Search of a Profession' *Social Work* (15) 2, April 1970 p 14

3. a client orientation, which 'emphasises primary attention to the needs of those served by the agency'.[1]

Most social workers, according to Rothman, tend to be orientated more towards bureaucratic concerns, if not professional concerns, rather than to client concerns. So in order to develop a radical orientation to community work, which treats the people in the community seriously, many community workers will have to develop a radical reorientation to social work.

Developing such a radical reorientation to social work is not easy. It's particularly difficult because the prospect of accountability of professionals to the people they work with, and the mutuality it implies, is often considered 'a dangerous form of role confusion', and 'the world in which we live, has no models to offer to those who want to work towards mutuality'.[2]

In spite of the difficulties, however, Concetta Benn and her colleagues deliberately developed a radical reorientation to their community work in the Family Centre Project in Melbourne.[3] Concetta and her colleagues systematically tried to reduce the status differential between the professionals and the people they worked with in the project, through a devolution of power that was enhanced by a participatory approach.[4]

Concetta Benn and her colleagues show us the way forward. We need not be conservative. We can be radical. As radical professionals, we can make a significant difference in our communities, in spite of our imperfections, by focusing on the people we work with, and facilitating a process of movement through the people we were with towards real power for the poor.

- Why is it important to be a radical community work professional?

✍ Record your reflections in your Working Notes.

Revolutionary professionals
10 minutes

A vocational professional is a revolutionary professional.

---

1 Rothman, J., *Planning and Organizing for Social Change*, Columbia University Press, New York, 1974
2 Nouwen, p 44
3 Benn, C., *Attacking Poverty Through Participation*, P.I.T. Press Melbourne, 1981, p 269
4 Liffman, M., *Power for the Poor*, Allen & Unwin, London, 1978, p 139

Robert Chambers suggests that if we are going to begin to do justice to the people we need to work with, we should develop a 'revolutionary profession'. This is not a profession made up of people who build 'road blocks' and defend the bastions of one ideology against another, but one whose members can break through barriers, and fight against the biases which discriminate against the disadvantaged in our society.[1]

Chambers outlines a number of preferences that affect our participation as professionals in the struggle to do justice to the people we need to work with. In our selection of projects, we tend to select nice 'clean' projects first and 'dirty', 'smelly' projects last.[2]

Project Preferences	
First	**Last**
Modern	Traditional
Large	Small
Complex	Simple
Regular	Irregular
High Profile	Low Profile
High Cost	Low Cost
Hard	Soft
Clean	Dirty
Nice	Smelly

In our selection of the time and the place we want to work, we tend to select 'easy' times and places first, and 'difficult' times and places last.

Time and Place Preferences	
First	**Last**
Accessible	Inaccessible
Convenient	Inconvenient
Urban	Rural
During office hours	Out of office hours
Day	Night

---

1 Chambers, R., *Rural Development: Putting the Last First*, Longman, London, 1983
2 Chambers, (adapted) p 173

During the week	Over the weekend
Dry	Wet

Chambers finally suggests that when we select the people we want to work with, we tend to select 'rich' people first, and 'poor' people last.

People Preferences	
First	Last
Rich	Poor
Fair	Dark
Male	Female
Adult	Child
Educated	Illiterate
Influential	Ineffectual

If we are to begin to do justice to the most disadvantaged, Chambers insists that we need to reject the dominant values of our society. We need not only to re-evaluate our professional preferences, but also actually reverse our professional priorities. We need to commit ourselves to a revolutionary option for the poor.

This revolution may be non-violent, but it is not without violence. The changes it requires are difficult! In spite of the difficulties, however, quite a few young professionals are doing their best to become fair dinkum revolutionary professionals.

Peter Stewart is a musician who works with disadvantaged groups round Brisbane, through street arts, so as to enable dispossessed people to articulate their rage and act out some of the possible solutions to the problems that enrage them.

Steven Yates and Emma Pritchard, a doctor and a lawyer respectively, have chosen to leave highly-rewarding positions in Brisbane to relocate to a low-profile town in central Australia, to help provide much-needed medical and legal services for Aboriginal communities.

Greg and Katie Manning are a wonderfully well-qualified Aussie couple, a do-it-yourself engineer, and a life-be-in-it physiotherapist, who have moved to India with their two children, Rebecca and Callum, to make themselves available to do community development work with their local counterparts in a city slum.

Peter Stewart, Steven Yates, Emma Pritchard, and Greg and Katie Manning show us the way forward.

> • How can we become a revolutionary community work professional?

✎ Record your reflections in your Working Notes.

Conclusion

10 minutes

The follow-up reading for this session is

> 'I Refuse to be Intimidated by Reality Any More', *Building A Better World*, Dave Andrews, Albatross, Sutherland, 1996. p 113-137 (Reading 16)

The set community tasks for this session are

- ❒ Meet with your learning partner and your community development support group.
- ❒ If the other people in your group would be open to it, share over a cuppa what you learnt in the session about a vocational framework for community work.

✎ Record your actions, reflections and conclusions in your Working Notes.

Session 17

Working within an Ethical Framework

Objectives

- To review your understanding of the importance of working within a vocational framework.
- To consider the importance of an ethical framework for community work.

Review

15 minutes

- ☐ Review your work from Session 16.
- ☐ Review the issues raised in course notes in the previous session, particularly your understanding of the importance of 'working within a vocational framework.
- ☐ Review the reading:

    'I Refuse to be Intimidated by Reality Any More', *Building A Better World*, Dave Andrews, Albatross, Sutherland, 1996. p 113-137 (Reading 16)

- ☐ Review the tasks:
    - ❖ How was your meeting with your learning partner and your community development support group?
    - ❖ What was the most important thing you learned while doing your community tasks for the last session?

✎ Record your reflections in your Working Notes.

An ethical framework for community work
90 minutes

The prerequisite of ethics

"Do unto others as you would have them do unto you"

According to Trevor Jordan,

> Ethics is about asking, 'what is right and wrong?' and 'what is good and bad?' and giving reasons for our answers.
>
> The terms 'ethics' and 'morality' can be used interchangeably. 'ethical' and 'moral' behaviour would be behaviour that is arguably 'right' or 'good'. 'Unethical' and 'immoral' behaviour is behaviour that is deemed 'wrong' or 'bad'. [1]

John Gardner states that

> no society can remain vital, or even survive, without a reasonable base of shared values ... [And] families and communities are the ground-level generators ... of ethical systems [which produce] and preserve ... these values. [2]

Amitai Etzioni says:

> Liberal friends ... express ... concern about the use of the term 'moral'. [People] don't like to be told about morals, said one, it sounds like preaching. Another suggested that the term reminds him of the Moral Majority. [3]
>
> I do not mean to preach, but to share a concern ... I am sorry if I remind people of the Moral Majority, because I believe that although they raised the right questions they provided the wrong ... answers.
>
> However, just as we should not give up on patriotism because some politicians wrap themselves with the flag when it suits their ... purposes, so we should not give up on morality because some abuse it to skewer [others]. [4]
>
> Communities speak to us in moral voices. They lay claims on [us as] their members. Indeed, other than the inner self, they are the most important sustaining source of moral voices [in our society]. [5]
>
> When I discuss the value of moral vo ices, people tell me they are very concerned that if they lay moral claims, they will be perceived as 'self-righteous'. If they mean by 'self-righteous' a person who

---

1 Jordan, T., *Social Ethics and the Justice System*, QUT Brisbane 1993, part 2 p 1
2 Etzioni, p 31
3 Etzioni, p 31
4 Etzioni, p 13
5 Etzioni, p 31

comes across as without flaw, who sees himself as entitled to dictate what is right [and wrong], who lays moral claims in a sanctimonious or pompous way—there is good reason to refrain from such ways of expressing moral voices.

[But] ... disinclination to lay moral claims undermines ... moral conduct in crucial situations.

During a conference on bone-marrow transplants, a psychiatrist argued that it was not proper to ask one sibling for a bone-marrow donation for another sibling, despite the fact that making such a donation does not entail any particular risk. His reason was that the sibling who refused might feel guilty, especially if, as a result, the brother or sister died.

A communitarian would argue that siblings should be asked in no uncertain terms to come to the rescue. If they refuse, they *should* feel guilty.[1]

Although it may be true that markets work best if everybody goes out and tries to maximise his or her own self-interest (though this is by no means a well-proven proposition), communities most assuredly do not. They need people who care for one another and for shared spaces and causes ...

Here, clearly, it is better to give than to take, and the best way to help sustain a world in which people care for one another is to ... 'do unto others ... as you would wish them to do unto you'.[2]

- Do you agree, or disagree with these ideas? State your reasons.

✎ Record your reflections in your Working Notes.

The simplicity of ethics

'We learned it all in kindergarten!'

On one level, 'doing to others as you would wish them to do to you' is a very simple matter. As Robert Fulghum says,

> *We learned it all in kindergarten!*
> *Most of what I really need to know*
> *about how to live,*
> *and what to do,*
> *and how to be,*
> *I learned in kindergarten.*

---

1 Etzioni, p.35
2 Etzioni, p.30

*Wisdom was not at the top
of the university mountain,
but there in the sandpit.*

These are the things I learned:

*Share everything.
Play fair.
Don't hit people.*

*Put things back here you found them.
Clean up your own mess.*

*Don't take things
that aren't yours.*

*Say you're sorry
when you hurt somebody.*

*Wash your hands
before you eat. ...*

Take a nap in the afternoon.

*When you go out into the world,
watch for the traffic,
hold hands and stick together.*

*Be aware of wonder.
Remember the little seed
in the plastic cup.
The roots go down
and the plant goes up.
And nobody really knows why,
but we are all like that.*

*Goldfish die.
So do we.*

*Everything you need to know
is in there somewhere.
The golden rule
and basic sanitation.
Ecology and politics
and sane living.*

*Think of what a better world
it would be if we all
had bickies and milk
about three o'clock
every afternoon and
then lay down for a nap.*

> *Or*
> *if we had a basic policy*
> *in our nation*
> *always to put things back*
> *where we found them*
> *and*
> *cleaned up our own messes.*
>
> *And it is still true,*
> *no matter how old you are,*
> *when you go out into the world,*
> *it is best to hold hands*
> *and stick together.* [1]

- **What are three of your simple 'kindergarten' rules for living?**

✎ Record your reflections in your Working Notes.

The complexity of ethics

'Not with my daughter you don't!'

But on another level 'doing to others as you would wish them to do to you' can be a very complex matter, as Dale Hardman recounts.

A balmy afternoon

It was a balmy spring afternoon in the Blintz County workhouse. The interviewing room was only half-separated from the cell corridors. The inmate looked out the dirt-specked window for some time, then returned his gaze to the social worker. 'Twelve more days. I could do 12 days on a bed of spikes. You're the reason I got 55 days knocked off my six months. I wouldn'ta got out unless you went to bat for me.'

Oscar De Curia only nodded, but inwardly he beamed because expressions of gratitude were infrequent among workhouse clients. 'I would like,' he said, 'to get some idea of your plans when you get out. Most guys need some help getting into a job or school or ... '

'Nah. I work for my old man putting up siding. I always got a job waiting.'

... De Curia had an impulse to suggest some vocational ed. courses, but instead he just nodded and said, 'Okay, then what about your social life?'

'That's all I been thinking about since I got my commutation.'

---

1 Fulgham, R. 'We Learned it All in Kindergarten.' *Kansas City Times,* Sept 17 1984

De Curia brightened a bit. At least here he didn't have to worry about imposing his own norms. Here he could relax, be more natural, more human.

'Chicks,' said the inmate. He leaned back and clasped his fingers behind his thick black curly hair. 'Chicks is my specialty. Take the average guy in here—for him sex is just quick service stuff: roll in the hay, be on your way. No art to it. No class. ... Like the soup commercial says: "To make the best you gotta begin with the best. Then prepare it tenderly ... carefully ... slowly ... " So I begin with the best. Nothing but fresh meat for me—very fresh. A virgin.'

'I see. Well, since there's not a lot of those around ... '

'Well, ya gotta know where to look. For one thing you gotta start young—maybe 14 or 15—so you find where they hang out.'

'Hmm.' De Curia opened his mouth to point out that a sex act with an adolescent would constitute a new violation, but he again bit his tongue and admonished himself that he must not be a moralist. And certainly this client was canny enough to know the law on this point.

'They hang out a lot around Whiffly Dip, especially on weekends. Skating rinks and bowling alleys is good hunting grounds. Always full of teeny chicks. ...There was one little chick I met at the Rollerama just before I got busted. A virgin, I'll bet my shirt. About 14. Real good skater.'

'Hmm.' De Curia resolved to be nondirective if it killed him, but his discomfort continued to rise.

'I only saw her two, three times before I got sent up. Skated with her each time. I know she likes me. I think she's the one I'll start with.'

'I see.' De Curia shifted uneasily as his tension mounted.

'Like I say, begin with the best. And she's the best. Long slender legs. Willowy. Little round bazoobs like ripe peaches. Long auburn hair, always in a ponytail. Her name was Irma Jean something.'

Every man has a sort of safety plug in his boiler; it melts at a lower temperature than the boiler and serves to prevent the boiler from rupturing. And here De Curia blew his plug. Out spewed his professional role, his persona, in a great gust and blast, and he stood before his client a very angry human being. 'Hey, wait a minute! That's my daughter you're talking about, you lecherous bastard!'

Oscar's conflict

It was several hours later that Oscar De Curia sat in his office, pondering his misdirected interview at the workhouse.

In ten years of practice he had held doggedly to the dictum of nondirection: the non-moralistic listener, eschewing judgments, never imposing his own norms, never playing God, never setting himself up as an ethical model for his clients' emulation.

... But now, suddenly, when these norms were violated close to home, his carefully cultivated professional posture had disintegrated and he had blown his cool, the interview, and the case. Although De Curia was not given to extensive self-contemplation, he was, in those brief and unaccustomed moments of introspection, essentially honest with himself. Perhaps these two facts were related: in introspection he usually came out the loser, due to a basic trait of honesty, so he indulged in it rarely.

Oscar had experienced similar interviews in the past, listening with composure to expressions of sexual exploitation, tales of assaults on persons or property, and threats of vengeance or power or violence. He had often felt a rising discomfort and a need to protest, and always, until today, he had successfully repressed such unprofessional impulses. But now, with his treasured, auburn-haired teenager as the proposed object ...

It was well beyond closing time when the janitor still at his desk pondering his conflict. Upon his return home, De Curia was unusually attentive to his daughter, but otherwise his manner was, for him, exceptionally subdued. His wife reckoned that he had either been fired or out philandering but that in either case he would shortly tell her ...

Generalising the problem

During the ensuing week, Oscar De Curia resolved that he would, at whatever cost, resolve his newly mounted conflict. One of his first acts was to request that his supervisor transfer the client who had torpedoed his cool.

... The supervisor had indeed encountered this knotty question before; he had mulled it over at considerable length and then shelved it. But Oscar would not be shelved. He was a persistent clod, and he insisted on answers. And answered he was. The supervisor said: 'Mm hmm.'

'Well, it's true, ain't it?' De Curia waxed ungrammatical only when be became emotional. 'From the time we enter graduate school we're admonished against imposing our own values on people. So I don't and look what happens! My own daughter is up for grabs!'

'Mm,' said the supervisor, thoughtfully.

'Tell me honestly, Jake,' (the supervisor encouraged this bit of familiarity) 'What would you do? You must have encountered this kind of incongruity before. How did you handle it?'

Jake ... glanced out his door, perchance to spot a client in need of his attention. A swatch of blue and a hank of white hair caught his eye. "Hey Dave!" yelled Jake, much as a man might yell when stranded on a sandbar by high tide.

Dave had been retired from the agency for several years now, but occasionally popped into see how things were going. These visits ... were usually welcome and especially so today.

'Come in Dave, and shoot the bull a spell,' said Jake with an outward show of camaraderie and an inward sigh of relief. 'Oscar and

I were just talking about lower-class norms. How they often impede therapy or progress, or whatever you wanna call it, but how we're not supposed to tamper with them.'

'So what did you tell him to do?' asked Dave.

… 'My friend,' said Dave, 'there is nothing in social service more frequently encountered than conflict regarding values. Every social worker I know runs into it daily and most of them, like you, never really come to grips with the realities of the problem. And every social worker I know, consciously or unconsciously, overtly or covertly, imposes their norms on the poor every day of their working life.'

'But you're different,' said Jake, with a noticeable edge to his voice.

'Only that I'm honest about it,' said Dave. 'I do it intentionally. Deliberately. In cold blood. Further, a half-dozen studies indicate that the more moralistic, value imposing workers have better success with their clients.'

… 'Then aren't you saying, in effect, that your values are better than those of the lower class?'

'Ah, now comes the stinger. I impose some middle-class values. There are quite a number of lower-class values that I prefer to middle-class ones.'

'For instance?'

'Comradeship. Closer, more intimate interpersonal relations. More egalitarian views; more emphasis on person than on status. More interpersonal good humour. More freedom of expression. More open expression of affection.'

'Affection?'

'Yes. Take one example. When was a kid I worked on a string of blue-collar jobs: ranches, mines, factories, railroads, construction. It wasn't uncommon to see two guys who were buddies standing around the fire at night or around the bar or bunkhouse, with an arm slung over the friend's shoulder. No one thought anything of it. Now suppose that on some white-collar job—let's say in an insurance office—you spot two guys at the water cooler with their arms round each other. You'd nudge your neighbour and say, "Hey, Fred! Lookit!" What a helluva culture when two people can't express honest affection without being considered gay.'

'Maybe there are more gays in the lower classes.'

'Fewer. I'll tell you another trait of the poor I'd consider keeping. When a husband and wife are at loggerheads, they are much more likely to have a good old hell-raising, whooping and hollering knock-down-drag-out battle. But in 20 minutes it's all over. You and me, when we're on the outs with the old woman, we turn on the deep freeze for about a month. We never speak or look at each other for weeks on end. Now I ask you honestly which is better for mental health?'…

Deciding on some functional norms

'Dave, you're not being consistent,' Jake said waving his hand. 'A minute ago you were the champion of good old middle-class values. Now you've changed sides. You can't play both sides at once. What do *you* want?'

Dave pondered this one briefly: 'First, I want [people] to be honest about when they impose norms, whether middle-class or lower-class. Second, want them to forget the infantile quibble about the norms of one class being better than those of another. I want ... '

'How do you decide which norms you are going to support, then? You gonna play God?'

'Functionality is how. First we gotta decide on objectives, social workers and clients in dialogue together. And this holds true whether it's one caseworker and one client or a [community] project involving 50 workers and 10,000 clients. We can agree that employment is a goal, or marriage stability or family planning or whatever, but we have to thrash it out and arrive at some consensus regarding our objective. Once the objective is agreed upon, my job is clear: If a certain cultural norm is functional, if it aids in achieving the agreed-upon objective, I will support it. If it's dysfunctional, if it's thwarting our objectives, then it's gotta go, and I'll do my damndest to see that it goes. And I couldn't care less whether the norm comes from the lower, middle, or upper class.'

'Meehl and McClosky', said Jake, 'consider that our job definition is to help the client achieve the client's end. Period. That doesn't leave room for negotiation about objectives.'

'I'll be damned if I'm gonna help that guy achieve my daughter's end,' said Oscar De Curia hotly.

'And I'll venture no worker worth [their] salt would,' replied Dave. 'In fact, I think they'd draw the line on about half the goals of our correctional clients. Plus a number of others. For instance, I won't help a client toward suicide, if that's his goal. Or to obtain heroin, or to bust out of jail or a hospital. Or to defraud the welfare office or desert his family or go AWOL. Or, in my case, to obtain an abortion. This is why I said we must first agree on objectives.'

'And if you and the client can't agree?'

'My personal guideline is this: I will never help clients accomplish something that I consider morally wrong, harmful to them or to me or to others. And I won't help a client to rendezvous with any teenager, not your daughter or anyone else's ... [1]

- What objectives do you consider 'morally wrong' for you?

✎ Record your reflections in your Working Notes.

---

1 Hardman, D. 'Not With My Daughter You Don't!' *Social Work* Vol.20 No.4 National Association of Social Workers, July 1975, pp 278-285

The principles of ethics

'Guidelines proven to have enduring, permanent value'

We can determine what Hardman calls 'functional norms' by applying the principles of what Covey calls 'natural laws' to our practice in particular situations.

> The reality of such natural laws becomes obvious to anyone who thinks deeply [about] the cycles of social history. These principles surface time and time again, and the degree to which people in a society ... live in harmony with them, moves them toward either survival and stability or disintegration and destruction.
>
> The principles I am referring to are not esoteric, mysterious, or 'religious' ideas. There is not one principle that is unique to any specific ... religion, including my own. These principles are a part of most every major religion, as well as enduring social ... and ethical systems.
>
> They seem to exist in all human beings, regardless of ... conditioning and loyalty to them, even though they might be submerged ... by such conditions or numbed by [incidents of] disloyalty to them.
>
> Principles are not practices. A practice that works in one circumstance will not necessarily work in another, as parents who have tried to raise a second child exactly like they did the first can readily attest.
>
> While practices are situationally specific, principles are fundamental truths that have universal application. They apply to marriages, to families, to private and public organisations of every kind. When these truths are internalised into habits, they empower people to create a wide variety of practices to deal with different situations.
>
> These principles are essentially unarguable because they are self-evident ... [They] are guidelines for human conduct that are proven to have enduring, permanent value. One way to quickly grasp the self-evident nature of principles is to simply consider the absurdity of attempting to live an effective life based on their opposites ... For example, the principle of fairness, out of which our whole concept of equity, [equality,] and justice is developed. Little children seem to have an innate idea of fairness, even apart from opposite conditioning experiences ... I doubt that anyone would seriously consider unfairness ... to be a solid foundation for lasting happiness and success. [1]

There are no short cuts. There are no quick fixes. Unless we practice these principles consistently we cannot expect to develop community.

---

1 Covey, S. *The Seven Habits Of Effective People*, The Business Library Melbourne 1994 pp.34-35

- What guidelines do you use as framework for ethical decision making?

✍ Record your reflections in your Working Notes.

The practice of ethics

'The ability to guide ourselves'

The bottom line is that we need to take what we have learnt as kids, and learn how to put these moral guidelines into practice as adults, so that we can get on with the job of trying to build a better world, without making matters worse in the process.

Recently, as part of a reform process started in Queensland as a result of the findings of the famous Fitzgerald enquiry into police corruption, we have been runnng a course on applied ethics for law enforcement officers. In this course there is a concern to restore 'the internalisation of commitments to a set of substantive values', through the lecturers' constant advocacy of personal integrity and social justice, and the students' continual assessment of case studies and current incidents. However, though it is easy to teach *about* community ethics and learn *about* community ethics in the classroom, it is difficult, if not impossible, to actually teach and learn community ethics anywhere but in the community itself. As Confucius said quite a few centuries ago:

> "I hear and I forget;
> I see and I remember;
> I do and I understand."

So we invite students from the colleges where we teach to come to our neighbourhood, for two to three weeks at a time, to practise some community ethics, by trying to live in community, ethically, with us and the disadvantaged people in our locality with whom we share our lives. Last month we had twelve students, some from university and some from seminary, come to live with us. As we have done this twice a year for the past eight years, probably close to two hundred students have gone through what we call our "community orientation courses".

We introduce them to Auntie Jean, an Aboriginal elder, who not only tells them the story of her people and their painful dispossession, but also takes them with her to meet her people, some languishing in their cells in a maximum security prison, and others in a human rights organisation, fighting for their release.

We introduce them to Father Kefle, an Eritrean priest, who shows them the scars of thirty years of civil war. They visit refugees, who have been torn away from their families, tortured by the very people who were supposed to protect them, forced to flee for their lives, and are now struggling to rebuild a life for themselves as strangers in a strange land.

Some of the students have never actually met an Aborigine or a refugee face to face before, let alone heard their story, or seen their struggle for themselves. These encounters confront the students with essentially ethical questions that we all have to answer one way or another.

- How do we, as members of a 'white' society, deal with our 'black' history?
- How do we, as members of the human family, respond to the desperate plea from our brothers and sisters, not just to address the superficial symptoms, but the underlying causes, of their lasting pain?
- And what are we going to do about it?

These questions call for answers from us: not just theoretical answers, but also practical answers. Answering these questions is a moral imperative that we can accept or reject, but cannot ignore.

One of the students on the last course who accepted the imperative for him to answer these questions, as honestly as he could, was a policeman. We'll call him Brad. He had been on the beat for many years. Brad said that he had become quite cynical about the public, like a lot of police who only ever related to people in their job as sources of information about 'criminals', or as potential or actual 'criminals' themselves. But when he took the opportunity to get out of uniform, and to meet people he'd stereotyped, face to face, as fellow human beings, he began to change.

The first stage of change was in terms of *perspective*. What we see depends on where we stand. Standing alongside the very people he had often been expected to take a stand against, helped Brad to see a totally different view of the struggle for justice on the streets. 'The critical interpretations of the most marginalised ... correct ... the blind spots in our own experience.'[1]

The second stage of change was in terms of *responsibility*. What we hear depends on who we listen to. Listening to people who continue to be dispossessed by the people that he usually listened to, helped Brad to hear a totally different side to the story of the history of our society.

---

[1] Wildung Harrison, B. 1985 p.250

'The very things I would like least done to me are the things that I do to others every day.' [1]

The third stage of change was in terms of *pain*. How we feel depends on what we do. Recognising that what he was doing as a police officer was often part of the problem, rather than part of the solution, helped Brad feel the impact of the issues in a way that he'd never felt before. 'The shock of recognition that one is the oppressed, and the shock of recognition that one is the oppressor, both are accompanied by pain.' [2]

The fourth stage of change was in terms of *responsiveness*. We have two options for managing the pain that comes from recognising the gap between who we are and who we are meant to be. One option is rationalisation: changing the ideal of who we are meant to be, so it is closer to the reality of who we already are. The other option is action: changing the reality of who we are, so that we come closer to the ideal of who we are meant to be. Choosing action rather than rationalisation helped Brad respond to the issues in a way that he had thought through, but had never thought he'd ever really put into action.

'Doing to others as you would wish them to do to you' began quite unceremoniously, but quite significantly, for Brad, by stopping when an Aboriginal caught his attention in the street, listening to him when he wanted to talk, and looking out for him when he asked for a packet of smokes like he would have done for any of his mates.

> At that point I join the action ... by having the courage to commit myself, or end up with a sense of guilt, because I am not doing what I know I should. I seek compensation in almsgiving ... hoping that way to buy some peace. But peace cannot be purchased. It is not for sale. Peace has to be lived. I cannot live my peace without commitment to men [and women], and my commitment to men [and women] cannot exist without [a commitment to] their liberation, and their liberation cannot exist without the final transformation of the structures that are dehumanising them. [3]

This was the stage of realisation Brad had reached when he completed our community orientation course. We spoke to him about how encouraged we were about the stages of change he had gone through so far. However, we cautioned him, saying that it would all be in vain unless he continued to take the change a stage further.

---

1 Lebacqz, K. 1989 p.173
2 ibid p.170
3 P. Freire in *Walk In My Shoes*, A. B. A. Melbourne 1977 p.92

The fifth stage of change is in terms of *practice*. Aristotle said, 'We are what we do repeatedly. Excellence, then, is not an act, but a habit.'[1] It is good to choose to do good. But it is not good enough if we choose to do good intermittently. We must choose to do good habitually. Amiel said,

> Moral truth can be conceived in thought. [We] can have feelings about it. [We] can will to live it. But moral truth may have been penetrated and possessed in all these ways, and escape us still ... Only those truths that have entered into ... our being itself, ... unconscious as well as conscious, are really our life.[2]

Only a really good life is a really good foundation for building a better world.

- What ethics have you "heard and forgotten"?
- What ethics have you "seen and remember"?
- What ethics do you "do and understand"?
- What have you learnt from your practice?

✍ Record your reflections in your Working Notes.

Conclusion

10 minutes

The follow-up reading for this session is

The Code of Ethics, Australian Institute of Welfare and Community Workers (Reading 17)

The set community tasks for this session are

☐ Continue with your community work.

☐ In the meantime, talk the Code over with as many people as you can in your community.

☐ Meet with your learning partner and your community development support group, and develop your own code.

☐ Write up your own code of ethics for community work.

✍ Record your actions, reflections and conclusions in your Working Notes.

---

1 quoted in Covey, p 46
2 ibid. p 317

Session 18

Working within a Cultural Framework

Objectives

- To review your understanding of the importance of working within an ethical framework.
- To consider the importance of a cultural framework for community work.

Review

15 minutes

☐ Review your work from Session 17.
☐ Review the issues raised in course notes in the previous session, particularly your understanding of the importance of 'working within an ethical framework.'
☐ Review the reading:
  The Code of Ethics, Australian Institute of Welfare and Community Workers (Reading 17)
☐ Review the tasks:
  ❖ How was your meeting with your learning partner and your community development support group?
  ❖ What was the most important thing you learned while doing your community tasks for the last session?

✎ Record your reflections in your Working Notes.

Living Community: Session 18

A cultural framework for community work [1]

90 minutes

'Can we all call our country our home?'

January 26th was just a week away. I didn't have much time if I was going to be able to organise the barbecue in our street for Australia Day.

As I crossed the street to talk to Spiro about having the party on the street outside his house where there is a bit of a natural cul-de-sac, I fantasised about the upcoming event, which I hoped would bring all my neighbours, many of them first generation migrants, from England, Ireland, Greece, India and the Philippines, together, as Australians, one and all, on Australia Day.

At the time it didn't seem like it was very unrealistic. Most of us had sent our kids to the same school, and used to turn up at the same school nights where a kaleidoscope of kids from more than fifty different countries would regularly bring the house down at the finale, by singing a stirring rendition of 'I Still Call Australia Home.' None of us left without a tear in our eye.

But, as soon as I ran my idea of an Australia Day barbecue by Spiro, I knew that there was no chance my dream for our community was going to come true that year.

When I asked him if we could have the barbecue in the street in front of his house, actually blocking his driveway for four or five hours, Spiro was more than happy to comply. Nothing was too much trouble for him.

But when I asked him to come to the barbecue with his family himself, he shook his head slowly but surely, and politely declined.

'Why won't you come, *theo*?' I asked him respectfully, using the common honorific for 'uncle', as I could see the hurt in his eyes.

'I work for the council all my life and I know how Australians are once they have a few drinks.'

'How's that?' I prodded.

'If I bring my wife, she feels left out. She doesn't speak much English. If they hear her speak in Greek, they tell her, "Speak in English!" When I say she doesn't speak much English, they tell us, "Go back to Greece!"'

'I've seen that kind of thing happen, and it must feel awful. But,' I persisted, 'this will be different. We are your neighbours, you know none of us will treat you like that. And this is your street, you have the right to speak your language in your street. And my wife would be more than happy to speak to your wife in Greek.'

He just shook his head and said, 'No. You have the barbecue. You can have it in front of my house. But I won't come.'

---

1 Adapted from D.Andrews, *Building A Better World*, pp 258-296

... He didn't come. And neither did any of my Aboriginal friends. Australia Day is 'Invasion Day' to them, a day of mourning. Not a day of celebration.

We still have a long way to go before everybody in our street really feels they can call Australia 'home'.

- Have you, your family or your friends ever had similar experiences?

✎ Record your reflections in your Working Notes.

Culture and Community

'What we consider good and bad manners'

Community development depends on resolving the issues that revolve around issues of cultural unity and diversity. Our culture is our routine of sleeping, bathing, dressing, eating, and getting to work. It is our household chores, and the actions we perform on the job, the way we buy goods and services, write and mail a letter, take a taxi or board a bus, make a telephone call, go to a movie, or attend church. According to Ina Corrine Brown,

> This is the way we greet friends or address a stranger, the admonitions we give our children, and the way they regard what we consider good and bad manners, and, even to a large extent, what we consider right and wrong ... All these and thousands of other ways of thinking, feeling, acting, seem so natural that we may even wonder how else one could do it.
>
> But to other millions of people in the world every one of these acts would seem strange, awkward, incomprehensible, and unnatural. These people would perform many, if not all, of the same acts, but they would be done in different ways that to them would seem natural, logical, and right.[1]

Ferdinand Toennics asserts that these differences, between 'us' and 'them', are so profound that it is only possible for us to develop community within a culture, with people like us, not between cultures, with people like 'them'.

Toennies argues that while the quality of interaction required to produce a society involves only transient, impersonal, unidimensional, secondary relationships, the quality of interaction required to produce a community involves permanent, personal, multifaceted, primary

---

1 Brown, I. *Understanding Other Cultures*, 1963

relationships. Community is only possible for people who have blood, place, and mind in common. Without these prerequisites of kinship, township, and mateship, Toennies thinks we don't have a chance to develop community.[1] According to this perspective, community is essentially *mono-cultural*.

Herman Daley and John Cobb contend that while the differences between 'us' and 'them' are profound, it is still possible for us to develop community between cultures, with people like 'them'. While the quality of interaction required to produce a community may be easier in homogeneous groups, those permanent, personal, multifaceted, primary relationships which characterise community, may be broader, deeper, higher, and wider in heterogeneous groups.[2] Community, according to this perspective, is potentially *multi-cultural*.

- What is the difference between a mono-cultural and a multi-cultural view of community?

✍ Record your reflections in your Working Notes.

Monoculturalism and Community Development

'To civilise the savages'

Until recently Australia, like most countries, has been resolutely monocultural in its community development.

Anyone is welcome as long as ...

- they are not robbing Australians of jobs;
- they do not lower the Australian standard of living (by imposing too much strain on our welfare system);
- they import things (especially their food) which enrich our culture;
- they leave their own cultural tensions behind, and do not import conflict into the Australian culture;
- they are largely assimilated (with some tolerance for the preservation of 'quaint' ethnic customs);
- they make the learning of the English language a top priority;
- and they are prepared to embrace the Australian way of life.[3]

---

1 Toennies, pp.12-29
2 Cobb and Daley, p 170
3 McKay, pp 155-156

At its best, this monocultural approach to community development has still managed to be quite hospitable. As a result, Australia now has, apart from Israel, a population with a larger percentage of overseas born people than any other country in the entire world. However, the monocultural approach has at its worst been guilty, not only of prejudice, but also of genocide.

Indigenous people have lived in Australia for some 40,000 years. They dwelt in small extended family groups which constituted some 500 semi-nomadic hunting and gathering communities who travelled around the country according to the rhythm of seasons and ceremonies. When the first migrants arrived, there were about 300,000 Aborigines and Torres Strait Islanders. After a hundred years of settlement there were over 3,500,000 migrants, and barely 50,000 Aborigines and Islanders left.

The first voluntary migrants were English, then Scottish, Welsh and Irish, followed by Europeans and Americans. This sequence of migration became a caste system that has dominated the cultural reality of the continent. In the 19th century, during the gold rushes, many Chinese migrated to Australia, only to run up against a wall of anti-Asian hostility.

Early in the 20th century the Australian government officially adopted what came to be known infamously as the 'White Australia Policy'. During this time, red and yellow, black and brown applicants were refused entry to Australia, but more than a million whites were welcomed as migrants. Only since the 1960s has the White Australia Policy been scrapped, the rights of indigenous people recognised, and migrants received from all over the world, regardless of their colour, race or culture.

Discrimination still exists. You only have to see the difference between the treatment of 'illegal' British backpackers and 'illegal' Afghan asylum-seekers, to know that prejudice is still alive and kicking in the 'Lucky Country'. But in spite of on-going prejudice, there is growing recognition that Australia is one country with many cultures. So to be an Australian is to be multicultural, whether we like it or not.

- What is a monocultural view of our community?
- What are its strengths?
- What are its weaknesses?

✐ Record your reflections in your Working Notes.

Multiculturalism and Community Development

'People should practise their own cultures'

Only recently has Australia tried to be more multicultural in its community development. Like most countries, it still has a long way to go. Most Australians are still struggling to come to terms with *demographic multiculturalism*: the fact that both the indigenous people of this country, and the migrants to this country, come from a variety of cultures.

> There seems little doubt that one reason for Australians' current reservations about the concept of multiculturalism is their perception that the racial balance of migration is shifting markedly towards Asian migrants and away from the traditional European sources of Australia's immigrants.
>
> The reality is that about 4% of Australians were born in Asia. If the present trends in immigration were maintained the proportion could rise to about 7% by the year 2021, according to Australia's Population Trends and Prospects (1990, Australian Government Printing Service).
>
> But the perception of the level of Asian migration is much higher than this—a perception that is possibly influenced by the visual evidence of large numbers of Asian tourists as well as Asian migrants themselves.
>
> It is the perception of the fast-growing Asian immigrant population that has most sorely tested Australians' willingness to embrace the idea of positively encouraging ethnic diversity.
>
> When confronted with an ethnic group which is regarded as being so obviously different from the Australian mainstream, Australians begin to wonder whether their multiculturalism can extend this far. [1]

While most Australians are still trying to come to terms with demographic multiculturalism, some Australians are trying to move on *social and political multiculturalism*.

The advocates of social multiculturalism argue that we should not only recognise the fact that people come to this country from a variety of cultures, but also value the fact that when they come to this country they bring their various cultures with them. The advocates of political multiculturalism argue that it is not enough for people to bring their various cultures with them. To have any impact on this country, they need to not only have a presence in this country, but also have some power in this country.

Some Australians believe the advocates of social and political multiculturalism are going too far. Researchers Jupp and Kabala say:

---

[1] McKay, H. op cit p.160

Multiculturalism, in political terms means 'the acceptance of organised interests based on ethnic[ity] as a legitimate element in the policy making process alongside other interests'.

[The] implementation of multiculturalism illustrates how democratic processes and the legal system in Australia can be circumvented by powerful interest groups.[1]

But some Australians believe they are not going far enough. Aboriginal leader Pat Dodson says:

> If you listen to the rhetoric of multiculturalism you hear phrases like 'Many different people fitting together to make a whole', 'the Multicultural Australian Nation.'
>
> The Australian nation-state is always built in as the unifying concept before we start seeking diversity. As if the framework itself is unproblematic!
>
> In *Multiculturalism for All Australians* it says '…the council does not believe the encouragement of Australian cultures, including Aboriginal cultures, weakens the Australian peoples' sense of identification, as long as they occur within the appropriate multicultural framework.'
>
> Who defines 'the appropriate multicultural framework'? Not us! When the rhetoric refers to 'inclusion,' we would ask 'inclusion into what?' And the unspoken answer is, 'inclusion into political and social structures which are themselves culture specific … and exclusive![2]

Notwithstanding these principles, John Evans says: "… the principles of multiculturalism enunciated by the Australian Council on Population and Ethnic Affairs provide useful criteria for the change we seek.[3]

These measures for balanced multicultural community development include ensuring equality of opportunity and responsibilty, the unity of social and political cohesion, and the diversity of indigenous and migrant cultures.[4]

- What is a multicultural view of our community?
- What are its weaknesses?
- What are its strengths?

✍ Record your reflections in your Working Notes.

---

1 Jupp, J. & Kabala, M. *The Politics Of Immigration*, Bureau of Immigration Research, 1993, pp 18-19
2 Dodson, M. *Aboriginal and Torres Strait Islander People and Multiculturalism*, QUT Brisbane, 23/8/93 pp 9-10
3 Houston, J.(ed.)*The Cultured Pearl*, JBCE Melbourne, 1986, p 229
4 Australian Council on Population and Ethnic Affairs, *Multiculturalism for All Australians*, AGPS Canberra 1982

Becoming receptive as a community

'Being pro-majority and pro-minority'

Our attitudes to multicultural community can be expressed in four categories. The *assimilative* among us, who are 'pro-majority and anti-minority' in terms of relating to other cultures, would tend to say that the majority culture is good, and minority cultures should adjust to the majority culture. The *reactive* among us, who adopt the opposite 'anti-majority and pro-minority' view, would tend to say that minority cultures are good, and the majority culture should adapt to minority cultures.

The *receptive* among us, who are pro-majority and pro-minority, would tend to say that both cultures are good, and we need to work out a way forward together, which combines the best of both worlds. While the *alienated* among us, who are both anti-majority and anti-minority, would probably say 'to hell with everybody!'

The following tables illustrate the various perspectives.

Majority perspectives

	1. Assimilative	3. Receptive
Majority – Minority Relations	Us – Yes Them – No	Us –Yes Them – Yes
	2. Reactive	4. Alienated
Majority – Minority Relations	Us – No Them –Yes	Us – No Them – No

Minority Perspectives

	1. Assimilative	3. Receptive
Majority – Minority Relations	Us – No Them – Yes	Us –Yes Them – Yes
	2. Reactive	4. Alienated
Majority – Minority Relations	Us – Yes Them – No	Us – No Them – No

If we are assimilative, we will not be able to work for true diversity in the community, because everything we do will tend towards the ethnocentric hegemony of the majority culture. If we are reactive, we will not be able to work for true unity in the community, because everything we do will tend towards the ethnocentric fragmentation of minority cultures. If we are alienated, we will not be able to work for either true unity or true diversity, because everything we do will tend to be a counter-productive projection of our egocentric preoccupations.

It is only if we are receptive, committed to the good of both majority and minority cultures, and the need to work out a way forward together that combines the best of both worlds, that we can work towards true unity and true diversity between the cultures in the community.

We need to help our communities move from an assimilative attitude towards a receptive response, without becoming reactive—and alienating or alienated—in the process.

- What is a "receptive" approach to community?
- If we are in the majority culture what would being "receptive" mean for us?
- If we are in a minority culture what would being "receptive" mean for us?

✎ Record your reflections in your Working Notes.

Being community both ways

'The best of both worlds'

The receptive approach is currently demonstrated in Australia by Mandawuy Yunupingu, the leader of Yothu Yindi.

When most of us think of this indigenous rock band from northeast Arnhem Land at the Top End of Australia, we immediately think of 'the successful fusion of didgeridoo and clapsticks with synthesizer and sampler' that put Aboriginal music, including lyrics from an Aboriginal language, on the radio all round the world. But Mandaway Yunupingu and Yothu Yindi are concerned with a lot more than entertainment ...

> When the dance music remix of Yothu Yindi's *Treaty* finally burst into the Australian top 20, the sound of consciences being salved was almost audible. For years there had been veiled accusations of racism aimed at the Australian music industry, particularly commercial radio, concerning the lack of recognition given to Aboriginal musicians.
>
> Suddenly those accusations seemed to have less substance; a round of communal back-slapping ensued and the band's commercial success was followed by a plethora of awards for the single, its accompanying video clip, and the album from which it was taken, *Tribal Voice*.

For Yothu Yindi's leader, Mandawuy Yunupingu, this recognition is just reward for years of hard work and determination. Essentially optimistic, you get the impression he always felt commercial success was just around the next corner, despite the lack of precedents. Yet Mandawuy's outlook hasn't always been so positive.

'In my time I've been without hope,' he says. 'I was angry, I got into fights. I've turned to drinking, I've been locked up ... But I've changed now because I know my family is really strong and powerful. Instead of being angry and turning away, I'd rather challenge and find a positive solution.'

... Mandawuy's family is a remarkable one. His mother? 'She gave me a lot of insight into life. My mother taught me honesty, taught me all those behaviours one should have in order to be proud, in order to have a good solid basis to operate from.'

His father took on the tribal responsibilities in his early forties, and imbued in his children not only a strong sense of kinship but also strong political beliefs as the leader of the first land rights protest. 'He was into making sure that his tribe's pattern of living was always there, that it wasn't lost. That was the sense of leadership he gave us. And then he balanced that with the view of wanting to develop his ability to live in a contemporary sense.'

In 1963, Mandawuy's father, Munggarawuy Yunupingu, led the Gumatj clan in protest over the mining of bauxite on their land. They sent a bark painting outlining their concerns to the politicians in Canberra, asking that the miners leave. His father's political action made a strong impression on Mandawuy as a child. 'That was the biggest political milestone for me,' says Mandawuy. 'I saw him operate, the way he talked with men in power ... And he talked to us, to the family, about the important things of how not to sell out, how to be strong.'

Unfortunately, their protest was unsuccessful. 'Of course, he lost that case when he took it to the High Court, but then Mabo turned it around.'

His sons did not forget their father's protest. In fact, the broken promises of past governments are the subject of Yothu Yindi's hit song *Treaty*. [1]

... For his part, Mandawuy decided the future of his people lay in education. He became the first Aboriginal university graduate from his region of Gove, and is now the principal of the Yirrkala school, where he's pioneering a curriculum that emphasises both Yolngu (Aboriginal) and Bandala (European) learning.

This marriage of cultures is typical of the approach taken by Mandawuy and his Gumatj clan. Mandawuy is neither militant nor separatist; rather, he's a realist who believes that retaining Aboriginality

---

1 Yunupingu, M. 'The Yothu Yindi Family', *BIPR Bulletin*, April 1992, pp 26-27

does not mean rejecting the best of what other cultures have to offer. This is reflected not only in Mandawuy's approach to education and politics but also to music and technology.

'These days we're doing more compromising in terms of cultural situations, and you've got to do it because you're dealing with the commercial aspects of the music industry. As long as our values, beliefs and principles remain intact and I reckon we've got the strength to do that, then I think that's the way to go.

We may have made some compromises but we've retained the essence, our Yolngu integrity is not being threatened. In fact, we're enriching our culture.'[1]

These days, Mandawuy has his own family to look after. He and his wife have six children, all girls, aged 5 to 13. 'I like their company,' Mandawuy says proudly of his daughters. 'They are sweet girls, my girls.' Many of the things he wishes for them seem remarkably similar to the aspirations his own parents had for him. 'I would like to give them a little bit of balance in their life', he says. 'That is what I am striving to formulate for them in a way that they will grow with strength. I want to give them every possible way that is not going to be hard for them. This is what I am trying to do: open those barriers so they grow up with the best of both worlds.'

It seems impossible to overestimate the importance of family, or kinship, within Aboriginal society. Indeed, its entire social framework is based on kinship, a kinship of opposites similar to the Eastern Yin and Yang symbols.

> 'Everything in the Aboriginal world is divided into two aspects of reality', says Mandawuy. 'There is the *yindi* and *yothu*, the *yothu* and the *yindi*. They say mother earth is *yindi* and *yothu* are the people—her children. That's what we follow, that's what constitutes our law. And it's how we structure our pattern of living.
>
> 'My family is the Gumatj people. Everyone is related, everyone has an identity that is kinship. For me, I am the hawk, the crocodile and the kangaroo. These symbols tie the individual to the family and environment.
>
> ... 'When you start to live with people, you start to understand one another's differences and respect for their differences and you try to live like this', says Mandawuy. 'The way we have managed to structure our existence in Yothu Yindi is by applying things that are relevant, things that we believe should be part of today's society. Living with one another is one of those things. Not living with racism, not living with negative parts—they are the types of things we commonly reject. The momentum is to take what we think is the right way, and change attitudes.'

---

1 Hitchings, S. 'Mandawuy Yinupingu', *Australian Left Review*, June 1992 p 3

One day, he hopes, those attitudes will have changed sufficiently for black and white Australia to have reached reconciliation. He believes that the Aboriginal notion of kinship, of *yothu yindi,* is what is needed to achieve that aim. 'I'd like to formulate the yothu yindi kinship, that sort of pattern', he says. 'If they (the rest of the country) could relate to that, then BANG, we've got a big family!' [1]

- What does the "best of both worlds" mean to Mandawuy Yunupingu?
- How can we learn about being community "both ways"?

✎ Record your reflections in your Working Notes.

Thriving in a polyethnic community

'As the Rainbow People of God'

According to Desmond Tutu, not only do we need to survive in our polyethnic communities, but we also need to thrive in our polyethnic communities, as the Rainbow People of God. Here are some tips for not merely surviving, but thriving, in a polyethnic community: -

1) Meditate on the oneness of the human family

There aren't many races, there is only one race. Beneath the differences we are all the same. The most personal, is the most universal. We all want to love and be loved.

2) Celebrate heterogeneity rather than homogeneity

There is one whole, but there are many parts. The differences may seem quite superficial, but they are actually quite significant. The universal is not uniform, but multiform. We all want to live different ways, not to be forced to live the same way as everyone else.

3) Recognise the contradictions in our values

We need to be aware of any egocentricity that could subvert our work for unity, and any ethnocentricity that could subvert our work for diversity, that may be operating unconsciously in the way that we live our lives.

---

[1] Yinupingu, M. pp 26-27

4) Acknowledge the limitations in our knowledge

We need to be aware of our ignorance. We all have blindspots, which by definition we cannot see ourselves. So we need to listen to the feedback that we get from others, in order to see the way we live our lives as others see us.

5) Revel in the role of a learner at large

To start with, we need to keep our mouths shut, and our eyes and ears open. If we must speak, we need to ask open-ended questions, rather than make statements that close down discussion. A closed person cannot learn from anyone, not even a dear friend. But an open person can learn from everyone, even a complete stranger.

6) Delight in the whole world as a teacher

If we are willing to learn, the whole world will be willing to teach us. It can teach us not only a whole range of ways to talk, but also, with each new way of talking, can teach us a new way of thinking. Each new set of vocabulary gives us a new set of categories to be able to understand our world anew.

7) Relish developing another worldview

Our worldview isn't the only worldview. In spite of the propaganda of our various religions, none of us has a monopoly on verity. It can be really exciting to compare and contrast the vast array of perspectives that the worldviews of our numerous traditions provide.

8) Enjoy exploring the same world differently

We need to take every chance we can get to look at the world through another's eyes. In spite of our fears, we need to have the courage to step out into the unknown with others as our guide. Then we will we be able to experience a myriad of unexpected wonders inherent in our otherwise predictable world.

9) Rejoice in the possibility of synthesis

Together we can work towards a community world, that is a unique combination of all our cultures, the best of all possible worlds. Not single cropping, but companion planting. Not agriculture, but permaculture. Not ethnic cleansing, but inclusive living. Not mono-culture, but multi-culture. Not concrete jungle, but global village. We alone can do it. But we cannot do it alone.

10) Engage in the practice of *satya, ahimsa* and *tapasya* [1]

The first step towards a community world is *satya*. Satya means seeking after the truth in every situation. Without such seeking there can be no comprehension of the potential, let alone the realisation of the potential, that is intrinsic to every situation.

The second step towards a community world is *ahimsa*. Ahimsa means seeking a way forward together, with everyone who can help us, in a way that is not harmful to the welfare of anyone, whether they are part of the group helping us or not.

The third step towards a community world is *tapasya*. Tapasya means seeking a way forward together, and continuing to seek it, until we find it, accepting the pain of the painstaking process, as the price we are gladly willing to pay, in order to find a way to become the 'Rainbow People of God'.

- Which of these tips do you think might be most helpful to you in making the most of life in a polyethnic community? (Give your reasons.)
- Do you have any other suggestions that you would like to add to this list?

✍ Record your reflections in your Working Notes.

Conclusion

10 minutes

The follow-up reading for this session is

> 'Issues in Cross-Cultural Counselling' and 'The Principles of Cross-Cultural Practice' (Reading 18).

The set community tasks for this week are

- ❒ Keep on with your community work.
- ❒ In the meantime, read the set readings and make sure you discuss the issues they raise over a cuppa with at least two,

---

[1] Hindi terms

if not three, of the following people: an Aboriginal, an Islander, a migrant, and a refugee.

❐ Then meet with your learning partner and your community development support group to share your reflections on these conversations.

❐ Write up a list of the tentative conclusions that you have made about the cultural factors that you need to take into account in the community work that you do.

✍ Record your actions, reflections, and conclusions in your Working Notes.

Session 19

Working within a Legal Framework

Objectives

- To review your understanding of the importance of a cultural framework.
- To consider the importance of a legal framework for community work.

Review

15 minutes

- ☐ Review your work from Session 18.
- ☐ Review the issues raised in the course notes from the previous session, particularly your understanding of the importance of a cultural framework.
- ☐ Review the reading:

    'Issues in Cross-Cultural Counselling' and 'Principles of Cross Cultural Practice' (Reading 18)
- ☐ Review the tasks:
    - ❖ How was your meeting with your learning partner and your community development support group?
    - ❖ What was the most important thing you learned while doing your community tasks for the last session?

✎ Record your reflections in your Working Notes.

A legal framework for community work

90 minutes

Community development workers

Most community development workers are unpaid volunteers. Of the paid community development workers in Australia, most work under the Social and Community Services (SACS) Award.

You can access information about the SACS Award by contacting the Australian Services Union (ASU), which is the largest union representing community workers in Australia. The ASU web site is http://www.asu.asn.au/

Community development organisations and regulations

Most community development workers, paid or unpaid, decide to work together in community development organisations. Most of these organisations are informal associations. But increasing numbers of community development organisations are becoming formal, incorporated Associations, subject to increasing degrees of government regulation in regard to incorporation, insurance, permits, licences, copyright, occupational health and safety, and other issues.

Community development work in Australia is regulated by four spheres of government:

- At the local level: local government
- At the state level: State Government
- At the national level: the Commonwealth Government
- At the international level: the United Nations.

Each of these spheres of government has its own geographic focus and its own regulations. But these regulations are layered and overlap one another.

Local governments

Of immediate importance to the work of community workers in Australia are the **Shire** and **City Councils**. Like community workers, shire and city councils have a local focus, regulating local planning, health and safety.

- You can access information about Shire and City Councils through the Gov.Au national web site, https://www.gov.au/

- What local regulations do you need to know about?
- How would you go about getting the information you need?

✎ Record your reflections in your Working Notes.

State Governments

Of considerable importance to the work of community workers is **privacy legislation** and **freedom of information**. Queensland Privacy adopts the 11 Information Privacy Principles (IPPs) in the Commonwealth Privacy Act 1988.

- See these principles at the web site of the Department of Justice and Attorney-General, https://www.oic.qld.gov.au/annotated-legislation/ip/schedule-3

The **Queensland Freedom of Information Act 1992 (FOI Act)** gives people a right, subject to limited exceptions, to access documents held by ministers, state government.

Each of you needs to check for information about your own State Government legislation through their web sites.

- What state regulations do you need to know about?
- How would you go about getting the information you need?

✎ Record your reflections in your Working Notes.

The Commonwealth Government

The Commonwealth Government agency with the most impact on the work of community workers in Australia is the Commonwealth Department of Social Services, http://www.dss.gov.au. This department administers legislation about social security and family assistance. Also important are the Commonwealth Department of Health http://www.health.gov.au, and the Australian Safety and Compensation Council http://www.ascc.gov.au/.

- For information about social security law and programs, go to http://www.centrelink.gov.au/
- For information about family assistance law and programs, go to http://guides.dss.gov.au/family-assistance-guide

- You can access information about Health Law in Aged and Community Care at https://www.health.gov.au/health-topics/aged-care/about-aged-care/aged-care-laws-in-australia

- What Commonwealth regulations do you need to know about?
- How would you go about the task of getting the information?

✍ Record your reflections in your Working Notes.

The United Nations

Of utmost importance to the work of all community workers is the **United Nations Universal Declaration of Human Rights** adopted and proclaimed by General Assembly resolution 217A (III) of 10 December 1948.

See Appendix A for the text of the Declaration. Read it through and answer the following questions:

- How does this list of rights compare with your own guidelines?
- Which human rights are scrupulously upheld in your community?
- Which human rights need to be promoted more in your community?
- What responsibilities are required in order to guarantee human rights?

✍ Record your reflections in your Working Notes.

Community development and legal rights

The **Human Rights Commission**, http://www.humanrights.gov.au/ administers human rights and equal opportunity legislation:

- the Australian Human Rights Commission Act 1986
- the Racial Discrimination Act 1975
- the Sex Discrimination Act 1984
- the Disability Discrimination Act 1992

You can access their searchable database to resources on human rights, disability rights, sex discrimination, racial discrimination, and Aboriginal & Torres Strait Islanders at https://www.humanrights.gov.au/our-work

You can get legal information in each state from Community Legal Centres. Find out about your nearest community legal centre from the **National Association of Community Legal Centres** (NACLC): http://www.naclc.org.au/, email: NACLC@fcl.fl.asn.au

You can get legal aid in each state from **Legal Aid Offices**.

- **In the ACT:** Legal Aid Office ACT (1300 654 314).
- **In New South Wales:** Legal Aid NSW (helpline 1800 806 913, youth hotline 1800 10 18 10, TTY 02 9219 5037), Aboriginal legal services in NSW, Law Society (helpline 1800 357 300), community justice centres, and LIAC's and LawLink's sources of assistance in NSW.
- **In the Northern Territory:** Northern Territory Legal Aid Commission (1800 019 343) and NT Aboriginal Legal Service offices [from ATSILS].
- **In Queensland:** Legal Aid Queensland (1300 65 11 88), Aboriginal & Torres Strait Islander Legal Services, and the ATSI Women's Legal and Advocacy Service.
- **In South Australia:** South Australian Legal Services Commission (1300 366 424, TTY 08 8463 3691), Law Society and the Aboriginal Legal Rights Movement.
- **In Tasmania:** Tasmanian Legal Aid Commission (1300 366 611) and the Tasmania Aboriginal Centre.
- **In Victoria:** Victoria Legal Aid (1800 677 402), Law Institute of Victoria and the Victorian Aboriginal Legal Service.
- **In Western Australia:** Western Australian Legal Aid (1800 809 616, TTY 1800 241 216), Law Society of WA and the Aboriginal Legal Service of WA.

- What legal rights do you need to know more about?
- Where would you go to find out more information about them?

✐ Record your reflections in your Working Notes.

Conclusion

10 minutes

The follow-up reading for this session is

> 'United Nations Declaration of Human Rights' (Reading 19 or Appendix A).

The set community tasks for this week are

- ☐ Keep on with your community work.
- ☐ In the meantime, read the set readings and make sure you discuss the issues they raise over a cuppa with at least two people from your local community.
- ☐ Answer the following questions:

1. Which human rights are scrupulously upheld in your community?
2. Which human rights need to be promoted more in your community?
3. What responsibilities are required in order to guarantee human rights?

- ☐ Then meet with your learning partner and your community development support group and share your reflections on these conversations.
- ☐ Write up your own Declaration of the human rights you will take into account in the community work that you do.
- ✎ Record your actions, reflections and conclusions in your Working Notes.

Note: You will need to organise a learning partner to be with you in order to do the next session.

Session 20

Community Work Skill 1: Communicating

Preparation

You will need to organise a learning partner to do this session with you.

Objectives

- To review your understanding of the importance of working within a legal framework.
- To consider a series of basic community work skills, starting with communicating.

Review

15 minutes

- ❒ Review your work from Session 19.
- ❒ Review the issues raised in course notes in the previous session, particularly your understanding of the importance of working within a legal framework.
- ❒ Review the reading: United Nations Declaration of Human Rights (Reading 19)
- ❒ Review the tasks:
  - ❖ How was your meeting with your learning partner and your community development support group?
  - ❖ What was the most important thing you learned while doing your community tasks for the last session?

✍ Record your reflections in your Working Notes.

Developing community through communication

15 minutes

The importance of communication

Scott Peck says:

> If we are going to use the word 'community' meaningfully, we must restrict it to a group of individuals who have learned to communicate honestly with each other, whose relationships go deeper than their masks of composure and who have developed some significant commitment to 'rejoice together, mourn together', 'delight in each other' and 'make each other's condition their own'.[1]

The case study of Martha's Vineyard

In a small, relatively isolated community on Martha's Vineyard, about every tenth person used to be born without the ability to hear. Everybody in the community—hearing and non-hearing alike—spoke a unique sign language brought from England when they migrated to Massachusetts in 1690. In the mid-twentieth century, with increased mobility, the people ceased to intermarry and the genetic anomaly disappeared.

But before the memory of it died—and the sign language with it—historian Nora Groce studied the community's history. She compared the experience of the non-hearing people to that of the hearing people.

She found that 80% of the non-hearing people graduated from high school as did 80% of the hearing. She found that about 90% of the non-hearing got married, compared to about 92% of the hearing. They had about equal numbers of children. Their income levels were similar, as were the variety and distribution of their occupations.

Then Groce did a parallel study on the Massachusetts mainland. At the time, it was considered to have the best services in the nation for non-hearing people. There she found that 50% of non-hearing people graduated from high school compared with 75% of the hearing. Non-hearing people married half the time while hearing people married 90% of the time. 40% of the non-hearing people had children while 80% of hearing people did. Non-hearing people had fewer children. They also received about one-third the income of hearing people and their range of occupations was much more limited.

How was it, Groce wondered, that on an island with no services, non-hearing people were as much like hearing people as you could possibly

---

1 S. Peck, *The Different Drum,* Rider and Co London 1988, p 59

measure, yet thirty miles away, with the most advanced services available, non-hearing people lived much poorer lives than the hearing?

The one place in the United States where deafness was not a disability was a place with no services for deaf people. In that community, all the people adapted by signing instead of handling the non-hearing people over to professionals and their services. That community wasn't just doing what was necessary to help or to serve one group, but doing what was necessary to incorporate everyone.

- What strikes you about this case study?
- What was the difference in the health statistics between the two communities?
- What was the reason the researcher gave for the difference?

✍ Record your reflections in your Working Notes.

The difficulties of communicating
20 minutes

One-way and two-way communication

- For this exercise you will need two pieces of paper and a pen, and the help of your learning partner.
- ☐ Make a mental note of the time.
- ☐ Then, making sure that your learning partner can't see Figure 18, study it for a minute. *Without allowing any questions,* try to describe the boxes in the diagram so that your learning partner can draw them on their first piece of paper.
- ☐ When you are finished, note the amount of time that it took.
- ☐ Without showing them the diagram, ask your learning partner to estimate how many squares they have drawn correctly in relation to the others. Write this number next to the recorded time.
- ☐ Now make a mental note of the time again and study Figure 19 for a minute. Then, without showing the diagram, but *inviting and answering questions for clarification,* try to describe the boxes in the diagram so that your learning partner can draw them on their second piece of paper.

Community Work Skill 1: Communicating

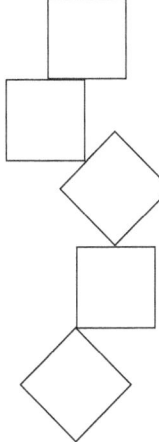

Figure 18

☐ When you are finished, repeat the procedures for Figure 19 as for Figure 18: noting the amount of time that it took, ask your learning partner to estimate how many squares they have drawn correctly in relation to the others, and write the number again, next to the recorded time.

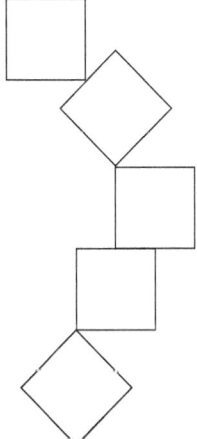

Figure 19

☐ Record the actual numbers of correct squares on the papers next to the estimates made by your learning partner.
☐ Discuss the results: the time taken, the accuracy estimated, the accuracy achieved, and the reasons for these results.
✎ Record your reflections in your Working Notes.

Two-way communication is always better than one-way communication. Extending the right to others to ask questions and seek clarification is critical to two-way communication. Also critical is clearly answering the questions asked of us. Two-way communication may take twice as long, but it can halve the hassles we often have in trying to understand one another.

Attentive and reflective listening

35 minutes

A prisoner taps messages on a prison wall.
'Can anybody hear me?'
There is complete despair when nobody is there to hear.
But, oh the joy, when somebody hears and replies -
'I can hear you'. [1]

Attentive listening skills

Note that we need to be in an environment with minimal distractions to listen attentively. Attentive listening also needs us to:

1. Adopt an appropriate posture:
    - standing or sitting close
    - leaning towards the other
    - looking into their face
    - maintaining eye contact
    - showing keen interest
2. Listen silently, and not interrupt:
    - nodding understanding
    - encouraging to continue
3. Set aside significant time for people

☐ Speak for 2 minutes on a personal topic of interest while your learning partner listens attentively. When you have finished, give some feedback to your learning partner on what you noticed about how attentive, or inattentive, they were. Then change roles and repeat the exercise. [2]

---

1 Anthony de Mello
2 K. Shields, p 51

- What did you feel was inattentive behaviour?
- What did you feel was attentive behaviour?
- What do you need to work on to be more attentive?

✍ Record your reflections in your Working Notes.

Reflective listening skills

Good listening is reflective. In order to listen reflectively we need to do the following:

1. Use short phrases to indicate understanding. For instance, *'You sound like you're frightened…'*
2. Ask open-ended, personalised questions for further understanding. For instance, *'How does that affect you?'*
3. Summarise the essence of the speaker's statements in their own language so that they can affirm our version of their words. For instance, *'It sounds like you're scared you might make a mistake.'*
4. Be careful not to add to what the speaker has said, nor to put words or ideas into their mouths.

☐ While holding your pen, speak about a personal matter you are really concerned about. *'I feel freaked out about my work because I often don't know what to do.'*

☐ Have your learning partner listen attentively, and reflect back to you what they heard you say you were feeling—not by just parroting, but sensitively paraphrasing what you said. *'It sounds like you feel nervous because you're scared you might make a mistake.'*

☐ If you feel satisfied that you were heard, pass the pen to your learning partner, who then takes their turn to speak about a personal matter that they are really concerned about.

☐ However, if you do not feel satisfied you have been heard, hold on to the pen, and try again until you feel assured by their reflective listening that you have been truly heard.

☐ Then change roles and repeat the exercise.[1]

---

1 K. Shields, p 51

After you have both had a turn, answer the following questions:

- What did you find most challenging about reflective listening?
- Which aspect of reflective listening do you need to work on more?

✎ Record your reflections in your Working Notes.

Some tips on listening

- Listening takes time.
- Listening requires courtesy.
- Listening attends to the whole person.
- Listening observes the body as much as the voice.
- Listening is about understanding—that is under-standing. We cannot understand anyone if we look down at them. We can only understand someone if we look up to them.
- Listening occurs at a surface level—what people are saying.
- Listening occurs at a deeper level—what people are feeling.
- In order to listen respectfully we need to listen deeply to feelings.

- Which of these tips would you underscore as particularly important for you to work on?
- What other tip(s) of your own would you add to this list?

✎ Be sure to record your tips in your Working Notes.

Speaking

35 minutes

Communication isn't easy. Consider the possible mistakes we can make in a conversation.

> *There's what you meant to say.*
> *There's what you actually say.*
> *There's what they heard you say.*
> *There's what they thought they heard you say.*

There's what they want to say about what they thought they heard you say.
There's what they actually say about what they thought they heard you say.
There's what you heard them say about what they thought they heard you say.

And so on.

Effective speaking skills

☐ Make a list of controversial subjects for discussion.
☐ With your learning partner, pick a subject from the list that you would like to talk about.

Stage One – Articulating our perspective

☐ Pick a topic, and taking one side of the controversy, express your views for one minute as passionately and as persuasively as you can. Then ask your learning partner to take the other side of the controversy and speak against your views for one minute as passionately and as persuasively as they can.
☐ Talk about your results in articulating your views and your partner's results in articulating contrary views.
☐ Repeat the exercise with another topic, but this time ask your learning partner to speak first.
✎ Record your reflections in your Working Notes.

Stage Two – Advocating the perspectives of others

☐ Now reverse roles.
☐ Take a minute to advocate your learning partner's views, as passionately and as persuasively as you can.
☐ Then invite your learning partner to take a minute to advocate your views, as passionately and as persuasively as they can.
☐ Talk about how you both went in advocating other's views.
✎ Record your reflections in your Working Notes.

Stage Three - Advancing our own and other perspectives

- Finally both give a one-minute speech that presents both sides of the argument in a single presentation, as passionately and as persuasively as you can.
- Talk about your result in advancing a balanced perspective.
- Record your reflections in your Working Notes.
- Answer the following questions:

> - How can you articulate your own views passionately but respectfully?
> - How can you advocate other's views both sincerely and persuasively?
> - How can you advance an integrated perspective genuinely?

- Record your reflections in your Working Notes.

Note that effective speaking is
- personal: it comes from ideas we've made our own.
- passionate: it comes from the love in our hearts.
- persuasive: it comes from the logic in our heads.
- genuine: it is authentic, honest, and vulnerable.
- sincere: it is respectful especially of opponents.
- story-based: it uses examples to make our ideas come alive.

Conclusion

10 minutes

The follow-up reading for this session is:

> 'Communication' in Trevor Tyson, *Working With Groups*, Macmillan, Melbourne, 1989 pp 72-84 (Reading 20)

The set community tasks for this session are:
- Meet with your learning partner and your community development support group.
- Share what you learnt in this session about communicating. Talk about ways in which you could all listen more attentively and reflectively, and speak more effectively.

☐ Look for opportunities to listen—really listen—to people in your community this week.

☐ Look for opportunities to speak up in your community this week—for yourself, for others, and for yourself-and-others.

✎ Record your actions, reflections, and conclusions in your Working Notes.

Note: You will need to organise two learning partners to be with you to do the next session.

Session 21

Community Work Skill 2: Negotiating

Preparation

You will need to organise two learning partners to be with you to do this session.

Objectives

- To review your communicating skills.
- To consider the next in a series of basic community work skills: negotiating.

Review

15 minutes

- ☐ Review your work from Session 20.
- ☐ Review the issues raised in the last session, particularly your communicating skills.
- ☐ Review the reading:

    'Communication' in Trevor Tyson, *Working With Groups*, MacMillan, Melbourne, 1989 pp 72-84 (Reading 20)
- ☐ Review the tasks:
    - ❖ How was your meeting with your learning partner and your community development support group?
    - ❖ What was the most important thing you learned while doing your community tasks for the last session?

✍ Record your reflections in your Working Notes.

Negotiating deals between parties

25 minutes

The art of negotiating

Negotiating is the art of

- Turning disagreement into agreement
- Mediating a peace deal between parties in a dispute
- Brokering an arrangement acceptable to all parties

Typical tasks for negotiating in community work are

- Negotiating entry to a community organisation
- Negotiating access to community resources
- Negotiating support for a community program
- Negotiating settlement of a community dispute

> - What are some areas of negotiation that are needed in your community?

✑ Record your reflections in your Working Notes.

The role of the negotiator

The negotiator's role in the negotiation process is to

- Establish contact with the relevant parties
- Approach the enemies as potential allies
- Establish communication between parties
- Help the parties understand one another
- Clear up any misunderstandings
- Enable both sides to relate as human beings
- Mediate a deal between the parties
- Broker an arrangement acceptable to all parties

> - With which of these roles are you most familiar?
> - What is actually involved in fulfilling the role?

✑ Record your reflections in your Working Notes.

Consider the place of the negotiator

The negotiator works between two parties, at the interface between people; between people and groups; between groups; and between groups and a system of some kind or other.

If we are to work in this role, we need certain qualities:
- A thorough knowledge of both parties
- Respect of and acceptance by both parties
- Access to the networks of both as well as being able to work in the gap in between

We need to be careful that we don't just run messages back and forth between the two parties, but get down to the task of setting up a process of serious negotiation between them.[1]

> 1. How can you acquire knowledge of both parties?
> 2. How can you become acceptable to both parties?
> 3. How can you avoid running messages back and forth?
> 4. How can you set up a serious process of negotiation?

✍ Record your reflections in your Working Notes.

The pressure on the negotiator

The negotiator works between two parties, each of whom wants the negotiator to work for them. Often this leads a negotiator to feel as if they are working for two masters who are at cross-purposes. If we are not careful, this can drive us crazy.

Tony Kelly and Sandra Sewell, experienced community workers, say that "to survive this situation we need a firm self-identity and an astute political sense" so we don't get played off against one side or the other.[2]

We need to be clear about
- Who we are
- Who we are working with
- Who we are working for

Who are we?

- We are *mediators*, not spin doctors or hatchet merchants.

---

[1] Kelly, T. & S. Sewell, *With Head Heart And Hands*, Boolorong Brisbane 1988, p 91
[2] Kelly and Sewell, p 91

Who are we working with?
- We are working with *both parties*, not working for one against the other.

Who are we working for?
- We are working for *both parties*, not working for one against the other.

- Who are you?
- Who are you working with?
- Who are you working for?

✎ Record your reflections in your Working Notes.

The cardinal rule of the community negotiator

The community negotiator's cardinal rule in the negotiation process is to consider the impact of any arrangement on the most vulnerable people in the community. If it's not 'good news to the poor', it's not good.

As Tony Kelly and Sandra Sewell say, 'If the starting point for the broker is not the poorest of the poor, he or she runs the risk of being co-opted by the *status quo* and becoming a public relations machine for the system'.[1]

- What is the difference between a corporate and a community negotiator?
- How important is concern for the poor to the welfare of the community?

✎ Record your reflections in your Working Notes.

Negotiating deals acceptable to all parties

50 minutes

Vital negotiating skills can be acquired or improved using the following approach:[2]

---

[1] Kelly and Sewell, p 91
[2] Adapted from R. Fisher & W. Ury, *Getting to Yes*

Stage One

Separate people from problems

- People are humans
- Humans can act tough but all are vulnerable
- We need to be hard on issues but soft on people
- We need to relate to people and work on the problems, rather than treat people as problems and try to fix them.

> - What happens when you treat people as problems and try to fix them?
> - How can you separate the people from the problems, relate to the people, and work on the problems?

✍ Record your reflections in your Working Notes.

Stage Two

Focus on interests rather than positions

- *Positions* are predetermined solutions
- If people stick to their own predetermined solutions, they are unlikely to think of a solution that's acceptable to other people

> - What are some of the positions, for example on the issue of decision-making—on the way people think decisions should be made in the community?

- We need to focus on *interests* rather than positions
- Interests are people's fears and desires
- We can find out people's interests by asking why they take a particular position on a particular issue

> - Why do people take their position on the decision-making issue?

- Usually each side has multiple interests
- We need to acknowledge the interests of each side

- Some interests may be in conflict, however many interests will be compatible
- We need to consider both conflicting and compatible interests

- What are their interests in the leadership issue?
- What ones are in conflict with others in the group?
- What ones are compatible with others in the group?

- People need to set aside their predetermined solutions, and find solutions that address as many interests as possible

- Will people set aside their position on decision-making for the sake of discussion?
  (If people say 'yes' - proceed. If people say 'no' - ask them to observe.)

✍ Record your reflections in your Working Notes.

Stage Three

Invent multiple options for mutual benefit

- Don't look for a single solution
- Look for as many solutions as possible
- Don't decide what is possible beforehand—do that later
- Brainstorm as many wild and wonderful options as possible
- To brainstorm effectively, make the atmosphere informal
- Discourage criticism, but encourage creativity

- What are all the different ways people could organise your community that could address the concerns they have about decision-making?

- Record all the ideas in full view
- Put ticks against the most promising ideas

- What ideas do you think are most promising?
- Can you improve on these ideas?
- What other ideas have you seen, heard, or read about that might be other ways you could address your concerns about decision-making?

- Identify shared interests
- Then identify options that address these shared interests

- What would you say are shared interests?
- What options address those shared interests?

- Underline (in pencil) the option that people think would be most likely to meet most of their needs

- What option is most likely to meet most of your needs?

- Draft a tentative agreement, and keep working on the draft until it is finally acceptable to all parties
- ✎ Record the draft agreement in your Working Notes

Stage Four

Set up objective criteria for assessment

We need to agree on how to assess whether the agreement is workable in practice. The criteria need to be fair, simple and practical, and acceptable to all the parties in the dispute.

- What criteria can people agree on to use to assess whether the agreement is workable in practice, or not?

We need to constantly assess whether the way we run our group is safe, accepting, respectful, inclusive, and just. We also need to assess the impact of the way we run our group on the most vulnerable people in the community.

> - Is the agreement 'good news to the poor', i.e. to the most vulnerable people, or not?

- If it is—okay! If it is not—then we need to negotiate another agreement.
- If we can do that—okay! If we can't do that, then we need to have in mind a viable alternative to a negotiated agreement.
- ✎ Record your reflections in your Working Notes.

A viable alternative to a negotiated agreement

If we have trouble negotiating an agreement that is acceptable, we need to have in mind a viable alternative. We need to help each party think about a bottom-line, fall-back position they can live with, if the negotiating process falters, or fails. This fall-back position will:

- Save them from being pressurised
- Strengthen their hand in negotiation
- Give them a basis for assessing agreements
- Give them a way out in case they need to get out

> - If you couldn't come to an agreement on the leadership style you would like for your group, what would you do?
> - Could you cope with the consequences of that choice?

- If so—okay! If not, then we need to think of another viable alternative.
- ✎ Record your reflections in your Working Notes.

Conclusion

10 minutes

The follow-up reading for this session is

> 'Organisation' Trevor Tyson, *Working With Groups,* Macmillan, Melbourne, 1989, pp 24-57 (Reading 21)

The set community tasks for this session are

- ☐ Meet with your learning partner and your community development support group.

Living Community: Session 21

☐ Share what you learnt in the session about negotiating. Talk about ways in which you may need to negotiate some agreements in the community.

- Are there any issues you need to negotiate or re-negotiate?
- Are there any issues that may need to be negotiated in the near future?
- How would you negotiate agreements round these issues in your community?

☐ Look for opportunities to negotiate informally, if not formally, around small but significant issues that will come up in your community this week.

✎ Record your actions, reflections and conclusions in your Working Notes.

Note: You will need to organise two learning partners to be with you to do the next session.

Session 22

Community Work Skill 3: Facilitating

Preparation

- You will need to organise two learning partners to be with you to do this session.
- You will also need to get three hundred drinking straws and one hundred pins.

Objectives

- To review your negotiating skills
- To consider the next in a series of basic community work skills: facilitating.

Review

15 minutes

- ☐ Review your work from Session 21.
- ☐ Review the issues raised in the last session, particularly your negotiating skills.
- ☐ Review the reading:

    'Organisation' Trevor Tyson, *Working With Groups*, Macmillan, Melbourne, 1989, p 24-57 (Reading 21)
- ☐ Review the tasks:
    - ❖ How was your meeting with your learning partner and your community development support group?
    - ❖ What was the most important thing you learned while doing your community tasks for the last session?

✐ Record your reflections in your Working Notes.

Facilitating growth and change

The importance of meetings [1]

10 minutes

Meetings are an important part of any enterprise labouring for personal growth, social change and community development. They are times when we can share information, give each other some support and accomplish joint tasks together. They are times when we can laugh and cry, think up ideas and get down to work.

However, as we all know, there can be good meetings and bad meetings.

- ❒ Brainstorm a list of the characteristics of the kind of meeting we all feel is worthwhile—the kind of meeting we feel is worth going to ourselves! Write down this list of suggestions on the left-hand side of a piece of paper, and save it for later in the session.

Note that a good meeting includes

- Most of the participants turning up
- The feeling it is a meeting of real people
- A high level of energy and enthusiasm
- A sense of involvement in the decisions
- Some commonly agreed group goals
- Clear processes for reaching those goals
- Clear roles for facilitating those processes
- A good facilitator
- Other similar things

- ❒ Keep this list, as we will come back to it later.

The importance of facilitating

5 minutes

A facilitator plays a role in the group that's similar to a chairperson. They help the members make decisions and carry out tasks. They take responsibility to remind the group of its purpose and monitor group maintenance and group function. They suggest processes and encourage

---

[1] V. Coover et al., *Resource Manual For A Living Revolution*, New Society Publishers, Philadelphia, 1978, p 61

participation. While the word 'chairperson' is used in corporate groups, in community groups we use the word 'facilitator'.

As we all know, there can be good and bad facilitators.

- ☐ Complete the statement 'a good facilitator always …' three times, indicating three qualities of a good facilitator.
- ☐ Then read out your statements one by one, to the two others in your group.
- ✍ Record your reflections in your Working Notes.

Different views on facilitating

50 minutes

The statements on good facilitators may be indicative of different styles of leadership. Some may reflect a 'full-on' or directive style; some may reflect a 'laissez-faire' or non-directive style; while some of the statements may reflect a 'fair-go' or democratic style of leadership.

Note these different styles of leading/facilitating -

- A 'full-on' directive style
- A 'laissez-faire' non-directive style
- And a 'fair-go' democratic style

Rather than debate the merits and demerits of these styles of facilitating, explain to the group that you are going to put them to the test in an exercise. The group goes through this exercise three times, each time with a different facilitator and a different set of instructions.

- ☐ Give each person in your group a letter: A,B, or C. Each of the people is to lead the group in carrying out a task.

A. 'Full-on' directive leader

- ☐ Person A should take Handout 1 (on page 247) and read the instructions silently. No one else should see them.
- ☐ Person A follows the instructions in Handout 1.
- ☐ After ten minutes A should call a halt to the construction. Leave the structure and move to another part of the table for the next part of the exercise.

B. 'Laissez-faire' non-directive leader

- ☐ Person B takes Handout 2 (on page 248) and read the instructions silently.

Living Community: Session 22

☐ Proceed as for A.

C. 'Fair-go' democratic leader
☐ Person C should take Handout 3 (on page 249) and read the instructions silently.
☐ Proceed as for A and B.

When time is up, assess all the structures in terms of height, strength and beauty. Then answer the following questions, bearing in mind that they concern the roles people played, not the people themselves.

1. How did A facilitate the group? How did B facilitate, and C?
2. What was the group like when A facilitated the group? when B, and C facilitated?
3. How did people participate when A facilitated the group? when B, and C facilitated?
4. How well did the group perform when A facilitated the group? when B, and C facilitated?
5. Was any behaviour of the group related to the way the facilitator was behaving?

✍ Record your reflections in your Working Notes.

Then each facilitator in turn should discuss how they felt playing their role in the group:

1. What was the role that you were asked to play?
2. What did you like about the role?
3. What didn't you like about the role?
4. How do you think it affected the group?
5. How do you feel it affected you?

✍ Record your reflections in your Working Notes.

Then each of the group members should discuss how they felt about the process.

1. How did you feel about the facilitator of the group?
2. How did you feel about other people in the group?
3. How did you feel about your own particular work?
4. How did you feel about the structure the group made?

- ✎ Record your reflections in your Working Notes.
- ❏ Finish the exercise with a discussion on the merits and weaknesses of the three styles of facilitating.
- ❏ Compare and contrast the 'full-on' directive leader with the 'laissez-faire' non-directive leader and the 'fair-go' democratic leader.
- Note that a good 'fair-go' democratic leader is usually the best facilitator, because
   1. They help the members make decisions and carry out tasks.
   2. They take responsibility to remind the group of its purpose.
   3. They monitor both group maintenance and group function.
   4. They suggest options but let the group make their own decisions.
   5. They encourage the participation of all the members in the group.
   6. They help the group to realise it is their group and they are in charge.
   7. They encourage the group as a whole to do the best that it can.

The selection of a facilitator

10 minutes

In regular meetings, it is helpful to encourage people to either share the role or rotate the role of facilitator. In this way, as many people as possible can learn how to facilitate meetings in the community.

However, on occasion there are meetings that we expect to be very difficult to deal with. It may be a large meeting, an emergency meeting or a meeting where some kind of trouble is anticipated. In these circumstances, it is crucial to choose an experienced facilitator.

- What would you look for in an experienced facilitator?

✍ Record your reflections in your Working Notes.

An experienced facilitator:
- Has the time and interest to prepare well for the meeting
- Has the energy and courage to deal with the meeting
- Has more concern for the process than for the outcome
- Can facilitate the process in spite of pressure not to
- Can encourage participation from all the participants

Facilitating function and maintenance

Facilitating the group function of the meeting

20 minutes

There are two parts to facilitating the group function of the meeting: preparing for a meeting, and running the meeting.

a) Preparing for a meeting[1]

- What do we need to do to prepare for a meeting?

✍ Record your reflections in your Working Notes.

In preparing for a meeting, the facilitator needs to:
1. Make sure people are informed about the meeting
2. Ask for suggestions of items to put on the agenda
3. Make sure the setting for the meeting is appropriate
4. Put a proposed agenda on the table for discussion
5. Gather the necessary writing and recording materials
6. Have an alternate facilitator in case of an emergency

---

1 V. Coover et al, p 63

b) Running the meeting[1]

- **What do we need to do to run the meeting?**

✍ Record your reflections in your Working Notes.

In running the meeting the facilitator needs to
1. Make sure that an agenda is agreed upon
2. Have priorities and times allocated for items
3. Take care that a recorder is also nominated
4. Start on time—with energy and enthusiasm
5. Keep the group focused on one task at a time
6. Regulate the discussion so that it is inclusive
7. Encourage the louder people to hold back a bit
8. Encourage the quieter people not to hold back
9. Make sure the discussion is getting the job done
10. Slow down the conversation if it is moving too fast
11. Speed up the conversation if it is moving too slowly
12. Sum up the meeting and provide satisfying closure

Facilitating the group maintenance of the meeting

40 minutes

- ☐ Review the characteristics of a good meeting you listed above, at the beginning of the session.
- ☐ Divide the right-hand side of the paper into two columns, and put 'task' on the top of the first and 'relationship' on the top of the second.
- ☐ Place a tick in the appropriate column next to each characteristic, according to whether it is a 'task' or a 'relationship'.
- ☐ Then answer the following question:

- **Which is more important – task or relationship?**

✍ Record your reflections in your Working Notes.

---
1 Shields, p 96

There are usually there are a lot more characteristics listed under 'relationships' than 'tasks'. Thus while both tasks and relationships are very important, people feel relationships are more important than tasks. Facilitating maintenance in a group is essentially about facilitating group relationships.

Maintaining the meeting[1]

- What do we need to do to maintain the meeting?

✍ Record your reflections in your Working Notes.

In maintaining the meeting, the facilitator needs to

1. Host – welcoming participants – greeting them by name.
2. Initiate – opening up discussion – by making suggestions.
3. Diffuse – reducing any tension – by laughing or crying.
4. Affirm – increasing sense of respect – by being friendly.
5. Encourage – inviting other's ideas – by being receptive.
6. Listen – attending to their opinions – by being accepting.
7. Clarify – eliminating any confusion – by giving examples.
8. Mediate – reconciling differences and finding similarities.

❑ Reflect on a meeting you attended recently (that you did not facilitate yourself)

- What were some of the roles the facilitator played in order to maintain the group?
- What effect did playing these roles have on the group?
- Were there any roles he or she may have played – but didn't?
- What effect did not playing these roles have on the group?

✍ Record your reflections in your Working Notes.

Affirming people is essential to maintaining relationships. In the process of doing some of the exercises in this session, you have criticised one another about the roles that you have played. So it might be helpful to finish this session by affirming one another.

---

1 Coover et al, pp 46-47

- ☐ At this point each person should take a moment to share what they liked about this session and the part they were able to play in the group.
- ☐ After each person has spoken, someone else should reflect on what they said, noting something they like - and would like to affirm - about them.

Conclusion

10 minutes

The follow-up reading for this session is

'Leadership', Trevor Tyson, *Working With Groups* Macmillan, Melbourne, 1989, pp 85-96 (Reading 22)

The set community tasks for this session are

- ☐ Meet with your learning partner and your community development support group.
- ☐ Share what you learnt in this session about facilitating. Talk about ways in which you could facilitate some of the meetings in the community.

- How could you prepare better for meetings?
- How could you run community meetings better?
- How could you maintain community meetings better?

- ☐ Look for opportunities to facilitate meetings better in your community this week.
- ☐ Also look for opportunities to affirm people every time that you meet with them.
- ✎ Record your actions, reflections and conclusions in your Working Notes.

Living Community: Session 22

Handout 1

Briefing for A: 'Full-on' directive facilitator

Your job is to be a dictator. Display this style of leadership without informing your group of what you are doing. Just do it.

The task of the group is to build a structure out of the straws and pins. The structure will be judged for its height, strength and beauty. The structure is to be constructed entirely according to your ideas.

Do not tell the group your ideas about what the finished structure will look like, just give them the work to do.

Don't let them decide what to do.

Don't take any suggestions from anyone. You give the orders.

Don't allow the members to talk with each other. If they have something to say, have them say it to you.

Feel free to criticise or praise their work as you like.

Handout 2

Briefing for B. 'Laissez-faire' non-directive leader

Your job is to be laid back and let it happen. Display this style of leadership without informing your group of what you are doing. Just do it.

The task of the group is to build a structure out of the straws and pins. The structure will be judged for its height, strength and beauty. The structure is to be constructed from the member's own ideas.

You should be friendly but not take any initiative at all. Only say something if the members ask you something. Even then you should not direct the group in any way.

You can tell the group what the task is but don't make any suggestions about what is to be done or how it is to be done. Let the members decide for themselves what to do.

Don't criticise or praise anyone's work.

Handout 3

Briefing for C. 'Fair-go' democratic leader

Your job is to be a democratic facilitator. Display this style of leadership without informing your group of what you are doing. Just do it.

The task of the group is to build a structure out of the straws and pins. The structure will be judged for its height, strength and beauty. The structure is to be the product of the thinking of the whole group.

You should encourage a thorough discussion of what the task is and how to do it by the whole group. As much as possible allow the people to decide how to divide up the work among themselves.

During the discussion, you should act as a moderator. When a suggestion is made, ask whether the others in the group support it or not. You should encourage the group to come to consensus before decisions are made.

You should encourage members to talk with each other as they go, consulting, clarifying and checking with each other as they need to.

You can criticise or praise people's work if you give a reason for it.

Session 23

Community Work Skill 4: Supporting

Objectives

- To review your facilitating skills
- To consider the next in a series of basic community work skills: supporting

Review

15 minutes

> ☐ Review your work from Session 22.
> ☐ Review the issues raised in the last session, particularly your facilitating skills.
> ☐ Review the reading:
>
> > 'Leadership', Trevor Tyson, *Working With Groups*, Macmillan, Melbourne, 1989, pp 85- 96 (Reading 22)
>
> ☐ Review the tasks:
> > ❖ How was your meeting with your learning partner and your community development support group?
> > ❖ What was the most important thing you learned while doing your community tasks for the last session?

✍ Record your reflections in your Working Notes.

Supporting people in development

The importance of support

5 minutes

It is not easy working for community development. Even when we are working *with* people, we may not feel supported *by* people. At one stage, we may find ourselves being able to support others more than they can support us. At another stage, we may find ourselves in unresolved conflicts with the very people that we work with.

Jan McNicol, a community worker from Brisbane, says: "Without a support network for the things I am on about", it is "harder for me to maintain my truth" and keep going. [1] We all need to make sure that we get the support we need.

☐ Answer the following questions:

- How can you make sure people get the support they need?
- How can you make sure you get the support you need?

✍ Record your reflections in your Working Notes.

There are many ways of getting and giving support in community development: [2]

- Phone check-ins
- Net connections
- Networking parties
- Clearness meetings
- Senior mentors
- Peer monitors
- Personal coaches

Support options for people

Phone check-ins

10 minutes

Many community workers are working in communities whose people do not have a deep understanding of what they are doing. So these workers look for support from people outside their community, who are doing the same kind of work.

Support from other community workers can be as near as the phone. It's just a matter of ringing up an appropriate person, and asking for a few minutes of time to chat on the phone. It is important when calling, to give assurance to the person on the other end of the phone that this matter will only take a few minutes of their time. If it is an unscheduled call,

---

1 Shields, p 104
2 Shields, p 115

it is important to say that you would be happy to phone back at a more convenient time if it's not convenient for them now.

A phone check-in involves a person just talking about the last day/week/fortnight/month, how it has gone, and how they feel about it. Generally a phone check-in will last for only two or three minutes. It shouldn't go any longer than five minutes. The purpose of the check-in is for a hearing, not counselling.

> 1. Do you have someone you call for a phone check-in?
> 2. If you do have one, how is it going with them?
> 3. If you don't have one, how could you get one?
> 4. Who could you support with a simple phone check-in?

✍ Record your reflections in your Working Notes.

Internet connections

10 minutes

In their search for support, community workers sometimes cannot find it on the end of a phone. The internet, through email and the World Wide Web, helps them to access wider networks. Many workers now use the internet for vital professional support.

Internet connections have some disadvantages. They may widen the 'digital divide' between those with good Internet access (the cyber-rich) and those without (the cyber-poor). They create virtual connections rather than real connections; and at worst they can reduce personal communication to impersonal information exchange.

But internet connections have the great advantage is that they can be accessed anytime of the day, anywhere in the world. This gives people access to wider connections, more conversations, more information and the potential for mobilisation of people round a particular cause of concern.

> - Do you have community work internet connections?
> - If you do, what are they and how well do they work?
> - If you don't, where would go to find some?
> - What Net connections could you share with others?

✍ Record your reflections in your Working Notes.

Some helpful Internet connections are
- The Community Tool Box, http://www.ctb.lsi.ukans.edu
- Community Work Consultants & Trainers, http://www.communitypraxis.org
- Community work resources, books and articles, http://www.lastfirst.net
- Local Government Community Services Association, http://www.lgcsaa.org.au
- Global Development Research Centre on Community, http://www.gdrc.org

Networking parties

10 minutes

A networking party is an opportunity for us to get together with the people we know who have a common interest in community work. All you need to do is invite a group of people to your place, who share your interest in community work.

Provide drinks and munchies and a comfortable, welcoming atmosphere. Then settle in for a night of sharing what you do, what you need, and what you can do to help meet one another's needs. This may lead to developing an informal or a formal support network of some kind or other.

- Have you ever had a networking party?
- If you have, how did you organise it and how did it go?
- If not, how would you go about organising one?

✎ Record your reflections in your Working Notes.

Clearness meetings

10 Minutes

A clearness meeting is a process through which a community worker asks for feedback from people they trust and respect. It is a process in which clarity is sought, not permission or approval. It is meant to enable the worker to make a good decision.

A clearness meeting can be called any time by people who feel the need for help in considering a decision that they are asked to make.[1]

The worker seeking clearness needs to prepare for the meeting by considering by themselves the decision they want to make. They need to take time out, meditate, and write down their thoughts and feelings about the decision they are considering. Then they should invite a few friends who know them well, to come to a meeting to reflect on the decision together. The best way is to meet with three to five friends for two to three hours in a relaxed atmosphere after a meal together.

A facilitator (not the worker) needs to be selected to guide the process. They should outline the purpose of the meeting—to help the worker seek clarity, not permission or approval. Invite the worker to share their thoughts and feelings about the decision they are considering. Invite the other people present to reflect on what they have seen and heard asking probing questions and making helpful comments. Invite the worker to respond to these reflections. Finally give people the opportunity to affirm the worker and call for clarity. If the worker feels the need for any further help, they should say so.

- Have you ever had a clearness meeting?
- If you have, how did you organise it and how did it go?
- If not, how would you go about organising one for yourself or for someone else?

✎ Record your reflections in your Working Notes.

Senior Mentors

10 minutes

Senior mentors are people who are older than us, the kind of people that we would like to be like when we get to their age. We need to encourage people in community work to find older people who are role models, and arrange to meet with them regularly to discuss their work.

Senior mentors may not be called 'community workers' or have any formal qualifications, but they need to be good models of just, compassionate community work.

Once people have found a person who could be a senior mentor, they need to talk with them about the possibility of meeting regularly to discuss their community work. Regular but not too frequent meetings

---

1 Coover et al., pp 123-124

seem to work best. Meeting once every month or so is usually helpful for a worker, but not too much pressure for the mentor.

The meetings need to be relaxed affairs, flexible enough to talk about anything and everything to do with people's community work. The worker may or may not get some advice from their mentor. The most important thing is that they can discuss issues in the context of support from an experienced person.

- Do you have a senior mentor in your community work?
- If you do have one, how are you getting on with them?
- If you don't have one, who could be one for you?
- Could you be a senior mentor for someone you know?

✍ Record your reflections in your Working Notes.

Peer monitors

10 minutes

Peer monitors are people about the same age as us, in more or less the same stage of life, in the same community, who are interested in the community work we are doing. We need to encourage people in community work to find peer monitors, to whom they can be accountable in regard to specific issues.

Everyone has personal issues that may affect their work. If you always turn up late, people will get angry with you. If you get angry in return, people will turn away from you. You need to deal with these personal issues, and you need to be accountable to ensure you deal with them well. When it comes to dealing with personal issues, accountability should be mutual, rather than hierarchical, so as not to be depersonalising. Hence to provide support with these issues, we need to encourage people to have peer monitors rather than senior mentors.

Accountability is simply answer-ability. It means answering the question about 'how we are going' fully, freely, and truly. People need to find peer monitors who will not be scared to ask them the hard questions, and wise enough not to accept dishonest answers.

Once people have found a potential peer monitor, they need to ask them about meeting regularly to discuss their personal issues. If they are in the same community, it will be easy for them to meet regularly. They should meet as often as they need. Usually people need to meet more frequently earlier and less frequently later on.

The meetings can be very informal, on the run, at the corner, before or after church. The only thing that matters is that the question about 'how we are going' is asked and answered—fully, freely, and truly.

The worker may or may not get some advice from their monitor. The most important thing is that they are held accountable for dealing with their issues in the context of support from a counterpart.

- Do you have a peer monitor in your community work?
- If you do have one, how are you getting on with them?
- If you don't have one, who could be a monitor for you whom you could monitor?

✍ Record your reflections in your Working Notes.

Personal coaches

25 minutes

A personal coach is not so much an expert as a trainer who helps a person realise their potential and maximise their work performance. They are more concerned with helping the person to learn, than with teaching them. Rather than teaching, they seek to help the worker learn, leaving the responsibility for learning with the learner. The personal coach aims at developing internal motivation rather than the external motivations of advising or directing or instructing.

The sequence suggested for a session with a Personal Coach has four different headings and spells out the word GROW.[1]

> G = Goals: setting goals for the session
> R = Reality: checking to explore the current situation
> O = Options: what options or alternatives for action exist
> W = What is to be done, When, by Whom, and the Will to do it.

Goals

Goals relate to achievement, so here we are looking at what we want to achieve or get out of a particular coaching session. We could ask questions like:

- What would you like to get out of this session?
- What would you like to achieve in the half hour we have?

---

1 Whitmore, J., *Coaching For Performance*, Nicholas Brealey Publishing, London.

- What would be the most useful thing for you to take away from this session?

It is the learner who sets the goals. It is crucial for him to have 'ownership' of the goals he sets for himself.

Reality

Having defined the goals, we now need to clarify the situation, i.e. What is the actual situation now? We could use questions like:

- What is happening now?
- Who is involved?
- What have you done about this so far?
- What results did that produce?
- What are the major difficulties in finding a way forward?

Options

The aim of this stage is to create as many options or alternatives as possible. It is important to accept all ideas and to build an environment where people will feel safe to make suggestions.

Once a full list has been produced, it will be necessary to analyse all options to select the best solution, i.e. analyse the benefits and costs of each option. Possible questions to use are:

- What options do you have?
- What else could you do?
- What if … ?
- Would you like another suggestion?
- What are the benefits and costs of each?

What will you do?

The aim of the final phase of the training sequence is to convert a discussion into a decision. It should produce an action plan. The questions to use at this point are:

- What are you going to do?
- When are you going to do it?
- Will this action meet your goal?
- What obstacles might you meet along the way?
- Who needs to know?
- What support do you need?

- How and when are you going to get that support?
- What other considerations do you have?

All of the above questions are designed to encourage the person to set their *will* to do it, to actually take action. The *'w'* is for *'will'!*

☐ Rate on a 1-10 scale the degree of certainty you have that you will carry out this action. If the person rates the chances as less than 7 out of 10, you may have to start again.

> - Do you have a personal coach in your community work?
> - If you do have one, how are you getting on with them?
> - If you don't have one, is there a thoughtful person who could one for you?
> - How could you take more of a coaching approach in your work with others?

✎ Record your reflections in your Working Notes.

Supportive colleagues you can refer people to

5 minutes

Earlier, we encouraged you to make a map of some of the local people, groups, and organisations that you believed that you would be able to cooperate with.

☐ Take a few minutes to look at that map again, to remind yourself of the support that is local, available, and accessible—for you, and for the people you are working with.

☐ Write a list of the key people that you may want to refer to, and/or refer others to.

☐ Keep one copy of this list handy in case of emergency. Keep another copy of the list in your Working Notes.

Conclusion

10 minutes

The follow-up reading for this session is:

> 'Groupwork', Trevor Tyson, *Working With Groups,*
> Macmillan, Melbourne, 1989, pp 106-132 (Reading 23)

The set community tasks for this session are:
- ☐ Meet with your learning partner and your community development support group.
- ☐ Share what you learnt in the session about the importance of supporting people in community work. Talk about ways in which you can support one another by phone check-ins, internet connections, networking parties, clearness meetings, senior mentors, peer monitors and personal trainers.
- ☐ Look for a way to get some support, and to give some support to somebody else.
- ✎ Record your actions, reflections and your conclusions in your Working Notes.

Session 24

Community Work Skill 5: Researching

Objectives

- To review your supporting skills
- To consider the next in a series of basic community work skills: researching.

Review

15 minutes

> ❑ Review your work from Session 23.
> ❑ Review the issues raised in the last session, particularly your supporting skills.
> ❑ Review the reading:
>
>   'Groupwork', Trevor Tyson, *Working With Groups*, Macmillan, Melbourne, 1989, pp 106-132 (Reading 23)
> ❑ Review the tasks:
>   ❖ How was your meeting with your learning partner and your community development support group go?
>   ❖ What was the most important thing you learned while doing your community tasks for the last session?

✐ Record your reflections in your Working Notes.

Reflecting on your community

What kind of community are you in?

15 minutes

☐ Circle the kind of community you feel most at at home in: –

- Family
- Friends
- Factory
- Office
- College
- School
- Church
- Club
- Other ...

☐ Circle the following statements that are true of the kind of community you feel most at home in: –

- Small
- Youthful
- Ageing
- Inward-orientated
- Outward-orientated

- Are there any other distinctive characteristics of your close community?

☐ Fill in the specific stories behind these general descriptors:

1. What is the history of your close community?
2. What are the events that have changed it?
3. What are the various groups in your close community?
4. What are the major issues your close community is dealing with?
5. How is your close community likely to change in the future?

✎ Record your reflections in your Working Notes.

What kind of locality you are in?

15 minutes

☐ Circle the following statements that are true of your locality: –

- Rural area
- Urban area
- Inner suburb
- Outer suburb
- Old suburb
- New suburb

- Stable
- Growing
- Declining
- Homogeneous
- Heterogeneous

- Are there any other distinctive characteristics of your locality?

☐ Fill in the specific stories behind these general descriptors:

1. What is the history of your local community?
2. What are the significant events that have changed it?
3. What are the various groups in your local community?
4. What are the major issues your locality is dealing with?
5. How is your locality likely to change in the future?

✎ Record your reflections in your Working Notes.

What are the similarities and differences?

10 minutes

☐ Consider the similarities and differences between your close community and your local community.

1. Does your close community reflect the range of people in your local community?
2. How similar or different are the age profiles of your close and local communities?
3. How similar or different are the class profiles of your close and local communities?

4. How similar or different are the ethnic profiles of your close and local communities?
5. Are there any other similarities or differences between your communities?
6. What do these similarities or differences between your communities signify?

Researching your community

What things do you need to know?

10 minutes

The kinds of things people generally need to know include:
- The people in your communities
- The characteristics of the people
- Their faith, values, and lifestyles
- Their style of life and quality of life
- The boundaries of the communities
- The organisation of the communities
- The various groups in the communities
- The various facilities in the communities
- The various resources in the communities
- The relationships between the communities

- What things do you need to know about your communities?

✍ Record your reflections in your Working Notes.

How would you get to know these things?

15 minutes

The ways people usually get to know these kinds of things include:

Observing their communities
- Walking around them
- Stopping, looking and listening to them

- Considering the significance of what they see and hear in them

Interviewing key people in their communities
- Talking with leaders
- Talking with workers
- Talking with neighbours, colleagues, family and friends
- Talking with people whom no one else would usually talk to

Surveying the people in their communities
- Asking general questions about the community
- Asking specific questions about themselves
- Testing opinions by polling people in them

Accessing the data on their communities
- Local street directories
- Regional telephone directories
- Local agency reports
- State Government reports
- Commonwealth Government reports
- Census reports
- Other reports from the Australian Bureau of Statistics

> - How can you get to know the kinds of things you need to know about your communities?

✎ Record your reflections in your Working Notes.

What do you want to do with the things you learn?
15 minutes

Some of the things people want to do with the things they learn include:
- Developing a profile of their close community
- Developing a profile of their local community
- Comparing their close and local community profiles

- Talking to their close community about their relationship to the local community
- Developing a proposal for further involvement with the locality

- **What do you want to do with the things you have learnt about your communities?**

✍ Record your reflections in your Working Notes.

Conclusion

10 minutes

The follow-up reading for this session is

'Suggestions for a Study of Your Hometown' Robert Lamb, in *Tactics and Techniques of Community Practice*, Fred Cox, John Erlich, Jack Rothman, John Tropman; Peacock, Itasca, 1977, p 17-23 (Reading 24).

The set community tasks for this session are

☐ Meet with your learning partner and your community development support.

☐ Share what you learnt in this session about researching. Talk about where you want to go from here with your research; what things you want to know about your communities; how you can get to know these things; what you want to do with the information; and what you will do about it this week.

✍ Record your actions, reflections, and conclusions in your Working Notes.

NOTE: You will need to organise at least two learning partners to be with you to do the next session.

Session 25

Community work skill 6: Planning (A)

Preparation

You need at least two learning partners to be with you to do this session. You will also need a stack of 100 filing cards, or equivalent size pieces of paper (12.5 x 7.5 cm or 15 x 10 cm).

Objectives

- To review your researching skills
- To consider the next in a series of basic community work skills: planning.

Review

15 minutes

> ❐ Review your work from Session 24.
> ❐ Review the issues raised in the last session, particularly your researching skills.
> ❐ Review the reading:
>> 'Suggestions for a Study of Your Hometown' Robert Lamb, *Tactics and Techniques of Community Practice*, Fred Cox, John Erlich, Jack Rothman, John Tropman; Peacock, Itasca, 1977, p 17-23 (Reading 24)
> ❐ Review the tasks:
>> ❖ How was your meeting with your learning partner and your community development support group?
>> ❖ What was the most important thing you learned while doing your community tasks for the last session?

✎ Record your reflections in your Working Notes.

Analysis

The first phase of planning is analysis.[1] There are four steps to this phase: –

- Participants analysis
- Problems analysis
- Objectives analysis
- Alternatives analysis

☐ Pick a community or part of a community, with problems you would like to address.

Participants analysis

10 minutes

The first step is to identify all the people who have an interest in the plan.

☐ List all the possible participants—anyone who might be impacted positively or negatively by the plan.

☐ Prioritise the most important participants—those who would be impacted most by the plan, for better or worse.

☐ Consider what these people might bring to the planning table: not only their problems, but also their capacity to solve their problems—their interests, connections and resources.

✐ Record your reflections in your Working Notes.

Problems analysis

35 minutes

The second step is to understand the range of problems that people face in the community.

☐ Write down approximately 10 problem statements on 10 separate cards, one on each card.

A problem statement should be framed *negatively* - but as accurately and as specifically as possible. Don't exaggerate or generalise.

As a starting point, select one focal problem for the analysis. This is not necessarily the core problem but a convenient place to start. Circle the problem statement on this card in red and place it in the centre of a table.

---

1 Adapted from *Project Planning For Development,* Olive, Durban, South Africa

Now think about the relationship of the other problems to this focal analysis. Are they inter-connected? Are they causes, or effects, of the focal problem? Organise the other cards around it in terms of cause and effect, the causes below it and the effects above it, so the pattern of the cards begin to take the shape of a 'problems tree' *(Figure 20)*.

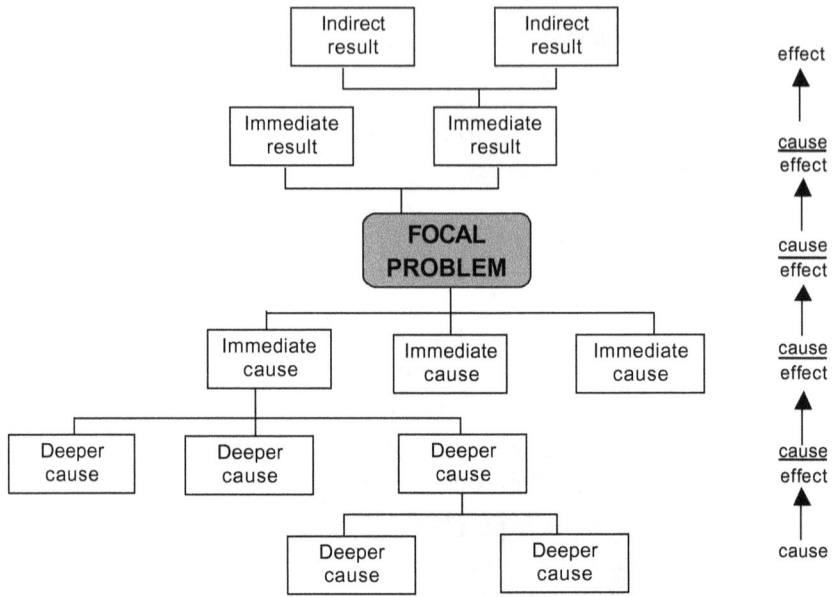

Figure 20: Problems Tree

Developing a problems tree allows you to visualise both the range of problems you face and the interrelationship between them.

Add more cards if needed to complete the cause and effect logic. If you have an effect, you need to look for its cause. If you have a cause, you need to look for its effect. Some cards will represent both a cause and effect. For example, a card stating 25% of the women in this community report being beaten by their partners, is the effect of multiple causes—inequality of power, misuse of power, lack of respect, poor communication skills, insufficient training in non-violent dispute resolution, and so on. But it is also a cause with multiple effects—physical harm, domestic terror, personal injury, social alienation, family fragmentation, and so on.

- ☐ Take away cards that are repetitive.
- ☐ Rewrite cards that are vague.
- ☐ Review the problem tree to make sure everyone present agrees with the problem analysis.
- ✎ Record your reflections in your Working Notes.

Solutions Analysis

30 minutes

The third step is to identify objectives or desired improvements, and the relationships between these desired improvements, indicating means and ends.

- ☐ Restate all the problem statements in the problem tree *as positive, desirable* and *realistic* conditions. They should be stated as outcomes described as if they have already happened. (eg. 100% of women in this community report they are not being abused by their partners)
- ☐ Reword the focal problem as an outcome and circle it with red just as you did for the problem. Build your solutions tree, in the same way, putting your focal solution in the same place as the problem. As you add solution cards to the tree, check the causality. Does this solution need to be in place in order to make your focal solution possible? Or is your focal solution going to lead to these other solutions?

Developing a 'solutions tree' allows you to visualise the range of potential improvements and the relationship between them.

- ☐ Review the cards to make sure they are realistic. Reword them if necessary.
- ☐ Add or delete cards to ensure the means-to-end logic is valid.
- ☐ Place the cards on a paper, and draw connecting lines to show the means-ends relationships between the outcomes.

The 'solutions tree' should look very much like the 'problems tree' but framed in positive rather than negative terms. See Figure 21.

For example: the card stating that 100% of women in this community report they are not being abused by their husbands is the effect of multiple causes - equality of power, use of power, use of the power of assertion rather than aggression, mutual respect, rich communication skills, sufficient training in non-violent dispute resolution, and so on.

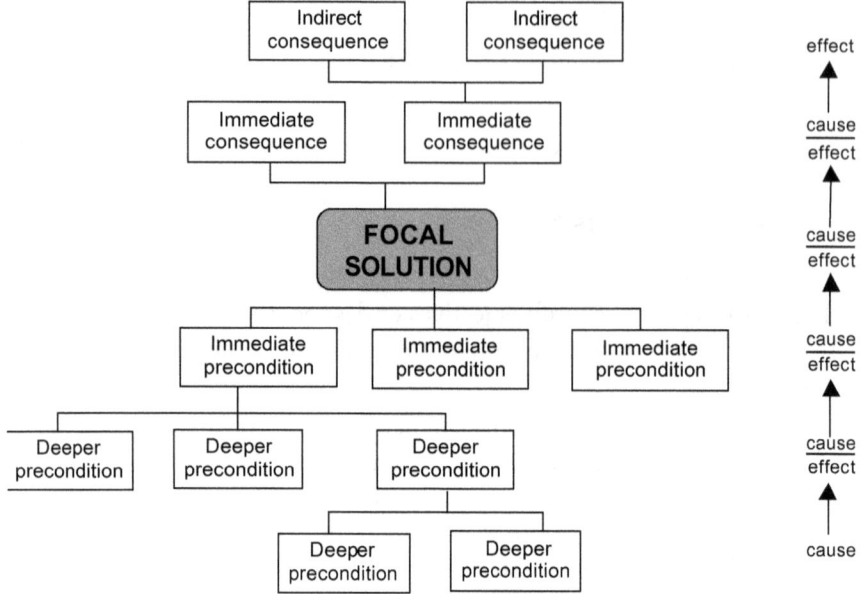

Figure 21: Solutions Tree

But it is also a cause with multiple effects—physical health, domestic peace, personal safety, social integration, family intimacy, and so on.

✎ Record your reflections in your Working Notes.

Alternatives Analysis

20 minutes

The fourth step is to identify alternative ways of impacting on the problems identified, assessing the feasibility of the alternatives and selecting a strategy.

- ❑ Study the range of solutions on the 'solutions tree'. Each card should represent an solution objective that could be achieved.

- ❑ Identify the different 'means-ends ladders' that present themselves in the 'objectives tree' and outline these with a pen. These represent different options for different strategies; some may overlap. See Figure 22.

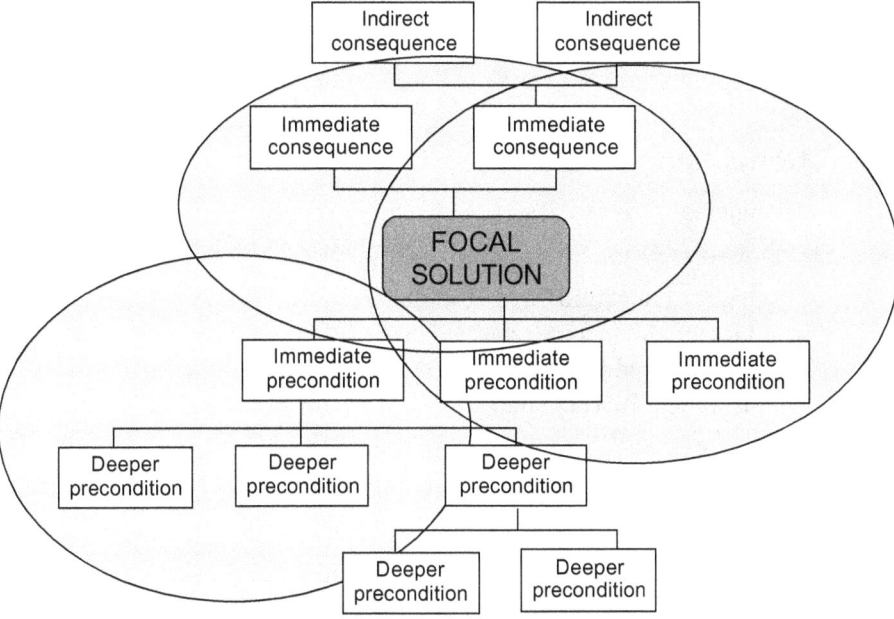

Figure 22: Alternatives Tree

☐ Eliminate the strategies that are
  - unethical
  - unrealistic
  - beyond your capacity at the moment
  - or being conducted by another group in your area.

☐ Select a strategy and discuss the implications for different participants. The matrix below is a simple tool that can help with the selection.

Options/ Alternatives	Positive implications	Negative implications
Advocating equality of power	Ethical, realistic, possible	A direct immediate threat to traditional culture
Training in non-violent dispute resolution	Ethical, realistic, possible	None

☐ Keep a copy of the trees and the matrix in your Working Notes.

Note: Keep the cards and a copy of your matrix for the next session.

Conclusion

10 minutes

The follow-up reading for this session is:

> 'Policy Issues and Organisational Relations' Yeheskel Hasenfield, in *Tactics And Techniques Of Community Practice*, Fred Cox, John Erlich, Jack Rothman, John Tropman, Peacock, Itasca, 1977, p 69-70 (Reading 25).

The set community tasks for this session are:

☐ Meet with your learning partner and your community development support group.

☐ Share what you learnt in this session about planning. In your group, work through the four steps in analysis for planning: participants analysis, problems analysis, solutions analysis and alternatives analysis.

☐ Consider whether there might be a wider group of participants with whom you can work through these steps. If appropriate, plan to do so this week.

✎ Record your actions, reflections and conclusions in your Working Notes.

NOTE: You will need to organise at least two learning partners to be with you to do the next session.

Session 26

Community Work Skill 6: Planning (B)

Preparation

You will need to have at least two learning partners to be with you to do this session.

Objectives

- To review your analytical skills
- To consider the next in a series of basic community work skills: designing.

Review

15 minutes

- ☐ Review your work from Session 25.
- ☐ Review the issues raised in the last session, particularly your analytical skills.
- ☐ Review the reading:
    'Policy Issues and Organisational Relations' Yeheskel Hasenfield, in *Tactics And Techniques Of Community Practice*, Fred Cox, John Erlich, Jack Rothman, John Tropman, Peacock, Itasca, 1977, p 69-70 (Reading 25).
- ☐ Review the tasks:
    ❖ How was your meeting with your learning partner and your community development support group?
    ❖ What was the most important thing you learned while doing your community tasks for the last session?

✐ Record your reflections in your Working Notes.

Design

5 minutes

The second phase of planning is 'design'.[1] There are four steps to this phase:

- Project Frame
- Project Elements
- Project Assumptions
- Project Indicators

We will consider using the project approach for this. The project then becomes the 'box' in which planned community development is packaged.[2]

The main advantages of the project approach

- It provides a new, neat and tidy organised program.
- It requires clear objectives, outputs, inputs and activities.
- It encourages a systematic approach to community development.
- It facilitates the control of funds invested in the project by donors.

The main disadvantages of the project approach

- It encourages the idea of adopting a new, neat, tidy, but maybe irrelevant program.
- It discourages the idea of continuing with and building on existing activities.
- If the design is flawed, then the program will be flawed. No matter how well organised the program may be, it will only be as good as the thinking that has gone into its design. Garbage in – garbage out.
- It focuses on investment concerns and facilitates investor control, which may undermine ownership of the program by local people.

---

1 *Project Planning For Development*
2 Adapted from *Project Planning, Monitoring & Evaluation Training Course* by Bernard Broughton ACFOA 1996

Project frame

30 minutes

The first step is to identify a framework for project planning. The Logical Framework or 'logframe' approach was developed during the late 1960's as a tool for development project planning.

	Project Elements	Indicators	External Factors or Assumptions
Objectives {	Development Objective/Goal		
	Immediate Objective/ Project Purpose		
Project Area {	Results/Outputs		
	Activities		
	Inputs		

Figure 23. The Logical Framework approach

The Logical Framework approach is rather jargon-bound, and it is important to understand what the commonly-used terms really mean. A brief explanation of the terms is given below.

- **Project elements:** the narrative description of the program at each of the five levels of the hierarchy used in the Log Frame.
- **Development goal:** the program objectives to which the project is designed to contribute (e.g. reduced violence).
- **Immediate objective:** what the project is expected to achieve in development terms within the community (e.g. reduced domestic violence in church families) Note that there may be more than one objective.
- **Outputs or results:** the specific results and tangible products produced by undertaking a series of tasks or activities (e.g. reduced incidents of domestic violence in church families). Note that each objective usually has a number of outputs.
- **Activities or procedures:** the specific tasks undertaken to achieve the required outputs (e.g. workshops on dealing with domestic violence)

- **Inputs or resources:** the resources required in order to do the work (such as personnel, equipment, and materials for workshops).
- **Risks:** conditions which could affect the success of the project, but over which the project manager has no direct control (e.g. price changes for the hire of personnel).
- **Pre-requisites:** conditions for successful program implementation and prior obligations that need to be fulfilled by agencies involved in the project before things can start (e.g. community group formation).
- **Means – ends relationships:** Constructing the Project Description of the matrix involves a detailed breakdown of the chain of causality implicit in project design. Each level of the hierarchy requires the completion of other elements if results are to be achieved. This can be expressed in terms of
    - *If* inputs are provided, *then* activities can be undertaken;
    - *If* activities are undertaken, *then* outputs will be produced;
    - *If* outputs are produced, *then* objectives will be achieved,
    - *If* objectives are met, *then* the project will have contributed towards achieving the overall development goal.

Figure 24. The elements of project planning [1]

---

[1] *Project Planning for Development*, p 76

It is important therefore that inputs are sufficient to allow activities to be undertaken, and so on up the hierarchy. It is usual, however, to start constructing the matrix from the goal down, before working back up the hierarchy to ensure that resources are sufficient to undertake the required activities.

It is useful to standardise the way in which the hierarchy of project objectives are described in the matrix. In particular, this helps the project planner to recognise more easily what is an objective, an output, or an activity/input.

Thus the following convention can be used: to describe goals and objectives in the infinitive ('to do something'), describe outputs in the future perfect ('something will have been done'), and describe activities/inputs in the present ('do something'). For example:

1. **Goal** - Reduce domestic violence

2. **Objective** - Reduce domestic violence by 50% over three years in the community

3. **Outputs**
    - 250 incidents of domestic violence in families will have been identified
    - 60 families with a history of domestic violence will have been trained in alternative dispute resolution
    - 60 families with a history of domestic violence will have begun to practice alternative dispute resolution

4. **Activities**
    - Identify families with a history of domestic violence
    - Counsel need for training in alternative dispute resolution
    - Recruit capable trainers in alternative dispute resolution
    - Organise workshops on alternative dispute resolution
    - Run workshops on alternative dispute resolution

5. **Inputs**
    - Two counsellors
    - Two trainers in alternative dispute resolution
    - Local facility for workshop venue
    - Training costs, etc.

- Before you move on, check that you understand the terms by asking one another to answer the following questions - and give examples.
  ❖ What is a goal?
  ❖ What is an objective?
  ❖ What is an output?
  ❖ What is an activity?
  ❖ What is an input?

Project elements

35 minutes

The second step is to connect the analysis with elements of the project.

Start with the development goal

☐ Look at the Alternatives Tree from the previous session, at the alternative you selected as your project strategy. Study those cards you outlined as being part of the means-ends strategy.

☐ Identify which card expresses the benefit the people will experience—the broader social or economic goal to which the project can contribute. This becomes the development goal.

- What is your development goal?

Immediate objective

☐ Identify a card at the next level down, which expresses how people in your community will act differently to bring about your goal. This becomes your immediate objective.

- What is your immediate objective?
- What is the relationship between your goal and your objective?

✍ Record your reflections in your Working Notes.

Results

☐ Look at your immediate objective and ask the question: 'What must the project deliver for it to achieve this objective?'

☐ Brainstorm and write up ideas on cards. Your agreed conclusions will form the outputs or results of the project.

- What results must the project deliver for it to achieve its objective?

Activities

☐ Take each result and generate a list of all the activities needed to achieve it. Set out these activities and number them in a logical order of sequence.

- What Activities are needed to deliver these Results?

Inputs

☐ Look at your activities and ask the question -'What does the project need in order for it to run these activities?'

☐ Brainstorm and write up ideas on cards. Then come to consensus on the inputs or resources for the project.

- What does the project need in order for it to run these activities?

☐ Check that
- these resources are relevant, necessary, and sufficient.
- the resources are quantified and costed correctly.

✎ Record your reflections in your Working Notes.

Project assumptions

10 minutes

The third step is to consider the assumptions made in planning the project.

Completion of each step in the framework is no guarantee of achieving the next step upwards. The levels of the framework are held together by assumptions – factors outside the project's control. The higher the level of the output or objective, the less control can be levered by the project itself.

- ☐ Identify assumptions which could influence the success or failure of the project.
- ☐ Write these assumptions on cards, wording them positively, not negatively.
- ☐ Then assess the importance and probability of these assumptions for achieving the immediate objective of the project's logical framework.

> - How important are your assumptions to the success of the plan?
> - How likely is it that the assumptions you are making are valid?
> - How can you design the project to minimise the dependence on these assumptions?

- ✍ Record your reflections in your Working Notes.
- ☐ Run all the assumptions you are making in your plan through the planning guide and questionnaire opposite. This is a procedure for assessing the importance and likelihood of your assumptions—and for identifying 'killer assumptions' that may be fatal planning flaws.

Community Work Skill 6: Planning (b)

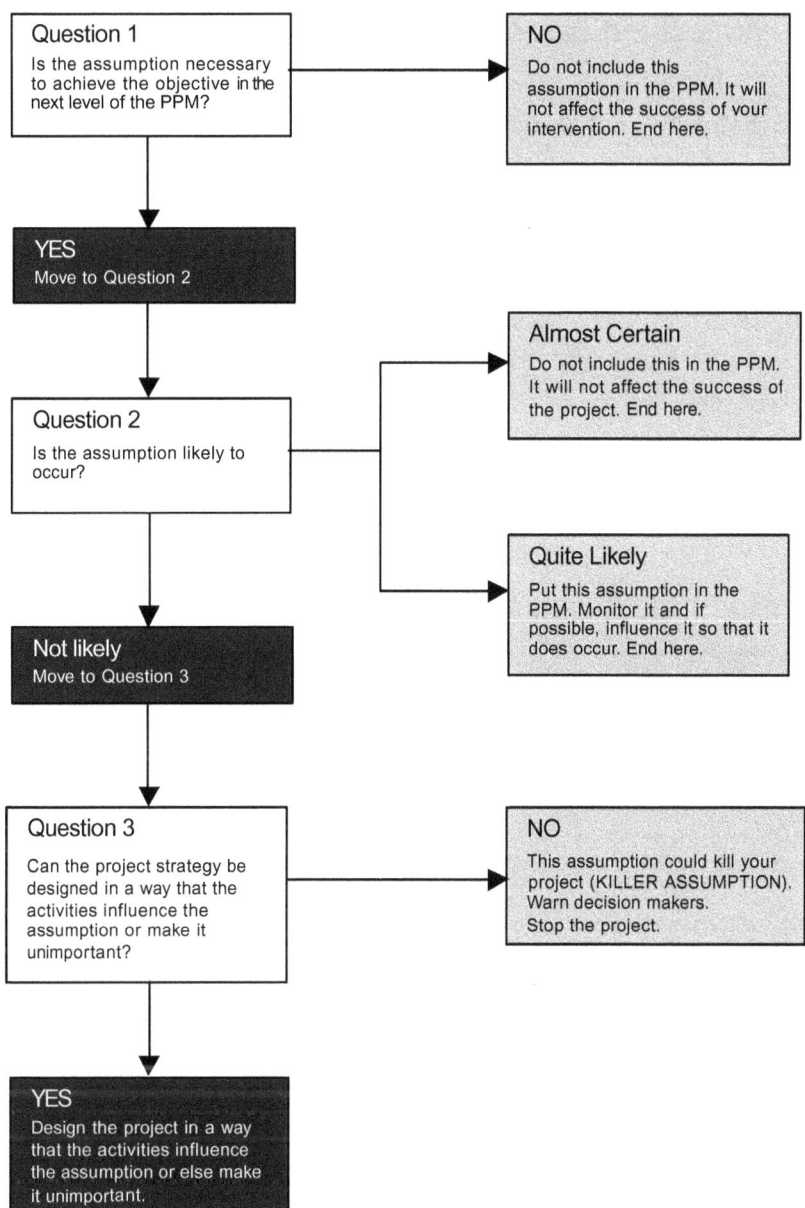

Figure 25. Project assumptions planning guide [1]

✎ Record your reflections in your Working Notes.

---

[1] *Project Planning*, p 66

Project indicators

15 minutes

The fourth step is to identify indicators for monitoring project planning. It is important to specify each of the objectives in detail.

A simple acronym used to set objectives is called **SMART**:

- Specific – Objectives should specify what they want to achieve.
- Measurable – You should be able to measure whether you are meeting the objectives or not.
- Achievable - Are the objectives you set, achievable and attainable?
- Realistic – Can you realistically achieve the objectives with the resources you have?
- Timely – Can you achieve the set objectives in the necessary time frame? [1]

- **What are the specific objectives of the project?**

For each specific objective, you need to identify appropriate indicators. These indicators should be

- Independent
- Attainable
- Factual
- Plausible
- Verifiable

- **What are the best indicators for each specific objective?**

✐ Record your reflections in your Working Notes.

---

1 http://www.learnmarketing.net/smart.htm

Last but not least, it is important to identify how evidence will be checked. The sources of information for verification need to be cited.

1. What information is needed?
2. By when is it needed?
3. In what form is it needed?
4. Who should provide it?
5. Is that possible or not? (If not, try again!)

- ✍ Record your reflections in your Working Notes.
- ☐ Keep the cards and the pieces of paper for the next session.

Conclusion

10 minutes

The follow-up reading for this session is

'How to Organise a Community Action Plan'
Jack Rothman, *Tactics And Techniques Of Community Practice*, Fred Cox, John Erlich, Jack Rothman, John Tropman, Peacock, Itasca, 1977, p 70-80 (Reading 26)

The set community tasks for this session are

- ☐ Meet with your learning partner and your community development support group.
- ☐ Share what you learnt in this session about planning. Work through the four steps in analysis for planning the Project Frame, Project Elements, Project Assumptions and Project Indicators in your group.
- ☐ Consider whether there might be a wider group of participants with whom you can work through these steps. If appropriate, plan to do so this week.
- ✍ Record your actions, reflections and conclusions in your Working Notes.

Session 27

Community Work Skill 7: Budgeting

Objectives

- To review your design skills
- To consider the next in a series of basic community work skills: budgeting.

Review

15 minutes

> ☐ Review your work from Session 26.
> ☐ Review the issues raised in the last session, particularly your project design skills.
> ☐ Review the reading:
> > 'How to Organise a Community Action Plan'
> > Jack Rothman, *Tactics And Techniques Of Community Practice*, Fred Cox, John Erlich, Jack Rothman, John Tropman, Peacock, Itasca, 1977, p 70-80 (Reading 26)
> ☐ Review the tasks:
> > ❖ How was your meeting with your learning partner and your community development support group?
> > ❖ What was the most important thing you learned while doing your community tasks for the last session?

✎ Record your reflections in your Working Notes.

Project budgets

20 minutes

The budget should be a realistic estimate of the costs of the inputs or resources involved in operating the activities of the project.

Cost estimates should be broken down into logical categories such as:
- Salaries
- Supplies
- Materials
- Equipment
- Travel
- Telephone
- Postage

- ☐ Look back on your Working Notes to see how you answered these questions about inputs or resources in the last session.

> - What inputs or resources for the project did you say you needed?

- ☐ Check that these resources are relevant, necessary and sufficient, and that they are quantified and costed correctly
- ☐ Write out a simple budget for your project. On the left hand side, list your costs; on the right hand side, list your income.
- ✎ Record your reflections in your Working Notes.

Budgets need to be realistic, achievable, measurable, and adequate (that is, not in deficit). If the budget is in deficit, the big question is:

> - How are you going to get the income you need to run the project?

Project funds

20 minutes

Most community projects do not get external sources of funding. We have to rely on internal sources of funding: that is, we have to fund our own projects!

- ☐ Check the budget to see whether you have listed your own voluntary contributions as income or not. If you did, it's great to recognise the value of your voluntary contributions in terms of time, money, expertise and materials! If you did not, it's about time you recognised their value.
- ☐ Make a list of all voluntary contributions of time, money, expertise and materials—and assign a total monetary value in the right hand column of your budget.

❏ Check whether the budget is still in deficit or not. If the budget is not in deficit—good! If the budget is still in deficit, the next question is:

> • Are there any other ways you can reduce the cost of the project?
> • Are there any other ways you contribute more to the project yourselves?

❏ Review and if necessary revise the budget again.

✍ Record your reflections in your Working Notes.

If the budget is still in deficit, the next question is:

> • Are there any other ways you can get funds for the project?

The two usual ways of getting funds from other sources are *fund-raising* and *funds-sourcing*.

Fund-raising

20 minutes

If we choose to raise funds, we need to choose between raising them ourselves, or employing a professional fund-raiser. Most of us who need to raise funds, however, don't have the funds to pay a professional. So we have to do it ourselves.

But we need to ask ourselves, 'How much time and effort do we really want to invest in fund-raising?' It is often easier to cut the costs or increase our own contributions than to tackle fund-raising on top of everything else.

> • How much time and effort do you really want to invest in fund-raising?

✍ Record your reflections in your Working Notes.

Once we have decided how much time and effort we want to invest, then we need to consider our fund-raising options. Whether we choose a traditional fund-raiser, like a cake stall, or a modern fund-raiser like a three-course meal, it still involves investing our voluntary labour in generating activities to raise funds. The quickest way to raise funds is to ask twenty people you know, to give a small specified amount towards a small specific project.

Fund-raising is usually very slow. But if it is done well, it can play a significant role in raising more awareness about our project, and encouraging more ownership of the project. Lots of people can contribute towards a project through a fund-raising event, and through the fund-raiser, find out about other ways they can become more involved in the project.

- What fund-raisers could you put on to raise funds for your project?

✍ Record your reflections in your Working Notes.

Funds-sourcing

45 minutes

If we choose to source funds, we need to remember that all funds from other sources come with strings attached, and there is usually very little room to move for negotiating or renegotiating the terms.[1] So we need to choose a source of funds that has terms acceptable to us.

1. What conditions for external funds are acceptable to you?
2. What are unacceptable to you?

Once you have decided on the terms you can and can't accept, you need to look for a funding source with terms that are consistent with your conditions. The options include government grants and contracts, philanthropic foundations, development organisations and corporate sponsorships. An internet search of "funding sources for Australian community organizations" will give you a number of suitable options.

Government grants

Governments recycle resources from the community and as such are a major source of funds for the community. Community needs always exceed the resources available from the government, so government agencies allocate resources according to a certain set of criteria.

---

1 Adapted from S.Kenny, *Developing Communities for the Future*, Nelson Melbourne, 1994, pp 189-201

Most government agencies require a detailed application for funding, and submissions are ranked on the basis of conformity to government guidelines, past performances and policy priorities.

> • What government funds do you know of, that you could get for your project?

✎ Record your reflections in your Working Notes.

Philanthropic foundations

Many community groups access charitable trusts. However, in Australia the number of charitable trusts are comparatively small and competition for funds is great.

Charitable trusts vary greatly in their philosophy. Not all are sympathetic to community development but many support community development projects. Most charitable trusts also require a detailed application for funding.

> • What philanthropic funds do you know of, that you could get for your project?

✎ Record your reflections in your Working Notes.

Development organisations

Development agencies are also a significant source of community funding. Most development agencies in Australia have a focus on addressing issues related to poverty.

Development agencies tend to have a priority on supporting projects in poorer communities overseas. However, they will occasionally support projects in poorer communities in Australia, especially projects working with indigenous people. Most development agencies also require a detailed application for funding.

> • What development agency funds do you know of, that you could source for your project?

✎ Record your reflections in your Working Notes.

Corporate sponsorships

Some community groups access corporate sponsorships, though many community groups tend to be suspicious of corporations and corporate sponsorships. Anyone seeking corporate sponsorships would need to be happy to be publicly associated with the company sponsoring them.

- What corporate funds do you know of that you could get for your project?

✎ Record your reflections in your Working Notes.

- What are the funding options that might be helpful for your project?
- Which ones would you consider as the top ten funding opportunities?
- How would you rank the top ten, from 1 (the most beneficial) to 10 (the least beneficial)?

☐ Consider the possibilities of securing funding from these sources.

- Nominate the most beneficial source of funds for which you are likely to be eligible.

✎ Record your reflections in your Working Notes.

Conclusion

10 minutes

The follow-up reading for this session is

'Financial Management', William Lawrence with Bernard Klein, *Tactics And Techniques Of Community Practice*, Fred Cox, John Erlich, Jack Rothman, John Tropman, Peacock, Itasca, 1977, p 299-308 (Reading 27)

The set community tasks for this session are

☐ Meet with your learning partner and your community development support group.

- ☐ Share what you learnt in this session about budgeting and work through the budgeting process with your group. Consider fund-raising options together.
- ☐ Consider your nomination for most likely external funding option. Try to get as much information about it as you can and report back to your community development support group about it next week. Do not talk about it to the wider community, lest you raise unrealistic expectations.
- ✎ Record your actions, reflections and conclusions in your Working Notes.

Session 28

Community Work Skill 8: Reporting

Objectives

- To review your budgeting skills
- To consider the next in a series of basic community work skills: reporting.

Review

15 minutes

- ☐ Review your work from Session 27.
- ☐ Review the issues raised in the last session, particularly your budgeting skills.
- ☐ Review the reading:
    'Financial Management', William Lawrence with Bernard Klein, *Tactics And Techniques Of Community Practice*, Fred Cox, John Erlich, Jack Rothman, John Tropman, Peacock, Itasca, 1977, p 299-308 (Reading 27)
- ☐ Review the tasks:
    ❖ How was your meeting with your learning partner and your community development support group?
    ❖ What was the most important thing you learned while doing your community tasks for the last session?

✎ Record your reflections in your Working Notes.

Applications

45 minutes

Every community group that goes looking for outside funding, has to learn the skills of preparing, writing, and submitting applications for the funds. These skills are crucial to your success in securing funding.

Preparing applications [1]

If we want to write a funding application for a project, we need to remember that applying is a competitive process, so we need to prepare the application very carefully. Applications are all about *packaging* our plans in the most attractive way that we can in order to get the funding we need for our project.

The integrity and credibility of the plan are important, but so is the delivery of the package of the plan. It needs to attract the attention of the agency from which we are seeking our funding.

- ❒ Obtain information about the funding rounds and processes of the agency we want to apply to be sure of our approach.
- ❒ Check if the organisation has any guidelines for writing applications.
- ❒ Seek information on priorities for funding, such as whether particular issues or types of organisation are given preference.
- ❒ Make sure that we know our field; what other organisations are doing in this field; and whether other organisations are applying as well.
- ❒ Seek an opportunity to meet with representatives of the agency, but do not be too pushy. If it is appropriate, meet them over lunch, but the emphasis should be on matters that are relevant to the application.

Meeting with representatives of the agency is very important

- To open up a channel of communication with the funder
- To make sure we are approaching our preparation correctly
- To put a personal face to an impersonal application

After talking with a representative from the agency, answer the following questions:

- What were you able to find out about your most likely funding option?
- How relevant was it in reality as a funding option for your project?

If it isn't relevant, reject it and look at alternative sources. If it is still relevant, then consider other options and try again.

---

1 Kenny, p 199

Writing applications [1]

If the agency has any guidelines for writing applications, it is imperative that we follow their guidelines in our writing. If the agency has no guidelines, we need to get whatever materials we can to give us a clue as to the appropriate language and style for writing our application.

- ☐ Make sure to detail:
  - The title of the project
  - The rationale for the project
  - The objectives of the project
  - The strategies of the project
  - The management of the project
  - The plan for evaluation of the project
  - The actual budget for the project

Note that we should put in a realistic budget including details such as award rates, not inflating costs, but indicating where we are prepared to cut back.

Remember that the application needs to be clear, brief and easy to read and that it should be written in the language and style of the funder, not our own.

- ☐ Check that you:
  - ❖ Identify the project objectives in terms of the funder's criteria
  - ❖ Describe the project activities in terms of the funder's criteria
  - ❖ Package the project so as to meet the funder's expectations

- Why is it so important to write in the language of the funder?
- What are the dangers of packaging your project for the funder?
- How can you package the project both honestly and attractively?

✍ Record your reflections in your Working Notes.

---

[1] .Kenny, p 202-3

Note:

Applying for funding is very competitive. Even in applying, we need to try to minimise the competition in the process as much as we can. If we hear that other groups in our area are applying for the same funding, we should talk with them about either writing a joint application—as agencies implementing a single project together—or writing complementary applications, so that there is no overlap between the objectives and activities of the different agencies.

Submitting applications

The way that we submit our funding applications is crucial to our chances of getting funding. It is quite acceptable to submit an application to more than one funding agency at the same time, as long as we indicate this to each of the agencies. However, we need to tailor each application to the specific expectations of each of the funders.

Wherever possible we should deliver the submission by hand and give it to the representative of the agency whom we have already got to know personally. If we cannot deliver the submission by hand, then we should phone beforehand to let them know we are sending it in, and phone afterwards to make sure that they have actually received the application.

After they have received our application, we should ask our contact to look it over and let us know whether or not they think it has covered everything necessary. If they think not, ask them to send it back with any suggestions that they may have to improve it. Then we need to re-write it and re-submit it as soon as we can.

Note:

All applications should be submitted with a covering letter from our project, and supporting letters for the project from other groups and agencies in our area. Both the covering letter and the supporting letters should state:

- Why our project is important to our area at this time
- What we hope to accomplish through the project
- Who will be helped through the project
- Why the project should be funded

- **What kind of covering letter would you write for your project?**

✍ Record your reflections in your Working Notes.

Evaluation

50 minutes

☐ Write the answers to the following questions on cards and put them on the table:

- What is evaluation?
- Why is it important?
- Who is it for?

✎ Record your reflections in your Working Notes.

Formalising evaluations

If we fund our project ourselves, we may well be satisfied with informal evaluation. If others fund our project, they will expect regular, formal evaluation reports from us. They are less concerned with the dynamics of evaluation, and more concerned with the indicators. Their concern is whether or not the evaluation report is accurate.

We need to be sure that our indicators for the objectives of our project are really SMART: Simple, Measurable, Achievable, Realistic, and Timely.

- What are the SMART indicators of the objectives of our project?

✎ Record your reflections in your Working Notes.

These indicators of the objectives of our project should be
- Independent
- Attainable
- Factual
- Plausible
- Verifiable

- What are the best indicators we could use for each specific objective?

✎ Record your reflections in your Working Notes.

Last but not least, we need to provide evidence to support these indicators. This evidence may include:

- Observations
- Interviews
- Anecdotes
- Records
- Minutes
- Accounts
- Inventories
- Documents

> - What would be the best kind of evidence for your indicators?
> - How could you get it? How could you keep it?
> - How could you best use it in a formal report to a funder?

✎ Record your reflections in your Working Notes.

Framing evaluations

We can frame our informal evaluation in our own terms, but we need to frame our formal evaluation in the same terms as our application—in the funder's terms. If the agency has any guidelines for writing an evaluation, it is imperative that we follow their guidelines in our writing. If the agency has no guidelines, we need to get whatever materials we can, to give us a clue as to the appropriate language and style for writing our evaluation.

We should make sure we spell out the project's

- Title
- Rationale
- Objectives
- Indicators of the objectives
- Evidence for these indicators
- Strategies
- Management
- Plan for evaluation
- Actual budget
- Activities
- Accounts
- Accomplishments

Note:

We need to package the report so as to meet the funder's expectations. We need to ensure that the evaluation is clear, brief and easy to read, and that it is written in the language and style of the funder, not our own. It is important to identify everything in terms of the funder's criteria: project objective, indicators, evidence for the indicators, activities and accounts. We should also account for, and justify, changes in the budget.

- How could you package a report on your project in these terms?

✍ Record your reflections in your Working Notes.

Appreciating evaluation

Appreciative Inquiry is an approach to evaluation that is 'valuing' rather than 'de-valuing'.[1] According to Appreciative Inquiry:

1. Evaluation should begin with appreciation of 'what is'.

'The basic principle assumes that every social system "works" to some degree and that it is a primary task of research to discover, describe and explain those social innovations, however small, which serve to give "life" to the system and activate members' energies.'

2. Evaluation should always be provocative, taking the best of 'what is' and generating challenging images of 'what might be'.

'Appreciative knowledge of what is (in terms of peak social innovations in organising) is suggestive of "what might be" and can be used to generate images of realistic developmental opportunities that can be experimented with.'

3. Evaluation should always be collaborative, including the members, not just the management of the organisation, in an open ongoing dialogue.

'There is an inseparable relationship between the process of the inquiry and its content. A collaborative relationship between the researcher and the members of an organisation is, therefore, deemed essential.'

4. Appreciative inquiry does not avoid underlying issues: on the contrary, it gladly embraces the mysteries of life. It is unashamedly spiritual.

'Organisation is a miracle of cooperative human interaction of which there can be no final explanation. There simply are no organisational theories that can give account for the life-giving essence of cooperative existence.'

---

1 Adapted from 'Appreciative Inquiry in Organizational Life' by David Cooperrider and Suresh Srivastava, *Research in Organizational Change and Development* Vol 1 pp 129-160, JAI Press 1987

5. This perspective is not seen as dis-empowering, but as empowering.

'The re-enchantment of the world gives rise to "a consciousness" where there is a sense of personal stake and partnership with the universe.'

- How do you respond to these statements?
- How do they compare with your own views?

✍ Record your reflections in your Working Notes.

Evaluating appreciatively

According to Appreciative Inquiry, research in sociology shows that 'when people study problems, the number and severity of the problems they identify actually increase'; but 'when they study human ideals, peak experiences and best practices, these things—not the problems—tend to flourish.'

So it is important to shift the focus of evaluation from the problems and gaps, toward the accomplishments. Instead of asking 'What hasn't worked?' we need to say, 'Describe a time things were going really well round here. What conditions were present at those moments and what changes would allow more of those conditions to prevail?'

There are five phases in the Appreciative Inquiry process.

Phase One: Definition

This is not a definition of the problem, nor a definition of a solution, but the definition of 'what they would like to learn more about'.

Phase Two: Discovery

Through multiple formal interviews and informal conversations, seek peak experiences and best practice examples on the topic.

Phase Three: Dream

Then generalise from these specific examples generating images of how the group might be able to function at its best.

Phase Four: Design

Develop individual and collective options that the group thinks might be worth experimenting with in order to function at its best.

Phase Five: Delivery

Experiment with options that might be able deliver more best practice innovations celebrating any success at all, no matter how big or small.

- How do you personally respond to this approach to evaluation?
- What do you think that, at its best, it could do for your project?

✍ Record your reflections in your Working Notes.

Note that **anyone** can do appreciative inquiry!

☐ The next time you have a few moments with your partner, say 'You know I'm curious as to what you think are the really good times we have had together. Could you tell me what stands out to you?'

☐ The next time you evaluate a colleague's performance, take them aside and ask them to tell you about the times when they felt they were most effective in their work—and then ask them what they think they could do to increase the frequency of those times in the future.

☐ The next time you have someone in an organisation to talk with you, ask them to describe what they believe the organisation does best, and offer any ideas as to how the organisation could do more of its 'best' in the future.

Note:

The learnings that surround the appreciative inquiry process begin to shift the collective image that people hold of the organisation. In their daily encounters, members start to create together compelling new images of the future. These images initiate small ripples in how employees think about the work they do, their relationships, their roles and so on. Over time these ripples turn into waves. The more positive questions people ask, the more they incorporate the learnings they glean from those questions in daily behaviour, and ultimately in the organisation's infrastructure.

And that

Unlike many behavioural science approaches, appreciative inquiry does not focus on changing people. Instead it invites people to 'engage in building the kinds of communities they want to live in.' It assumes that people are 'competent adults - capable of learning from their experiences and from the experiences of others.'[1]

Conclusion

10 minutes

The follow-up reading for this session is:

> 'Writing for Effect: Correspondence, Records and Documents', John Tropman and Ann Rosegrant Alvarez, *Tactics and Techniques of Community Practice*, Fred Cox, John Erlich, Jack Rothman, John Tropman; Peacock, Itasca, 1977, p 377-391 (Reading 28)

The set community tasks for this session are:

- ❒ Meet with your learning partner and your community development support group.
- ❒ Share what you learnt in this session about writing applications and evaluations. Consider whether you need to write a report of your work.
- ❒ Begin preparing a 10-minute report on the work you've done during this course. The report should be framed around
    - the tasks you attempted
    - strategies you tried
    - the things that worked out best
    - the things that could have gone better
    - the lessons that you have learnt
- ❒ This report should demonstrate an understanding of community work within the framework of your own spirituality, theoretically and practically. The more honest, authentic and creative it is, the better the presentation will be.

---

[1] These quotes are from Bernard Mohr, 'Appreciative Inquiry: Igniting Transformative Action', in *The Systems Thinker*, 12.1 (Waltham, MA: Pegasus Communications, Feb. 2001) pp 1-5

- ❏ Also look for opportunities to practise appreciative inquiry at home and at work, in the church community and in the local community, this week.
- ✍ Record your actions, reflections and conclusions in your Working Notes.

Session 29

Community Work Skill 9: Promoting

Objectives

- To review your reporting skills
- To consider the next in a series of basic community work skills: promoting.

Review

15 minutes

- ❐ Review your work from Session 28.
- ❐ Review the issues raised in the last session, particularly your reporting skills.
- ❐ Review the reading:

    'Writing for Effect: Correspondence, Records and Documents', John Tropman and Ann Rosegrant Alvarez, *Tactics and Techniques of Community Practice*, Fred Cox, John Erlich, Jack Rothman, John Tropman; Peacock, Itasca, 1977, p 377-391 (Reading 28)

- ❐ Review the tasks:
    - ❖ How was your meeting with your learning partner and your community development support group?
    - ❖ What was the most important thing you learned while doing your community tasks for the last session?

✍ Record your reflections in your Working Notes.

Promoting our vision with passion

35 minutes

Martin Luther King gave one of the great speeches of the 20th century to a great crowd in Washington promoting the civil rights struggle.

❐ Read the extract below or listen to the actual speech on **http://www.hpol.org/record.asp?id=72** (Dr. Martin Luther King: I have a dream – Real Audio and Transcript)

As you read and/or listen to 'I have a dream…' think about how you would answer this question: Why was this speech such a powerful inspiration to action?

'I have a dream…'

I say to you today, my friends,
that in spite of the difficulties and frustrations I still have a dream.

I have a dream that one day this nation will rise up and live out the true meaning of its creed:

'We hold these truths to be self-evident—
that all [people] are created equal.'

I have a dream that one day on the red hills of Georgia
the sons of former slaves and the sons of former slave-owners
will be able to sit down together at the table of brotherhood.

I have a dream that one day even the state of Mississippi,
a desert state sweltering with the heat of injustice and oppression,
will be transformed into an oasis of freedom and justice.

I have a dream that my four little children
will one day live in a nation
where they will not be judged by the colour of their skin
but by the content of their character.

I have a dream that one day the state of Alabama,
whose governor's lips are presently dripping with the words of interposition and nullification,
will be transformed into a situation where little black boys and black girls will be able to join hands with little white boys and white girls
and walk together as sisters and brothers.

I have a dream that one day every valley shall be exalted,
every hill and mountain shall be made low,
the rough places will be made plain,
and the crooked places will be made straight,
and the glory of the Lord shall be revealed, and all flesh shall see it together.

This is the faith I shall return to the South with.

With this faith we will be able to hew out of the mountain of despair a stone of hope.

With this faith we will be able to transform the jangling discords of our nation into a beautiful symphony of [fellowship].

With this faith we will be able to work together, pray together, struggle together, go to jail together, stand up for freedom together, knowing that we will be free one day.

This will be the day when all of God's children will be able to sing with new meaning:

'My country 'tis of thee,
sweet land of liberty, of thee I sing.
Land where my [ancestors] died,
land of the pilgrim's pride,
from every mountainside let freedom ring.'

When we let freedom ring,
when we let it ring from every village and every hamlet,
from every state and every city,
we will be able to speed up that day when all of God's children, ...
will be able to join hands and sing in the words of the old Negro spiritual,

'Free at last! Free at last!
Thank God almighty, we are free at last!' [1]

- **Why was this speech such a powerful inspiration to action?**

✍ Record your reflections in your Working Notes.

King eloquently articulated the deep longing in people's hearts. When James Baldwin heard these words he said:

> That day, for a moment, it almost seemed that we stood on a height and could see our inheritance; perhaps we could make [it] real, perhaps the beloved community would not forever remain [a] dream ...

They killed the dreamer, as they killed the dreamers who came before him. But they couldn't kill the dream of 'the beloved community'. The words that were heard that day are still heard today, echoing encouragement in the conscience of each succeeding generation as we consider the challenge to 'make it real'.

I have the audacity to believe that peoples everywhere
can have three meals a day for their bodies,

education ... for their minds, and ... freedom for their spirits.

---

1 Oates, S. *Let The Trumpet Sound*, New American Library, New York 1982, pp 260-262

> I believe that what self-centred [people] have torn down
> other-centred people can build up.
>
> I still believe that one day humanity
> will bow before the altars of God
> and be crowned triumphant over war
> and non-violent redemptive goodwill
> will proclaim the rule of the land.
>
> And every one shall sit
> under their own vine and fig tree
> and none shall be afraid.
>
> I still believe that we shall overcome.[1]

- **What can you learn from Martin Luther King about how you can promote your vision?**

☐ Write down as many ideas as you can come up with on separate cards, one idea per card.

☐ Spread the cards on the table and select one you want to work on.

☐ Why do you choose that one to work on? How do you intend to do it?

✍ Record your reflections in your Working Notes.

Promoting our mission with compassion

In this session we introduce you to two brilliant Australian examples of people who promoted their mission with compassion—Caroline Chisholm and Mary MacKillop.

Caroline Chisholm
30 minutes

> I'm not one of those who ask 'What will the Government do for us?'
> The question of the day is 'What shall we do for ourselves?'

Caroline was born into a wealthy rural English family in 1808. The Joneses were a religious family. Caroline's father brought his daughter up to stand by what she believed in, and her mother brought her daughter

---

1 Hope, A. and Timmel, S. *Training for Transformation*, Mambo Press, Gweru Zimbabwe, 1984, p 130

up to serve the poor. So the fun-loving young Caroline grew up with a serious faith, a strong mind and a social conscience.

Caroline's father died when she was young, and her hitherto wealthy family was suddenly plunged into desperate poverty. It was one thing for her to care for the poor; it was another thing for her to *be* poor herself. It was an experience Caroline never forgot.

When she reached a marriageable age, Caroline met Archibald Chisholm, an English officer in the Indian Army. He cut a dashing figure in his uniform and when she got the chance to talk with him, Caroline found Archy had substance as well as style. They decided to get married, but in an equal partnership, as opposed to the superior-subordinate relationships, which were more common in marriages of the time. Although Caroline, who was Protestant, agreed to become Catholic like Archy, it was only on the condition that she would be free to pursue any non-denominational philanthropic work that she felt called to 'without impediment'.

After their wedding Archy was recalled to India, and Caroline later followed him later to Madras. Upon her arrival the officers' wives drew her into their party circuit, but Caroline loathed the petty gossip that filled the empty lives of the *burri memsahibs*. Caroline's eye was caught more by the poverty than it was by the opulence. She immediately began to pray that God would show her a way to respond to the plight of the hapless child prostitutes that swarmed around the outskirts of the garrison town.

Caroline eventually decided that the only way she could save the poor kids from prostitution, or from marriages so degrading that they were almost as bad, was to start a school that could teach them marketable skills.

The officers and their wives were scandalised by Caroline's 'unbecoming' behaviour and told Archy to pull his wife into line or risk becoming a 'social outcaste'. But Archy refused to be bullied. He threw his lot in with the 'social outcastes' by personally underwriting the expenses of the school himself. So with Archy's support, Caroline set up a modern school in Madras. The school taught street children not only reading and writing, but also cooking and cleaning, budgeting and bookkeeping, and even nursing.

Some years later, due to ill health, Archy and Caroline applied to take long leave in Australia. They arrived in Sydney with their two children in 1838, and settled into a comfortable house in Windsor. After a couple of years Archy had to go back to his regiment; but they decided it was best for Caroline and the children to stay on at their new home in New South Wales.

Caroline thought she might open a school in Sydney as she had done in Madras. As she prayed about it, Caroline became convinced she needed to set the idea of a school aside for a while and get involved with the poor immigrant women, penniless widows and orphaned girls who slept in tents in the Domain or in the streets around The Rocks.

Many of the women that Caroline met told tragic tales of fleeing destitution in England by emigrating to Australia, only to fall into the hands of abusive crews on board the ships, and of unscrupulous brothel owners once the ships docked in Sydney harbour. Upon hearing these stories, Caroline made it her business to meet every ship as it came in. To start with Caroline took these women into her own home at Windsor. Then, when there were too many, she persuaded the wife of Governor Gipps to get her husband to make the old barracks on Bent Street available to her. She turned the rat-infested shed into an emergency shelter accommodating more than a hundred women at one time.

Caroline then accompanied the residents around town in their search for work. When she couldn't find enough jobs around Sydney, she set up voluntary committees all around New South Wales to act as employment agencies for her. She personally took her charges from Moreton Bay to Port Macquarie to secure proper employment for them. In the process Caroline secured employment for over 14,000 women. To protect the rights of these women, Caroline introduced employment contracts in triplicate to ensure the provision of good basic conditions in their place of employment.

When Archy returned in 1845, Caroline talked to him about the need to take her campaign to Britain in order to lobby the British Government directly. Archy agreed to return with Caroline to England to take the fight for the rights of migrants to their point of origin.

Back in England Caroline met with the Secretary of State, the Home Secretary, and the Land and Emigration Commissioners, providing them with detailed reports on human rights abuses and presenting them with specific policy options which they could adopt to address these issues. While waiting for these reforms to be adopted, Caroline went ahead and organised a society to aid migrants independent of, but in cooperation with the British Government. The central committee of the society she organised, under the high-profile presidency of Lord Ashley MP (Earl of Shaftesbury) and with the public support of Charles Dickens, set up a scheme to help poor migrants with everything from safe travel to personal loans.

Caroline did all she could to expedite family reunions for ex-convicts, who were separated from their wives and children for years. She lobbied for free passage for these reunions and for land reform to enable these families to get small farms of their own.

In 1854 Caroline joined Archy in Melbourne where, since 1851, he had been running the Aussie end of their operation. Back in Australia Caroline continued her relentless campaign through the press and the parliament for women's entitlements.

By 1866 the Chisholms had exhausted their considerable intellectual, emotional and physical resources. They had worked passionately, without pay, in the service of humanity for more than a quarter of a century. When they retired to England they were worn out. In 1877 Caroline died and her beloved Archy died a few months later. [1]

- What can you learn from Caroline about how to promote your mission? (Write down as many ideas as you can come up with on separate cards.)

Mary MacKillop

30 minutes

Never see a need without trying to do something about it!

Mary MacKillop was born in Fitzroy in 1842 into a Scottish migrant family. Mary was the eldest of eight children and their father, who had attended Scots College in Rome, educated the children at home. Having squandered most of the family fortune, the MacKillops were dirt poor.

At the age of fourteen Mary was sent out to work. By the age of sixteen, she had become the major family breadwinner. Even in her youth Mary showed herself to be a very capable person. At Sands & Kenny, the stationers where she worked, Mary was given a position of responsibility usually reserved for older employees.

At the age of eighteen Mary assumed the role of governess to her cousins in Penola, South Australia. There she met Father Julian Tenison Woods. Mary had already decided that she wanted to be a nun, so she asked Father Woods to be her spiritual mentor. Julian Woods and Mary MacKillop became close friends. They shared a vision for developing an Australian religious order that would serve the needs of the poor.

In 1866 they founded the Sisters of St. Joseph. This was an indigenous mission made up of small, mobile communities of two or three sisters caring for children in frontier towns, rural farms and roadside and railway

---

1 Adapted from S. De Vries, The Immigrants' Friend, *Strength of Spirit*, Millennium Books, Alexandria 1995, pp 91-110

camps. The itinerant lifestyle of the sisters was very simple. They took a vow of poverty to identify with the poor. Because they had no money, they were only able to survive by begging. The hierarchy of the church did not approve of the practice. However, mindful of her mission, Mary encouraged the sisters to carry on regardless.

Mary started Australia's first free Catholic school. At the time only the rich could afford to pay the fees to send their kids to school. The sisters provided education for the children of the poor, whether or not they could afford to pay the fees.

In 1867 Mary moved to Adelaide and it wasn't long before she and her sisters had seventeen schools up and running. Instead of supporting their efforts, the Bishop of Adelaide, who was a paranoid alcoholic, tried to clamp down on the congregation. When Mary resisted, he excommunicated her and discharged her sisters.

For Mary, being thrown out of the church was a terrible blow. She was totally devastated. But, in spite of the desolation, she was determined to maintain her faith. She refused to become bitter and twisted about the way she was treated. The Holy See sent a delegation to investigate the disturbance in the Antipodes; and as a result of their inquiries, they decided to back Mary against the Bishop. In 1872, when the Bishop lay dying, he apologised to Mary, absolved her from excommunication, and reinstated her and her sisters.

In 1873 Mary travelled to Rome. There she sought permission from the Pope for her congregation to run its own affairs free from the interference of the bishops in future. In the light of the quality of her work, her request was well received and the Josephites were given the independence for which Mary had fought. In 1875 Mary was elected superior-general of her order.

Under Mary's guidance the Josephites became the primary provider of Catholic education to Australian girls regardless of race, class or creed. Because they had a policy of being non-proselytising, the sisters enjoyed a lot of support from Protestants as well as Catholics in the communities where they worked around Australia.

In 1885 the Josephites again found themselves in conflict with the Bishops. The Holy See supported the congregation, but asked Mary if she would stand aside and let someone else (less controversial) lead the congregation for a while. So in 1888 Mary stood aside and Mother Bernard was elected to lead the order in her stead. In 1898 Mother Bernard died and Mary was elected again by the congregation to the lead the order into the twentieth century.

They not only taught students, but also taught the teachers who taught the students. They opened orphanages for those with no homes, and refuges for those fleeing violent homes. They provided family support and residential care services for those with intellectual, physical, psychological and developmental disabilities.

Mary died in 1909. And in 1995 this 'little battler', this 'feminist trailblazer' and 'ecclesiastical troublemaker', this 'extraordinary never-say-die pioneer of education for all' was appropriately recognised as our first 'fair dinkum' Aussie Saint.[1]

- What can you learn from Mary about how you can promote your mission? (Write down as many ideas as you can come up with on separate cards.)

☐ Spread the cards you wrote after reflecting on Caroline's work on the left-hand side of the table, and the cards you wrote after reflecting on Mary's work on the right-hand side.

☐ Then select a card from each side you want to work on.

❖ Why do you choose those cards? How do you intend to work on them?

✎ Record your reflections in your Working Notes.

Conclusion

10 minutes

The follow-up reading for this session is

'Fostering Participation' Jack Rothman, John Erlich, and Joseph Teresa, *Strategies Of Community Organisation*, Fred Cox, John Erlich, Jack Rothman, John Tropman; Peacock, Itasca, 1977, p 385-391 (Reading 29)

The set community tasks for this session are

☐ Meet with your learning partner and your community development support group.

☐ Share what you learnt in this session about promoting. Consider what action you might take together to promote your vision and your mission.

---

[1] Female Firebrands and Reformers https://www.oocities.org/eschiva/mckillop.html
Mary MacKillop and the Sisters of St. Joseph of the Sacred Heart https://www.sosj.org.au/our-foundress-mary-mackillop/marys-story/mary-story-beginnings/

❏ Continue your preparation of the 10-minute report on the work you've done during this course, that you can use to promote your mission. The report should be framed around:

- The tasks you attempted
- The strategies you tried
- What has worked out best
- What could have been better
- The lessons that you have learnt

This report should demonstrate an understanding of community work within the framework of your own spirituality, theoretically and practically. As Martin Luther King shows us, the more honest, authentic and creative it is, the better the presentation will be.

✎ Record your actions, reflections and conclusions in your Working Notes.

Session 30

Community Work Skill 10: Persevering

Objectives

- To review your promoting skills
- To consider the next in a series of basic community work skills: persevering.

Review

15 minutes

- ☐ Review your work from Session 29.
- ☐ Review the issues raised in the last session, particularly your promting skills.
- ☐ Review the reading:

    'Fostering Participation' Jack Rothman, John Erlich, and Joseph Teresa, *Strategies Of Community Organisation*, Fred Cox, John Erlich, Jack Rothman, John Tropman; Peacock, Itasca, 1977, p 385-391 (Reading 29)

- ☐ Review the tasks:
    - ❖ How was your meeting with your learning partner and your community development support group?
    - ❖ What was the most important thing you learned while doing your community tasks for the last session?

✍ Record your reflections in your Working Notes.

Meditation

60 minutes

Carl Jung says, "Any genuine personality [will] sacrifice [themselves] for [their] vocation."[1] But for that process to be life-affirming, rather than life-negating, self-sacrifice always needs to take place in the context of self-care and self-control.

Self-care

At the centre of the creative use of self is *self-care*.

> I am struck repeatedly by the degree to which people who are committed to 'good work', to making this world 'better' to live in, do not include themselves as valid environmental concerns ...
>
> If you are saving the world and killing yourself (even if only by self-neglect) you will not be effective in your work. The people whom you are trying to convince will not believe you.
>
> You can't abuse yourself and advocate that society should not abuse the environment.[2]

Katrina Shields explains the process of exercising self-care:

> (It) means, in the most simple sense, to attend to basic requirements—nourishing food, quality sleep, pleasant exercise and fresh air.
>
> However, taking care of ourselves extends well beyond this. Dealing with projects, people, and challenges on a daily basis (especially if it is done under pressure, with uncertainty and few external rewards) slowly drains our inner reserves.
>
> One way to 'top up' again is to nurture ourselves, perhaps by little treats and pleasures, deep relaxation exercises or meditation.[3]

- What are simple, practical, inexpensive ways you can care for yourself?

✐ Record your reflections in your Working Notes.

☐ Then reflect on the 'Ten Commandments for Community Workers' at the end of this chapter.

---

1 Jung, C., *Collected Works*, Princeton University Press 1967, vol.17, vii, pp167-187
2 Bryan, W., *Preventing Burnout in the Public Interest Community*, Northern Rockies Action Group, Paper NRAG Helena Vol.3 No.3, 1980
3 Shields, p 124

Self-control

At the circumference of the creative use of self is *self-control*.

> The essential problem in any situation of injustice is that one human being is exercising control over another human being and exploiting the relationship of dominance.
>
> The solution to the problem is not simply to reverse roles in the hope that once the roles have been reversed the manipulation will discontinue. The solution is for people to stop trying to control one another.
>
> All of us to one degree or another exploit the opportunity if we have control over another person's life. Common sense therefore dictates that the solution to the problem of exploitation cannot be through ... controlling others, but controlling ourselves individually and collectively. [1]

Stephen Covey explores the process of increasing self-control:

> We each have a wide range of concerns (from the welfare of our family through to the fate of the world). As we look at those things ... it becomes apparent that there are some things over which we have no control, [and do nothing about] and other [things over which we have some control and] can do something about.
>
> We could identify the former as a *circle of concern* and the latter as a *circle of influence*. [Increasing self control] depends on focusing our efforts on our circle of influence and gradually expanding those efforts to effect more and more of our circle of concern.
>
> We share in the spirit embodied in the prayer used in Alcoholics Anonymous,
>
> > 'Lord, give me the serenity to accept
> > the things I can't,
> > the courage to change
> > the things I can,
> > and the wisdom to know
> > the difference'.

- **How can we take greater control of ourselves, without controlling others?**

✍ Record your reflections in your Working Notes.

❏ Then reflect on the 'Guidelines for the Long Haul' at the end of this chapter.

---

1 Andrews, *Not Religion but Love*, p 32

Self-sacrifice

At the interface, in the community, between our selves and other selves, the creative use of self involves *self-sacrifice*. After years of often quite difficult experience with an intentional community, Art Gish wrote:

> It is important that we come to terms with our own selfishness. Unless we do that, our communities will be little more than reflections of the ... society we hoped to overcome. It is not enough to reject the selfishness of the larger society. The condition of our inner selves needs to be transformed.
>
> Community is not based on the extent to which we see the community fulfilling our own needs or the extent to which the interest of the total community matches our self-interest, but rather the extent to which we give up self in order to live [a] new life.
>
> Without this surrender, community is impossible. Each of us brings with us our own agenda from the past, our different patterns of living. To the extent that each of us insists on our own way community is impossible.
>
> Community is more than an association of independent individuals, for membership involves the very heart of a person's being in all its dimensions. One is not truly in community unless [one] is committed.
>
> Community always includes a price. It means giving up something else, being here rather than there, giving up other options. But the sacrifices are nothing in light of what is received. In fact, the ... higher the cost for us, the more valuable ... community will be for us.
>
> ... What we are talking about is ... a whole new world in which each individual lays down his/her life in love for each other. Renunciation of individual ego is no guarantee that a collective egoism will not take its place. The selfishness of 'mine' and 'thine' can be exchanged for the selfishness of 'ours' and 'yours'.
>
> So surrender, not only of each individual, but also of the total community, [is] demanded. Unless we are prepared to die for each other we are not [able] to live for each other.[1]

- **What would sacrificing yourself for the sake of community mean to you?**

✎ Record your reflections in your Working Notes.

❐ Then reflect on Angie Andrews' poem, *Who of you will join me?* at the end of this chapter.

---

1 Gish, A. *Living In Christian Community*, Albatross, Sutherland 1979, pp47-54 {edited}

Evaluation

30 minutes

Begin your evaluation of the course by looking at the course from a different angle. Ask yourself an intriguing question, such as

- If this course were a piece of fruit you tasted, what would you say it was?

Then move towards classic inquiry questions such as

- What was the best thing about this course?
- What is the one thing you will not forget?
- What would you do differently if you were to do it again?

Conclusion

40 minutes

The set community tasks for this session are

- ☐ Meet with your learning partner and your community development support group, and reflect on what you have accomplished.
- ☐ Decide whether you want to wrap up the group, or keep it going.
- ☐ If you decide to wrap up, celebrate your journey and say goodbye.
- ☐ If you decide to keep going, talk about how you can exercise more self-care and self-control, to sustain the self-sacrifice along the way.
- ☐ Copy the three 'posters' at the end of the chapter and display them round your house, office or factory where you can meditate on them regularly.
- ☐ Make sure you read: 'Survival Tactics' Katrina Shields *In The Tiger's Mouth*, Millenium Books Newtown 1991 p 119-137 (Reading 30) in the coming week.

Poster 1

Ten Commandments for Community Workers

Thou shalt learn to say NO as well as to say YES.

Thou shalt NOT let people's deadlines kill thee.

Thou shalt leave some things undone sometimes.

Thou shalt NOT be responsible for everything.

Thou shalt be as friendly as much as thou canst be.

But thou shalt NOT try to be everybody's best friend.

Thou shalt be good to one and all—even unto thyself.

Thou shalt NOT neglect thine own family or friends.

Thou shalt schedule time for thyself and thy supportive network.

Thou shalt relax regularly—and thou shalt NOT even feel guilty.

Poster 2

Guidelines for the Long Haul

~*~

Be constantly in touch with your soul.

Continually relate to reality soulfully.

Be accountable to one another.

Answer the hard questions as honestly as you possibly can.

Don't be responsible for everything,
but be responsive to everyone.

Never react; always respond;
as constructively as you can.

Don't try to do big things;
try to do little things with a lot of love.

Extend love unconditionally,
but trust only conditionally.

Don't have high expectations;
have high hopes with low expectations.

Cultivate seeds of hope in the grounds for despair.

Never forget
there's no salvation without grace,
and no grace without suffering.

Always remember
that strength is made perfect in weakness.

~*~

Poster 3

Who of you will join me?

by Angie Andrews

There is precious little acceptance in our society
of the changes in our bodies,
brought about by sacrifice, by the giving of life to others.
People want us to look unscathed, unscarred.
Without the sagging in our breasts,
the stretchmarks on our stomach,
the lines of strain and struggle.
People want us to look ageless, timeless.
With the model body of a young girl.
With long flowing hair,
fair skin, firm upright breasts,
tight muscled tummy, slim thighs, and long legs.
The image of the lithe and slender
is what men lust for.
The image of what men lust for
is what women strive for.
Where is the place for the beauty
derived from love and developed through sacrifice?
Where are the people who will celebrate
the signs of someone
who has given themselves to others
through touch, in tears, with love,
unnumbered times?
Who of you will join me
in forsaking the images we idolise in our society?
Who of you will join me
in turning away from the mirror
towards the door that leads to the needs of others?
Who of you will join me
in the risk of being worn out,
of being wrinkled, of being thrown away?
We are not fools,
who give what we cannot keep,
to gain what we cannot lose!

Appendix A

The UN Declaration of Human Rights

Article 1

All human beings are born free and equal in dignity and rights. They are endowed with reason and conscience and should act towards one another in a spirit of brotherhood.

Article 2

Everyone is entitled to all the rights and freedoms set forth in this Declaration, without distinction of any kind, such as race, colour, sex, language, religion, political or other opinion, national or social origin, property, birth or other status. Furthermore, no distinction shall be made on the basis of the political, jurisdictional or international status of the country or territory to which a person belongs, whether it be independent, trust, non-self-governing or under any other limitation of sovereignty.

Article 3

Everyone has the right to life, liberty and security of person.

Article 4

No one shall be held in slavery or servitude; slavery and the slave trade shall be prohibited in all their forms.

Article 5

No one shall be subjected to torture or to cruel, inhuman or degrading treatment or punishment.

Article 6

Everyone has the right to recognition everywhere as a person before the law.

Article 7

All are equal before the law and are entitled without any discrimination to equal protection of the law. All are entitled to equal protection against any discrimination in violation of this Declaration and against any incitement to such discrimination.

Article 8

Everyone has the right to an effective remedy by the competent national tribunals for acts violating the fundamental rights granted him by the constitution or by law.

Article 9

No one shall be subjected to arbitrary arrest, detention or exile.

Article 10

Everyone is entitled in full equality to a fair and public hearing by an independent and impartial tribunal, in the determination of his rights and obligations and of any criminal charge against him.

Article 11

(1) Everyone charged with a penal offence has the right to be presumed innocent until proved guilty according to law in a public trial at which he has had all the guarantees necessary for his defence.

(2) No one shall be held guilty of any penal offence on account of any act or omission which did not constitute a penal offence, under national or international law, at the time when it was committed. Nor shall a heavier penalty be imposed than the one that was applicable at the time the penal offence was committed.

Article 12

No one shall be subjected to arbitrary interference with his privacy, family, home or correspondence, nor to attacks upon his honour and reputation. Everyone has the right to the protection of the law against such interference or attacks.

Article 13

(1) Everyone has the right to freedom of movement and residence within the borders of each state.

(2) Everyone has the right to leave any country, including his own, and to return to his country.

Article 14

(1) Everyone has the right to seek and to enjoy in other countries asylum from persecution.

(2) This right may not be invoked in the case of prosecutions genuinely arising from non-political crimes or from acts contrary to the purposes and principles of the United Nations.

Article 15

(1) Everyone has the right to a nationality.

(2) No one shall be arbitrarily deprived of his nationality nor denied the right to change his nationality.

Article 16

(1) Men and women of full age, without any limitation due to race, nationality or religion, have the right to marry and to found a family. They are entitled to equal rights as to marriage, during marriage and at its dissolution.

(2) Marriage shall be entered into only with the free and full consent of the intending spouses.

(3) The family is the natural and fundamental group unit of society and is entitled to protection by society and the State.

Article 17

(1) Everyone has the right to own property alone as well as in association with others.

(2) No one shall be arbitrarily deprived of his property.

Article 18

Everyone has the right to freedom of thought, conscience and religion; this right includes freedom to change his religion or belief, and freedom, either alone or in community with others and in public or private, to manifest his religion or belief in teaching, practice, worship and observance.

Article 19

Everyone has the right to freedom of opinion and expression; this right includes freedom to hold opinions without interference and to seek, receive and impart information and ideas through any media and regardless of frontiers.

Article 20

(1) Everyone has the right to freedom of peaceful assembly and association.

(2) No one may be compelled to belong to an association.

Article 21

(1) Everyone has the right to take part in the government of his country, directly or through freely chosen representatives.

(2) Everyone has the right of equal access to public service in his country.

(3) The will of the people shall be the basis of the authority of government; this will shall be expressed in periodic and genuine elections which shall be by universal and equal suffrage and shall be held by secret vote or by equivalent free voting procedures.

Article 22

Everyone, as a member of society, has the right to social security and is entitled to realisation, through national effort and international co-operation and in accordance with the organisation and resources of each State, of the economic, social and cultural rights indispensable for his dignity and the free development of his personality.

Article 23

(1) Everyone has the right to work, to free choice of employment, to just and favourable conditions of work and to protection against unemployment.

(2) Everyone, without any discrimination, has the right to equal pay for equal work.

(3) Everyone who works has the right to just and favourable remuneration ensuring for himself and his family an existence worthy of human dignity, and supplemented, if necessary, by other means of social protection.

(4) Everyone has the right to form and to join trade unions for the protection of his interests.

Article 24

Everyone has the right to rest and leisure, including reasonable limitation of working hours and periodic holidays with pay.

Article 25

(1) Everyone has the right to a standard of living adequate for the health and well-being of himself and of his family, including food, clothing, housing and medical care and necessary social services, and the right to security in the event of unemployment, sickness, disability, widowhood, old age or other lack of livelihood in circumstances beyond his control.

(2) Motherhood and childhood are entitled to special care and assistance. All children, whether born in or out of wedlock, shall enjoy the same social protection.

Article 26

(1) Everyone has the right to education. Education shall be free, at least in the elementary and fundamental stages. Elementary education shall be compulsory. Technical and professional education shall be made generally available and higher education shall be equally accessible to all on the basis of merit.

(2) Education shall be directed to the full development of the human personality and to the strengthening of respect for human rights and fundamental freedoms. It shall promote understanding, tolerance and friendship among all nations, racial or religious groups, and shall further the activities of the United Nations for the maintenance of peace.

(3) Parents have a prior right to choose the kind of education that shall be given to their children.

Article 27

(1) Everyone has the right freely to participate in the cultural life of the community, to enjoy the arts and to share in scientific advancement and its benefits.

(2) Everyone has the right to the protection of the moral and material interests resulting from any scientific, literary or artistic production of which he is the author.

Article 28

Everyone is entitled to a social and international order in which the rights and freedoms set forth in this Declaration can be fully realised.

Article 29

(1) Everyone has duties to the community in which alone the free and full development of his personality is possible.

(2) In the exercise of his rights and freedoms, everyone shall be subject only to such limitations as are determined by law solely for the purpose of securing due recognition and respect for the rights and freedoms of others and of meeting the just requirements of morality, public order and the general welfare in a democratic society.

(3) These rights and freedoms may in no case be exercised contrary to the purposes and principles of the United Nations.

Article 30

Nothing in this Declaration may be interpreted as implying for any State, group or person any right to engage in any activity or to perform any act aimed at the destruction of any of the rights and freedoms set forth herein.

Appendix B

Readings

These readings are accessible on http://www.daveandrews.com.au/lcarticles/ Reading X.pdf. Each reading corresponds with its Session Number: e.g. Reading 14 is set for use in Session 14.

Reading 1: Our Ideal In The Real World, Dave Andrews, *Building a Better World*, Albatross, Sutherland, 1996, pp 52-68

Reading 2: On the Potential and Problems of Community, An interview with Robert Putnam on Radio National, ABC, 26.9.2001

Reading 3: **The Ottawa Charter For Health Promotion**, First International Conference on Health Promotion, WHO, Ottawa 21.11.1986

Reading 4: **Prison: The Community's Business**, Arlene Morgan, *People Working Together II,* A. Kelly & S. Sewell, Boolarong, Brisbane, 1986. pp 30-47

Reading 5: **A Potent Mixture of Faith, Humour and Courage**, Anthony Kelly, Arlene Morgan and Dierdre Coghlan, *People Working Together III,* Boolarong, Brisbane, 1997, pp 129-143

Reading 6: **An Honest Cop**, Mike Brown, *No Longer Down Under,* Grosvenor Books, Melbourne, 2002, pp147-162

Reading 7: **King of the Wharfies**, Mike Brown, No Longer Down Under, Grosvenor Books, Melbourne, 2002, pp 130-144

Reading 8: **Beginnings**, Kris Saunders and Teresa Scott, People Working Together II, A. Kelly & S. Sewell, Boolarong, Brisbane, 1986, pp 5-17

Reading 9: **Bringing People Together**, Dave Andrews, Building a Better World, Albatross, Sutherland, 1996, pp 214-226

Reading 10: **Journey Into The Acting Community**, David Thomas, *Group Work: Learning And Practice*, Nano McCaughan, George Allen & Unwin, Sydney, 1978, pp 167-181

Reading 11: The Settlement House: Mediator for the Poor, Buford Farris, Gilbert Murillo, and William Hale, The Practice Of Group Work, William Scwartz and Serapio Zalba, Columbia UP, New York, 1971, pp 73-95

Appendix B: Readings

Reading 12: **A Spirituality of Community**, Dave Andrews, *Building a Better World*, Albatross, Sutherland, 1996, pp 335-356

Reading 13: **Making Our Place in the Sun**, Anthony Kelly, Arlene Morgan and Dierdre Coghlan, *People Working Together III*, Boolarong, Brisbane, 1997 pp 7-34

Reading 14: **The Hotham Hill Neighbourhood Association**, John Goff, *People Working Together*, Les Halliwell, UQ Press, Brisbane, 1969, pp 123-131

Reading 15: **A Civilisation which is Still to be Created**, Dave Andrews, Building a Better World, Albatross, Sutherland, 1996, pp 297-311

Reading 16: **I Refuse to be Intimidated by Reality Any More**, Dave Andrews, *Building a Better World*, Albatross, Sutherland, 199, pp 113-137

Reading 17: **The Code of Ethics**, Australian Institute of Welfare and Community Workers

Reading 18: **Culture and Community**, 'Issues in Cross-Cultural Counselling' and 'The Principles of Cross Cultural Practice'

Reading 19: **Universal Human Rights**, United Nations Declaration of Human Rights, United Nations General Assembly (see Appendix A)

Reading 20: **Communication**, Trevor Tyson, *Working With Groups*, Macmillan, Melbourne, 1989, pp 72-84

Reading 21: **Organisation**, Trevor Tyson, *Working With Groups*, Macmillan, Melbourne, 1989, pp 24-57

Reading 22: **Leadership**, Trevor Tyson, *Working With Groups*, Macmillan, Melbourne, 1989, pp 85- 96

Reading 23: **Groupwork**, Trevor Tyson, *Working With Groups*, Macmillan, Melbourne, 1989, pp 106-132

Reading 24: **Suggestions for a Study of Your Hometown**, Robert Lamb, in *Tactics and Techniques of Community Practice*, Fred Cox, John Erlich, Jack Rothman, John Tropman, Peacock, Itasca, 1977, pp 17-23

Reading 25: **Policy Issues and Organisational Relations**, Yeheskel Hasenfield, in *Tactics and Techniques of Community Practice*, Fred Cox, John Erlich, Jack Rothman, John Tropman, Peacock, Itasca, 1977, pp 69-70

Reading 26: **How To Organise a Community Action Plan,** Jack Rothman, in *Tactics and Techniques of Community Practice*, Fred Cox, John Erlich, Jack Rothman, John Tropman, Peacock, Itasca, 1977, pp 70-80

Reading 27: **Financial Management,** William Lawrence with Bernard Klein, in *Tactics and Techniques of Community Practice*, Fred Cox, John Erlich, Jack Rothman, John Tropman, Peacock, Itasca, 1977, pp 299-308

Reading 28: **Writing for Effect: Correspondence, Records and Documents,** John Tropman and Ann Rosegrant Alvarez, in *Tactics and Techniques of Community Practice*, Fred Cox, John Erlich, Jack Rothman, John Tropman, Peacock, Itasca, 1977, pp 377-391

Reading 29: **Fostering Participation,** Jack Rothman, John Erlich, and Joseph Teresa, in *Strategies of Community Organisation*, Fred Cox, John Erlich, Jack Rothman, John Tropman, Peacock, Itasca, 1979, pp 385-391

Reading 30: **Survival Tactics,** Katrina Shields, *In the Tiger's Mouth*, Millenium Books, Newtown, 1991, pp 119-137

www.ingramcontent.com/pod-product-compliance
Lightning Source LLC
Chambersburg PA
CBHW050547160426
43199CB00015B/2571